Spiritually Transformative Psychotherapy

Spiritually Transformative Psychotherapy

Repairing Spiritual Damage and Facilitating Extreme Wellbeing

Steven R. Vazquez

ROWMAN & LITTLEFIELD
Lanham • Boulder • New York • London

Published by Rowman & Littlefield
A wholly owned subsidiary of The Rowman & Littlefield Publishing Group, Inc.
4501 Forbes Boulevard, Suite 200, Lanham, Maryland 20706
www.rowman.com

Unit A, Whitacre Mews, 26-34 Stannary Street, London SE11 4AB

British Library Cataloguing in Publication Information Available

Library of Congress Cataloging-in-Publication Data

Names: Vazquez, Steven R., 1947– author.
Title: Spiritually transformative psychotherapy : repairing spiritual damage and facilitating extreme wellbeing / Steven R. Vazquez.
Description: Lanham : Rowman & Littlefield, [2017] | Includes bibliographical references and index.
Identifiers: LCCN 2016039187 (print) | LCCN 2016039692 (ebook) | ISBN 9781442258112 (cloth : alk. paper) | ISBN 9781442258136 (pbk. : alk. paper) | ISBN 9781442258129 (electronic)
Subjects: LCSH: Psychotherapy—Religious aspects. | Spirituality.
Classification: LCC RC489.R46 V39 2017 (print) | LCC RC489.R46 (ebook) | DDC 616.89/14—dc23
LC record available at https://lccn.loc.gov/2016039187

™ The paper used in this publication meets the minimum requirements of American National Standard for Information Sciences—Permanence of Paper for Printed Library Materials, ANSI/NISO Z39.48-1992.

Printed in the United States of America

Contents

Acknowledgments

The quality of this book is due to the contributions of many people. Vicki Whitaker supplied countless hours of editorial and coaching help and her contributions are deeply appreciated. My office manager, Barbara Walker, has been of enormous help by typing and retyping this manuscript. Her assistance has been so helpful. My dear wife, Sue Anne, has been patiently understanding about my stacks of papers and books and she listened as I read through my chapters whether she wanted to hear them or not. She was always supportive of this endeavor.

This could not have been developed if it were not for the countless clients and colleagues who trusted me to use my intuitive processes in order to pursue spiritual states. I want to thank Dr. Andrea Silberman who volunteered for my first public demonstration of what came to be known as the Emotional Transformation Therapy® (ETT®) samadhi process. Donna Hoffmann read the entire manuscript and provided helpful feedback consistently. I thank Rev. Bill Dasch for reading the entire manuscript and providing helpful feedback. I also thank Karen Kucharen for her feedback on the book. Dr. Colin Ross saw this approach in action and has been a very supportive friend and colleague for years. I am thankful for the Forward he wrote for this book.

Many professional counselors have experienced and used these methods and showed that they were replicable. The spiritual journeys of Sylvia Lippman, Judy Boisseau, Carolyn Adkins, Deborah Owen, Holly Webb, Michael Webb, Laura Vogel, Lynn McCracken, Susan Ellis, Marci Holloway, Susie Hair, and Jerilee Merkle have informed and enlightened me. Thank you.

I am indebted to my own spiritual guides of Yeshua, Baba Muktananda, Jacob Boehm, Mother Meera, and Carlos Casteneda for their inspiration and help in understanding much of the spiritual realm of life.

I thank the dozens of cancer patients who allowed me to guide them through their journeys of physical and spiritual healing. I thank the many people who heard spiritual voices and messages as well as those who heard negative voices. I am thankful for clients who spoke in tongues, which helped me understand the phenomena of glossolalia. I am particularly grateful for hundreds of clients who went through profound spiritual awakenings in my presence.

Of course, the staff at Rowman & Littlefield that recognized the value of this manuscript will cause me to feel grateful for the rest of my life because they made this book possible. I am thankful for the three anonymous book reviewers who pushed me to improve the quality of this book to a higher level.

Finally, this book is replete with scientific research on religion and spirituality. The blossoming of hundreds of scientific research studies on various aspects of religion and spirituality has given most of the concepts validity. I thank those researchers for their efforts. Their research has brought a new understanding.

This book has been developing for many years and I am sure there are other people who contributed that I many not recall at the moment. I am so very grateful.

Foreword

Dr. Steven Vazquez and I have known each other for over twenty years. In the early 90s, I remember looking into one of his first-generation light devices. Although the device was interesting, its effect on me was minimal. Twenty years later, I watched him use his much-refined light device on participants at a workshop. Now I was impressed! People reported marked reduction in chronic pain after very short exposures to selected lights. One woman reported and demonstrated an increased range of motion in her neck. Placebo? Maybe. Suggestion? Maybe. But definitely worth studying.

As of the writing of this Foreword, *Spiritually Transformative Psychotherapy* is supported by many scientific studies referenced in this book, but the processes themselves are only now entering the research phase—2015. It is not manualized, and adequately designed treatment outcome studies have been described in a peer-reviewed journal only once. Some of the observations made—and the explanations given—by Dr. Vazquez in this book will be found incredible to the more pertinacious among us. Undoubtedly, scientists and academics without firsthand experience would minimize his results. Why then would I agree to write this Foreword? Going out on a limb is not an easy thing to do. Taking the heat and backlash, à la Dr. Oz, may be foolhardy, but I'm up for it.

The foundation of Dr. Vazquez's therapy method, ETT®, is built of many stones. Much of what he does is just good psychotherapy, as when he is doing individual grief work or couples counseling. This component of the foundation is good, solid psychotherapy, combining psychodynamic, cognitive, and systems approaches with emotionally focused therapy.

Another stone in the foundation is Dr. Vazquez's interest in spiritual matters, comparative religion, altered states of consciousness, paranormal phenomena, and related subject areas. Here, he operates as a scholar.

Again, though scientists may scoff, to me this reaction only demonstrates closed-mindedness.

The third, and to me most interesting foundation stone, is the light method. Dr. Vazquez's device generates light that can be varied in intensity, color, and hue. By trial and error, he has developed an extensive catalog of light settings that affect people in different ways—with variability from person to person.

What is so interesting about this? I look at Dr. Vazquez's theory as a testable scientific hypothesis, one that, if validated experimentally, could generate a whole new field of study. The theory states several things: (1) there are multiple nerve pathways in the brain leading from the retina to locations beyond the visual cortex, (2) these pathways have evolutionary utility and have been selected for (3) a wide range of brain-body physiological processes are regulated by incoming light, and 4) Dr. Vazquez's light device can be used to regulate these systems.

Using light to treat seasonal affective disorder is a mainstream, accepted treatment modality in psychiatry. Perhaps, we have just scratched the surface in this regard. Maybe Dr. Vazquez has opened a window into a wide and deep universe, in which a finely tuned light can be shone on the retina for a variety of purposes.

Dr. Vazquez's light treatment model is based on a set of scientifically testable hypotheses. Scientists have already studied how light stimulation applied in the brain could facilitate psychological changes through optogenetics. This involves activating brain cells by placing light-activating stimuli into the brain. However, ETT® achieves this by precise external visual stimulation. But it should be investigated, because if he is correct, this kind of light therapy could be a very useful gift to humankind. The brain physiology and neural pathways proposed in the theory could be investigated with the standard procedures of neuroanatomy, neurophysiology, and neuropsychology. Experiments could be done using functional magnetic resonance imaging (fMRI), electroencephalography (EEG), positron emission tomography (PET), single photon emission computed tomography (SPECT), or other brain-scanning techniques. Different light settings could be used in various sequences, one acting as a control condition for the other, using the standard research designs of experimental psychology with different self-report outcome measures such as Subjective Units of Distress (SUD) scales. For pain studies, analgesic and narcotic consumption during baseline and follow-up phases would be suitable outcome measures.

Now we get to the really extraordinary! In a clinical setting, Dr. Vazquez reports that patients using his interpersonal light treatment have had the biology of their cancer affected in a therapeutic fashion. Although psychosocial factors in cancer treatment have previously been scientifically documented, with patients showing an increased survival rate in response to psychosocial interventions, this takes therapy one step further.

A closed-minded refusal of experience and observation is not helpful. Dr. Vasquez's approach could be tested scientifically using the standard methodology and procedures of mainstream science. That should be done. The problem, of course, is, "Who is going to pay for it?" That is a political, cultural, sociological, and business problem—not a scientific problem.

This brings me to the ETT® samadhi process, another foundation stone of the book and of Spiritually Transformative Psychotherapy—and another set of extraordinary observations. These, however, should be documented scientifically by the time this book is published. Please check Appendix C for more information regarding research on ETT®.

So, for me, the correct attitude is similar to the principle of therapeutic neutrality I advocate in psychotherapy—I neither believe nor disbelieve what Dr. Vazquez is saying. But I think he has created something very interesting, very creative and, in reality, unique. I think his theory should be taken seriously and investigated seriously.

By the time this book is published, a series of studies will be underway or will have been completed which will provide more scientific evidence for the treatment model. The method will then be in transition from being non-validated to being evidence-based. A study nearly completed as of this writing is a 100-cases series treated with ETT®. Studies that should be up and running by the time of publication of the book include a neuroimaging study of the Samadhi process; a study of ETT for chronic pain at a major medical school; and a study on ETT for posttraumatic stress disorder (PTSD). These studies confirm my point that Dr. Vazquez's treatment method is based on a set of scientifically testable hypotheses.

Colin A. Ross, M.D.,
June 16, 2015

Introduction

The desperate search to "feel good" has become all-consuming. People suffering from chronic medical conditions will often try anything to feel good. The psychiatric drug industry makes billions of dollars selling people "feel good" medicine. For some of those who have been unsuccessful in finding anything to make them feel good, suicide has been their choice. While the need to escape emotional challenges prompts many of these behaviors; nonetheless, the quest is to feel good. Some people even pursue spirituality in order to feel good. The unfortunate paradox is that human beings possess the inherent capacity to feel good. This book is largely about new ways to access states of extreme well-being from within.

The widespread growth of mental health conditions in the United States and Europe has occurred in spite of the dominance of medication for these disorders. This has happened at the same time that fewer people affiliate themselves with a traditional religion and more people describe themselves as spiritual. The popular use of the Internet has made access to awareness of different religious and spiritual orientations more available than ever before. In addition, within the last two decades an impressive amount of scientific research has been applied to religious and spiritual experiences. Within this context of change, counseling and psychotherapy have entered the religious and spiritual domain, which is a complete departure from the previous separation between the two fields. Instead of imposing a particular religious position, more and more counselors support an individual's religious orientation or help the client explore this area when problems related to spirituality occur. This book is about how to support a person's spiritual orientation, if one exists, and when desired, deepen it, make it more powerful in meaningful ways while speeding up this characteristically long journey into a practical and deeper faith. This approach is particularly valuable for people who are spiritual but not involved in a traditional religion. However, even people without a spiritual orientation may benefit from an exploration into their deepest inner selves.

Virtually all the major religions advocate some form of prayer or meditation and engage in what I shall refer to as contemplative practices. Current research on these practices has scientifically verified that many of these practices can profoundly change the brain, especially certain forms of meditation. However, achieving the ultimate goal of any contemplative approach requires months or years of daily practice. These varieties of ultimate spiritual experiences include, but are not limited to, (1) direct contact with the divine or pure consciousness; (2) resolution of numerous medical conditions; (3) access to any and all experiences of ecstasy, peace, or euphoria—known to be produced temporarily by drugs; and (4) elevated abilities of a supernormal quality. Realistically, very few people will meditate daily for years to achieve these outcomes. However, this new approach offers availability of these profound benefits, and it does not require the length of time it takes with traditional methods.

One common practice ties together almost all the saints and religious leaders of different faiths who have described well-known spiritual experiences. All of them dedicated years of daily contemplative experiences to their quest: Jesus, Buddha, Saint Teresa of Avila, Mohammed, Yogananda, Saint Julian of Norwich, Guru Muktananda, and others. The Dalai Lama once said that he meditates four hours per day but that he would gladly meditate for less time if it would achieve the same outcome. Current evidence supports the idea that the ETT® samadhi process tends to accomplish the same goal as countless hours of meditation, but in substantially less time. In addition, this process can be modified to each person's religious or spiritual orientation. It can also be applied to the treatment of a wide variety of psychological issues and conditions.

To resolve distress, most people have not chosen contemplative practices but have opted for the quick fix provided by drugs, plant medicine, or technological approaches. While some of these approaches may provide a brief glimpse of the divine, they are only temporary, have significant side-effects, are frequently illegal, and sometimes potentially lethal. A far more beneficial approach, the one offered in this book, could be described as follows:

- wholly natural
- arising from the ancient wisdom of contemplative processes
- able to access ultimate psychospiritual experiences within a single session
- lasting for months
- causing no chemically induced side-effects

The usual reaction to these claims is that it sounds too good to be true. In this case, they are true; however, the process that produces these wonderful effects may also produce a disorientation that requires adjustments. Nonetheless, a renewal of contemplative approaches awaits those who have dropped out or never consistently engaged in contemplative prayer or meditation. Amplifying the speed of success will provide help for the millions who want to "feel good." This contemplative approach can complement other contemplative practices, replace them, or introduce the experience when none exists for a client.

Before a rapid contemplative process can bring about states of extreme well-being for the client, contamination of the process should ideally be avoided by unloading the unresolved emotions buried in the psyche. Although religion often addresses the need for forgiveness, the evidence—of violence, divorce, and medical consequences of resentment—suggests that conventional religious forgiveness has not worked well in many areas. The permanent and rapid removal of this type of distress is what the new ETT® method does best. It takes forgiveness to a new level.

The relationship between recovery from medical conditions and spiritual rebirth can often be found in the challenge of recovering from life-threatening illnesses. Scientific evidence concerning stress-related factors in medical conditions is abundant but rarely mentioned by most doctors. If it is mentioned, pills are offered as the remedy. With proper guidance, the excursion into the existential crisis of potential death opens the way for a possible spiritual rebirth. Contemplative practices can be a catalyst for this change.

One of the most important focal points of this book is that the outcomes of this amplified contemplative approach can be so extraordinary that few people are prepared for their outcomes. For example, literally hearing God's voice can make people think they are going crazy since hearing voices today is usually seen as a symptom of psychosis. These controversies will be thoroughly explored through scientific research, theory, and case examples. When the mind's potential is accelerated, extended human abilities can be produced. This journey usually requires guidance. To integrate and adjust to newly found capacities before their benefits are lost, a person usually needs a guidebook such as the one offered here.

The primary audience of this book consists of professional counselors, marriage and family therapists, psychologists, psychiatrists, social workers, and people who are mental health providers. Additionally, ministers, priests, pastoral counselors, spiritual directors, and rabbis will find it useful. It is specifically intended for mental health professionals who are trained in the method of Emotional Transformation Therapy® (ETT®). In fact, training in

ETT® is a prerequisite for its optimal use. Anyone going through spiritual experiences and needing more understanding will also find it valuable.

The book is designed to be read in sequential order with the first four chapters providing the basic foundation for the rest of the book. Chapter 1 is about the role of psychotherapy in religion and spirituality and it is replete with scientific findings on religion. It includes information on the ethical adaptation of counseling for people of varying religious/spiritual orientations, even atheists and agnostics.

Chapter 2 is a necessary foundation for the rest of the book because it describes the unique counseling method of ETT®. It is the use of this method that greatly impacts the speed and power of the counseling process. This form of interpersonal visual brain stimulation can be applied to a wide variety of psychological conditions and can provoke spiritual awakenings. The fundamentals of this new paradigm in counseling are supported by research, theory, and case illustrations. ETT® can provide an exceedingly rapid and in-depth process that facilitates long-term change through memory reconsolidation. This approach literally transforms distressing emotions, which facilitates rapid changes in dysfunctional cognition, behavior, and somatic symptoms.

Chapter 3 describes one of the most consistent and potent applications for ETT®—forgiveness. While forgiveness remains an important area of focus in almost every major religion, research shows that it is generally not very well understood or successful. This chapter provides supportive scientific research, theory, and case studies illustrating the use of ETT® for forgiveness. This chapter provides an entirely new level of understanding for accomplishing authentic forgiveness.

Chapter 4 reveals the ETT® samadhi process, a spiritually transformative contemplative procedure that is a foundation for the rest of the book. Using case examples, the introduction to this radically new contemplative process includes a description of its nature and the variety of states of extreme wellbeing that are possible.

Chapter 5 further describes the ETT® samadhi process in the context of known psychological, theological, and spiritual research. The ETT® samadhi process is compared to brainwave biofeedback, hypnosis, meditation, prayer, and elements of the near-death experience. Then the characteristics of the ETT® samadhi process are explored in the quantum physics context of time, space, and energy. Most importantly, the concept of psychological absorption and levels of states of consciousness are explored to explain the phenomena of samadhi.

Chapter 6 addresses the phenomenon of hearing voices and pursues issues concerning the differences and similarities between psychosis and spirituality. New research places conventional symptoms of hearing audibly clear voices internally in a new light. It also considers some psychotic states and spiritual states as part of an overarching transliminal state. The chapter is filled with documented research regarding these issues. How to understand both spiritual and psychotic voices and how to work with these voices are explored.

Chapter 7 focuses on how to counsel cancer patients for optimal outcomes. There is abundant scientific research on psychological, social, and spiritual aspects of the cause, duration, and treatment of cancer. This chapter translates these research findings into pragmatic counseling approaches, regardless of the medical treatment method that is being used. When potential death appears imminent, people often seek guidance for existential or spiritual issues. This opportunity for growth can turn the challenge of cancer into a "rebirth" experience. The chapter discusses how to use psychotherapy to increase both the quality of life and the survival rate.

Regardless of how great a spiritual experience has been, if a person's change negatively impacts relationships with people who matter most, it can become a problem. Chapter 8 examines the ways in which spiritual differences can produce conflict in couple relationships. Through numerous case studies and psychological theory, ways to constructively intervene in couple conflict are described. Integrating our inner spiritual world with our outer relationships world is the goal of this chapter.

The last chapter concerns the variety of extended human abilities, or "spiritual gifts," that may occur after spiritual awakenings. These extended abilities are explored through scientific research, cross-cultural evidence, theological perspectives, and case studies. These include phenomena such as unusual contact with elements of nature, glossolalia, prophecy, after-death communication, contact with angels, spiritual guides, Jesus or God, astral travel, telepathy, and spiritual healing. The role of counseling may be to soothe and normalize these occurrences when clients fear that they are going crazy. Guidance about how to keep people focused on their authentic spiritual paths regardless of the unusual nature of these "gifts" is provided.

In all of the case studies described in this book the client's names have been changed and identifying characteristics are eliminated to protect their privacy. However, all reports in case studies are completely true to the best of my recollection. Readers of this book should not attempt to use the methods and techniques described herein without being a licensed mental health professional and have undergone specialized training in some cases. An attempt was made to provide respect to all religious and spiritual points of view, and any bias shown has been unintentional.

Built on centuries of contemplative practice and a new form of psychotherapy, the method offered in this book has the power to amplify the intrinsic potential of the human experience. Combining old and new, this psychospiritual technology can relieve an apparently endless list of psychological and medical problems. The goal of expeditious relief becomes a possibility for many when it is no longer delayed by countless years of meditation. The sky is not the limit, the universe is.

Chapter One

Religion, Spirituality, and Psychotherapy

"My husband's death was expected, but then a year later my son committed suicide, my house burned to the ground, and finally, the next year my adult daughter died. I don't have anybody anymore. I can't stop crying, everyday for the last year. I can't sleep at night. How could a God let this happen? I don't think I believe in God anymore. I am not sure what I think about life after death, past lives, or any of that. I don't respect traditional religion enough to talk to a minister or priest, and I knew you from years before, so I came here. I just want to stop crying and to be able to sleep."

Lynette represents many people in today's society who are bright, aware, and knowledgeable and who might describe themselves as "spiritual but not religious." Nonetheless, spiritual issues arise in their lives, and often they do not want to explore their problems with a traditional religious authority. Fortunately, I was able to bring her grief to conclusion and facilitate normal sleep as she worked through her spiritual issues.

On October 9, 2012, I opened my local newspaper and found a front-page article reporting research by the Pew Forum on Religious and Public Life about religion in the United States (Zoll, 2012). It said that for the first time in the history of the United States, less than fifty percent of the population identified themselves as Protestant. For the first time the number of Americans who have no religion rose to over twenty percent. The only exception to the decline of church identification was the growth of nondenominational churches which were not classified as traditional Protestant. Simultaneously, recent research shows that the number of people describing themselves as spiritual, but not religious, has grown. These self-described spiritual people do not have access to churches in times of distress, which creates a need for another means of coping with distress that may involve spiritual issues.

On May 12, 2015, a major scientific survey of thousands of Americans found that there has been a decline in the number of people who identify themselves as Christians. The decline has been occurring in every major region of the United States, including the Bible Belt, as well as in every major ethnic group. Since 2007 the move from 78.4 to 71 percent is approximately a decline of about five million. The greatest loss has occurred in mainline Catholic and Protestant churches, while the number of atheists and agnostics has doubled (Pew Research Center, May 2015). At the same time the number of people who have dabbled in meditation has grown substantially, but only a tiny portion meditated regularly. This current trend may be interpreted as a loss of interest in traditional institutions but an increase in spiritual interest.

Some believe that the United States has undergone a change from a nation of spiritual dwellers to spiritual questers, a change that began in the 1960s. Spiritual dwelling refers to the sacred as a secure, rooted, stable force participated in through religious tradition in the local community. Spiritual questing, however, involves searching for the sacred by questioning religious institutions and looking for new spiritual practices and meanings. A third model involves the integration of spiritual dwelling and spiritual seeking. In the integration of these models of spiritual activities, the process of transformation is the focus of sacred quests, which involves exploration of dwelling and seeking (Wuthernow, 1998). Evidence suggests that there is a shift from dwelling to seeking in the general U.S. population, and if this continues, the general religious/spiritual landscape in the future will be one of spiritual consumers who will choose spiritual orientations based on what works best, not on what tradition must be followed. If prayer and meditation develop into forms that demonstrate better functional outcomes in daily life, these forms of practice are expected to increase.

These changes in U.S. demographics occurred in conjunction with the inclusion of religious issues and spiritual issues in the *Diagnostic and Statistical Manual for Psychiatric Disorders* IV—a move giving official recognition to spiritual and religious issues as foci in psychotherapy. Concurrently, a rising number of professional journals are combining religion and spirituality with psychology, and the number of professional books on these subjects has seen a rapid upsurge. In addition, the number of scientific studies on every aspect of religion or spirituality has recently grown exponentially. This is a major shift in which religious/spiritual matters have become the focus of scientific inquiry.

In order to discuss spirituality and religion, it is helpful to identify some general definitions of these terms in order to provide a consensus of their meanings. Cashwell & Young define spirituality as "the universal human capacity to experience self-transcendence and awareness of sacred immanence, with resulting increases in greater self-other compassion and love" (2011, p. 7). However, the relationship between spirituality and religion poses a high degree of varying opinions. Religion can be seen as "institutional and creedal, and is typically socially defined. Religion provides a structure for human spirituality, including narratives, symbols, beliefs, and practices, which are embedded in ancestral traditions, cultural traditions, or both" (Cashwell & Young, 2011, p. 9). In recent years, there has been a growing perception that spirituality is distinctly different from religiosity.

Even though religious and/or spiritual issues are now appropriate topics for psychotherapy, this does not mean that all therapists are automatically competent in these areas. In fact, research has shown that mental health professionals are significantly less identified with traditional religion than the general U.S. public (Delaney, Miller, & Bisono, 2007). Therefore, various professional mental health organizations have developed ethical standards and basic competency standards for mental health professionals who choose to conduct counseling on these topics. The following is a list of competencies developed and adopted by the Association for Spiritual, Ethical, and Religious Values:

Factor 1: Cultural Worldview

- The professional counselor can describe the similarities and differences between spirituality and religion, including the basic beliefs of various spiritual systems, major world religions, agnosticism, and atheism.
- The professional counselor recognizes that the client's beliefs (or absence of beliefs) about spirituality and/or religion are central to his or her worldview and can influence psychosocial functioning.

Factor 2: Counselor Self-Awareness

- The professional counselor actively explores his or her own attitudes, beliefs, and values about spirituality and/or religion.
- The professional counselor continuously evaluates the influence of his or her own spiritual and/or religious beliefs and values on the client and the counseling process.
- The professional counselor can identify the limits of his or her understanding of the client's spiritual and/or religious perspective and is acquainted with religious and spiritual resources, including leaders who can be avenues for consultation and to whom the counselor can refer.

Factor 3: Human and Spiritual Development

- The professional counselor can describe and apply various models of spiritual and/or religious development and their relationship to human development.

Factor 4: Communication

- The professional counselor responds to client communications about spirituality and/or religion with acceptance and sensitivity.

- The professional counselor uses spiritual and/or religious concepts that are consistent with the client's spiritual and/or religious perspectives and that are acceptable to the client.
- The professional counselor can recognize spiritual and/or religious themes in client communication and is able to address these with the client when they are therapeutically relevant.

Factor 5: Assessment

- During the intake and assessment process, the professional counselor strives to understand a client's spiritual and/or religious perspective by gathering information from the client and/or other sources.

Factor 6: Diagnosis and Treatment

- When making a diagnosis, the professional counselor recognizes that the client's spiritual and/or religious perspectives can (1) enhance well-being, (2) contribute to client problems, and/or (3) exacerbate symptoms.
- The professional counselor sets goals with the client that are consistent with the client's spiritual and/or religious perspectives.
- The professional counselor is able to (1) modify therapeutic techniques to include a client's spiritual and/or religious perspectives, and (2) utilize spiritual and/or religious practices as techniques when appropriate and acceptable to a client's viewpoint.

The professional counselor can therapeutically apply theory and current research supporting the inclusion of a client's spiritual and/or religious perspectives and practices. Note: The ASERVIC Competencies for Addressing Spiritual and Religious Issues in Counseling, Copyright© 2009 by the Association for Spiritual, Ethical, and Religious Values in Counseling. Reprinted with permission.

ADAPTING TO A CLIENT'S ORIENTATION

Several categories of religious/spiritual orientation require specific adaptations in a counseling relationship in order to provide optimum benefits. These include, but are not limited to, working with the following:

- people who are spiritual, but not religious
- people whose views are outside the therapist's religious/spiritual orientation
- people whose views are the same as the therapist's view
- people who are not religious, such as atheists or agnostics
- people who feel damaged by religious leaders or religious communities
- people who feel negatively affected by a religious tradition
- people who have destructive or dangerous religious views or behaviors

- people who have significant religious/spiritual conflicts with their spouse or close relationships
- people who attend psychotherapy for the purpose of seeking a spiritual direction or fulfillment

These different types of spiritual and religious orientation can challenge the adaptability of the therapist.

When the need for a confidant arises, often a minister, priest, or rabbi is, understandably, avoided by those seeking help. For example, issues of sexual affairs, sexual preference, or the anguish of depression may evoke a reluctance to disclose to church authorities. Some people fear that these issues risk how the religious authority might view the person after disclosure. In fact, many ministers, priests, and rabbis may not have much training, skill, or interest in the personal counseling role of their ministry. In recent years, these issues of psychological distress have motivated many churches to have specialized "family centers" that provide professional counseling, especially marriage counseling. Church counselors at family centers may or may not have a high level of skill. Being a member of a church and a licensed counselor for its population presents the issue of a dual relationship, a relationship outside of the licensure rules of most mental health professionals. As a result of these various problems, many people are motivated to look outside their churches for professional counseling.

HYPOCRISY AND RELIGION

The criticism that churches and religious people are hypocritical is often cited as a reason people leave religion. The existence of religious hypocrisy in certain groups may have some validity. As far as the impact of religion upon its participants, research has been done on "religious hypocrisy." In one study that included Protestant, Jewish, and Roman Catholics, people were divided into several groups:

- frequent attendees with strong religious motivation
- infrequent attendees with strong religious motivation
- frequent attendees with low religious motivation
- infrequent attendees with low religious motivation

Of the four groups, the frequent attendees without strong motivation showed the poorest psychological functioning, including the greatest sense of control by powerful others and chance, the lowest sense of efficacy, trust in others, personal control, and active coping skills (Pargament, Steele, & Tyler, 1979).

This study and others (Ryan, Rigby, & King, 1993) indicated that the incongruency between beliefs and behaviors, regarding the application of religious beliefs, has measured detrimental effects and confirms that hypocrisy is problematic. However, for those people who showed congruency, participation in religious institutions showed measured benefits.

These research findings do not support the contention that all people in Christian churches exhibit hypocrisy, although it was found to exist in some people. To assume that hypocrisy is the norm in all Christian churches is a generalization about all church participants that is not supported by research findings. This does not rule out that hypocrisy may exist pervasively in certain churches not included in the studies, but this idea is only speculation. The degree of hostility some people possess about church hypocrisy suggests psychological projection emerging from either internal incongruities or from previous negative experiences that remain emotionally unresolved. Sometimes people displace upsetting emotions, moving them away from people toward whom they do not wish to direct negative feelings and then re-directing the disturbance toward an institution such as religion. This is sometimes known as scapegoating or displacement. However, this process is often not conscious to the person, and only a form of psychotherapy designed to uncover this process can assist in correcting it. Nonetheless, this stereotyping of religion has often developed into a perceived "fact" by some people who believe they can cleverly detect what others "foolishly" fail to recognize.

From a psychological point of view, negative experiences with any type of group may cause people to conclude that a particular type of negative experience will always occur with the offensive group. As long as unresolved emotions are intact, there will be a need to avoid the encounter again. However, if psychotherapy could help to eliminate the unresolved emotions, those affected might be able to discern positive versus negative elements of a group without stereotyping everyone associated with such groups. Then, if participation in these religious groups offers benefits, the option to choose to participate may become a consideration. The problem may not be with religion per se, but with any group members who are incongruent with their beliefs and behaviors. The challenge of seeing beyond the stereotype of hypocrisy becomes even more difficult when those who exhibited hypocrisy have been parents or others whose behavior exhibited repeated incongruence and in an obvious fashion. Nonetheless, if other elements of religion may be of significant benefit, it is possible to resolve the hypocrisy disturbance to make religion of some type desirable as an option. The hypocrisy issue forces many people to look outside of religious institutions for help.

RELIGIOUS COPING

Abundant scientific research supports the idea that the majority of people seek comfort from religion or spirituality as a means of coping with stress. Statistically, it is clear that far more people seek help in the form of religion when under stress than the number of people who seek psychotherapy. This primarily takes the form of prayer, but may also be social support through churches (Koenig, George, & Titus, 2004; Shuster, Stein, & Jaycox, 2001; Tepper et al., 2001). Since religion is the major source of coping for most Americans and prayer is the major religious method for coping that people report as helpful, advances in meditation/prayer might tap into an important resource. With the continual decline in traditional church identification, how to fill the void for those in need of coping skills becomes an important question. While pharmaceuticals are widely used, they cannot replace the need for social support. For many people personal counseling can fill the void. Therefore, spiritual issues more frequently spill over into the psychological counseling domain. Since people tend to use prayer more than other religious means during a crisis, it would be valuable for psychotherapists to provide an inner process that can be shown to facilitate help during crises.

Developmental issues in religion or spirituality can be the source of internal conflicts which an adult client often fails to recognize. Religion is usually taught and explained to young children in ways that are age appropriate so that children can comprehend it. For example, moral issues may be explained in simplistic black and white terms because that is what they can understand. Imaginary characters and storytelling help children understand. In some faiths it is believed that children already know certain spiritual information that they tend to lose as they grow up. For example, in Tibetan Buddhism, it is assumed that past life experiences are recalled at a very early age but forgotten as children grow up. Nonetheless, children are too young to understand most religious concepts except in their most basic forms. There are several ways this can prove problematic. If a child is told that Jesus will always protect them while at the same time that child is being sexually abused by a parent, uncle, or another adult, the religious message may be interpreted as a lie. An adult whose religious activities never went beyond the age of nine or ten will be left with only a child's perspective of religion, a view that may appear ridiculous to an adult. Then the adult may tend to stereotype all religious ideas as simplistic and irrelevant to adult life. However, if a person has the opportunity to experience a mature religious philosophy that matches his or her age, it can appear realistic.

Many times young children will interpret religious language quite differently from the intended adult meaning. When psychiatrist Carl Jung was a child, he attended his uncle's funeral. When the minister said, "We give this body to Christ," little Carl thought Christ was a man-eater. This message caused great fear of Jesus and religion in general for many years. In a case of mine, a young mother was diagnosed with breast cancer. She was a devout Christian and prayed with her son every night. However, she noticed that her four-year-old son had become very "clingy" and often seemed frightened. I asked, "Please explain to me how you pray with him?" She reported that among other things they prayed that God would heal her cancer. I noticed that her voice tone was one of a pleading, frightened nature. Therefore, I told her that her son may be sensing her fear. Then I suggested that she focus prayers on hope and gratitude. She did this. Two weeks later she reported that her son was no longer clingy or frightened. Her four-year-old son was at a developmental phase that was highly influenced by the parent's experience. People exposed to religion during childhood and adolescence, who subsequently receive no other religious information as an adult, are likely to have distorted views based on their level of learning from an earlier age.

A NOTE ON THE MODEL OF TREATMENT USED

The rest of this chapter and the case studies in this book are unlikely to be understood completely without understanding the unique counseling method that was used to facilitate those changes. A more detailed description of the method used is described in the author's first two books, *Emotional Transformation Therapy* and *Accelerated Ecological Psychotherapy.* This Emotional Transformation Therapy® (ETT®) method routinely facilitates relief of emotional distress within minutes, which is often difficult for people to accept as fact without having had a direct experience of it. ETT® fosters spiritual experiences somewhat frequently as a by-product of its process without directly pursuing spiritual outcomes. As the development of this treatment evolved, this author learned to purposely target spiritual and religious issues, which led to the writing of this book. Most of the outcomes would sound too good to be true without a direct experience of this method. Therefore, this context for all the case studies described herein should be taken into account. Reading the two previous books on ETT® and the summary in Chapter 2 of this book may help the reader to accept the profound phenomena described in case studies recounted in this book.

THE DARK SIDE OF RELIGION

In my practice, I have encountered as many people who are angry at traditional churches and religion as I have encountered those who love their churches and would die for their religion. There is passion about the subject either way. Even those people who are atheists or agnostics may often feel strongly about spiritual or religious issues, so in this way it really matters to them. This fervor becomes a psychological issue because feelings, thoughts, and beliefs can bring distress or peace. The false separation between religion and psychotherapy has largely come to an end within the last decade in the United States.

John flew in to see me for a week of psychotherapy sessions. He was a bright young attractive man who was very successful in his business. John was gay but not currently in a relationship. After taking a brief history and discovering his symptoms, John told me about his sexual abuse history:

> I was an altar boy at my Catholic church where my family were devoted Catholics. I was raped by the priest on more than one occasion. He convinced me that I should cooperate because nobody would believe me if I told what happened. I was only fourteen and I felt scared not to go along with it (weeping). I need help because I am anxious all the time, have no self-confidence, and can't get those memories out of my mind.

John is one of several people I have counseled who were sexually abused by a minister, priest, or rabbi. John had eliminated anything religious from his life and had discarded any religious philosophy altogether. However, he responded very well to therapy and most of his symptoms abated within the brief time I saw him.

When sexual abuse, rape, or other intrusive behaviors are perpetrated onto members of a church, synagogue, or temple by a priest, rabbi, minister or others in church authority, the consequences can be devastating. The trauma sequelae from rape or sexual abuse are well known. However, when the perpetrator was a person in religious authority, it tends to also contaminate religious or spiritual resources as well as a personal relationship with God. As with all traumatic experiences, symptoms tend to be triggered by symbols or cues that are reminders of the trauma. Therefore, when the trauma is over, and even when it has been effectively processed in psychotherapy, religious or spiritual trauma tends to contaminate spiritual perspective and often remains compromised for the rest of the person's life, if not treated. Religious personnel are typically ruled out as a source for help by these survivors because of a generalized lack of trust for religious people. This situation places people in need for religious or spiritual repair, but help might be restricted to professionals outside of churches like psychotherapists skilled in these issues.

Religious cult abuse can be one of the most confusing and frightening experiences of all. I have worked with over fifty cases of people who claimed to be victims of satanic cult abuse, as well as many other people who reported being coerced into various religious groups where brainwashing was purported to have taken place. In many cases, I have little or no corroborating evidence of the accuracy of these recollections, but in other cases there is corroborating evidence that this occurred. Whatever the truth of the matter, it is the therapist's job to heal these people if that is why they entered treatment. These cult abuse victims have been responsive to ETT® (to be explained in Chapter 2) when all other forms of therapy were either partially successful or not helpful at all. These victims may generalize their fears to all religious figures, which often makes them seek help from a neutral religious guide. In other cases, these clients prefer religious help. However, religious figures are often ill-equipped to help this type of survivor. Therefore, psychotherapy that can be applied to reversing brainwashing can be particularly valuable for these people.

Many people believe that the religion of their particular church provides the right and only way to believe and that anyone outside of their church is wrong, evil, and an enemy. Although some people have learned to be politically correct in public, the mixing of faiths, as in interfaith marriages, can be very challenging. The news media reported a case in which a Church of Christ follower found out that his daughter was marrying a Baptist man, and then the father committed suicide. While the scientific research shows that an internally congruent religious belief provides many benefits, it can have serious risks when its inflexibility contributes to suicide or illness.

Many people suffer from unresolved issues about religion or spirituality that contribute to their mental health issues. In some cases, people's religious/spiritual (R/S) orientation or concepts about God do not provide enough skills or knowledge to help them effectively cope with life's challenges. A concept of God that is too small or narrow is not helpful. In other cases, R/S concepts are in conflict with other values. For example, adopting the belief that homosexuality is sinful while still participating in homosexuality produces a destructive inner conflict. Believing that anyone of a different denomination is condemned to hell, and thus wicked, can negatively impact relationships when that person is forced to work and/or be friends with those of different faiths. In this case, a narrow faith may make it difficult to live with others in a positive manner. In other cases if the experience of spiritual events does not match the religious belief, a person may become stagnated in inner conflict. In any of these instances, it may be helpful to explore confusing religious issues with a psychotherapist who is unbiased so that these issues can be explored without an agenda.

CLERGY FAMILIES

The families of clergy often suffer stressors different from other families. Children of clergy are often at risk. Clergy family members are often expected to be available to people in the congregation day and night, seven days a week (Darling, Hill, & McWye, 2004; Hileman, 2008; Hill, Darling, & Raimondi, 2003). This demand of time can leave the needs of the family unmet (Darling, Hill, & McWye, 2004). Other clergy family issues include the following:

- Clergy spouses feel unable to confide in members of the church community for political reasons, which places a greater burden on the family for coping (Hileman, 2008).
- Public scrutiny of the family places pressure on the family to appear perfect (Hileman, 2008).
- A lack of social support increases the likelihood that the marital relationship will be the primary means of coping.
- Boundaries between home and church are often absent, which may internalize as dysfunctional boundaries for children of clergy (Hileman, 2008).

These and other issues place members of clergy at risk. While evidence suggests substantial benefits for those people who participate in churches, the unique position of clergy families often makes family members vulnerable to psychological dysfunctions. Sometimes clergy family members might need the comfort of disclosing their issues to a skilled professional outside the church in order to feel safe and to avoid a negative political impact on people in the church.

FATHER GARY'S CASE

Father Gary was a fifty-five-year-old Episcopal priest who entered psychotherapy to talk through some issues. He was a bright, articulate, compassionate man who was plagued by migraine headaches. Fr. Gary was well liked by his parishioners and his family. However, several unfortunate events in the church did not go the way he wanted, and he was particularly disturbed by the dysfunction of his grown children.

In the course of our session, he became aware that he had intense anger at God. When I supported Fr. Gary to express his feelings, he let out a long and intense diatribe of anger at God.

I asked if he felt any discomfort about verbalizing such anger at God. He said no and that he believed God could handle it. Fr. Gary then said, "I certainly couldn't voice this anger where my parishioners could hear it." By the end of the session Fr. Gary felt much better. After his verbalization, he felt at peace with God.

A number of issues may arise when a person has a profound R/S awakening or when a person departs from the church that directly impacts the stability of his or her family. Although there is recent disagreement, Jesus never got married or had children, and the original Buddha left his wife and child to follow his spiritual quest. Spiritual role models for good marriages are somewhat lacking. When spiritual awakenings occur, it can affect one's family in a unitive or divisive manner. There has been a movement in some Christian churches to promote marriage reconciliation and to place "God first" in marriages. Both marriage and divorce are often affected by R/S orientation. Most often in my practice I have seen people who were disillusioned by some aspect of religion but who were still seeking direction for their spiritual path. Whatever they may find, it will affect their families. If religion or spirituality itself has become a factor in a relationship in which one partner is religious and the other is not, a counselor outside that church may be the most even-handed mediator.

In my local Dallas area, there are many counselors who call themselves "Christian counselors" or "faith-based counselors." The meaning of this phrase can range from those who use only Biblical scripture in their counseling to those conventional counselors whose religion is a Christian denomination. Since well-known figures in psychology like Sigmund Freud and Albert Ellis have denounced religion as pathology, many preachers warn their members about secular counseling. This warning causes many people to fear that secular counselors will attempt to change their religious values. While this can certainly happen, it is not the intention of this work to advocate taking a person's religious values away. However, if a person is projecting issues of avoidance, narcissism, shame, obsessive-compulsive disorder, or other dysfunctional conditions onto religion, religion can simply be the means through which these pathologies are acted out. In fact, if a person could be relieved of these adverse conditions, religious values could be lived at a more fulfilling level. Psychotherapy can enhance religious values.

MARY'S CASE

Mary was a friendly, forty-five-year-old married woman with sparkly eyes who came to therapy for the relief of several symptoms—generalized daily anxiety, negative self-perception, and some depression symptoms. She was an active member of a fundamentalist Christian church. She entered psychotherapy with dubious concern that professional counselors outside of her church might try to undermine her religious values. We used the ETT® method because of the speed and depth necessary to facilitate long-term healing. During the session, any mention of concepts outside the realm of her Christian philosophy caused her to object, a situation which I accepted and then sought a different direction. By the end of the first session she felt calmer, and her self-esteem had been elevated.

In the second session, it became clear that much of her distress revolved around her disagreement with her husband, but nonetheless her compliance and fear of speaking up dominated. It was more about her lack of communicating than his overbearing nature because he really didn't ask much. Her husband was invited to the third session, and I observed that her husband was flexible, but she remained conflicted within. Therefore, couple therapy brought little help. During her sessions I recognized that she would quote scripture or use religious concepts as a means to avoid anything uncomfortable. After a few sessions, Mary was sold on therapy and our bond because she had improved significantly.

In the fourth session, when she used her religion as an avoidance defense, I thought our bond was good enough to risk confronting her. Therefore, when she made her protest on the basis that a concept was against her religion, I said, "This has nothing to do with religion. You are misusing religious ideas for the purpose of avoiding issues that, if resolved, will ultimately help you. Please consider talking about this, so I can help you."

This was followed by a pregnant pause. I knew that either I had lost her as a client or our therapy would reach a new depth. Then Mary agreed. From that point on we achieved a new therapeutic depth, and in the next two sessions completely resolved her anxiety, depression, and mainly her poor self-esteem and ability to speak her mind. In fact, she was so giddy about her improvement that she told other church members. Their unified reaction was not surprising: "Why would you need to see a secular therapist when all you need to do is go to Jesus and God for your distress." Nonetheless, Mary boldly spoke and said that the counseling was good for her. Through all this psychotherapy Mary's religious values were left intact. Her improvement was so apparent that to my surprise, the minister of this large fundamentalist church "secretly" came to see me for counseling next.

For people who are highly committed to their church and to their religion, it may be valuable for the therapist to work in conjunction with their minister, priest, or rabbi. It is important to recognize the degree of authority each client gives to religion and work with it when appropriate. Of course, this is done only if desired by the client, the religious authority, and the counselor (McMinn et al., 1998). In some cases, the counselor's role is to support the client's interaction between the client and his or her church. In other cases, the minister, priest, or rabbi is delighted to turn over much of the counseling and inner work to the therapist because he or she may not have the time or interest in conducting the amount of spiritual counseling needed. Sometimes church authorities themselves need counseling from outside their churches.

REV. LIA'S STORY (MARY'S MINISTER)

Reverend Lia was a fifty-year-old, married woman who was a highly successful senior minister of a large Christian fundamentalist church. She had never attended professional counseling before. Rev. Lia came to see me because of the changes she had seen in Mary. Rev. Lia had an external locus of control, meaning everything and everybody outside of her had an excessively strong bearing on her experience, and she was a strong "caretaker." She responded well and talked about many things she had never confided to anyone before. Rev. Lia's distress improved but was not all resolved. At one point I stated that I knew she conducted public prayers and prayed with other individuals in need, but asked if she ever prayed alone. She said that she never prayed alone on her own behalf. I recommended that she pray alone on a daily basis for her homework and she agreed. The psychological concept at work was that she needed to improve her internal awareness through a process within her beliefs and reduce her source of distress. It's ironic that it took a "secular counselor" to provide this fundamentalist preacher with the antidote of prayer! As I saw her in future sessions, therapy worked well and she completed counseling with all symptoms resolved.

In recent years, a response to this yearning for a deeper spiritual experience within Christian churches has activated the development of certification and training focused on practices of "spiritual direction" and "spiritual formation." Spiritual direction is largely a practice of one-to-one help for people who wish to deepen their relationship within the divine and/or grow spiritually. This can occur in frequent regular meetings or in a retreat format. Spiritual formation concerns the growth of the whole person by focusing on the inner life, relationships, and spiritual practices. Spiritual directors often focus on elements of spiritual formation. Partially in response to the influx and popularity of Eastern practices that drew many people away from traditional Christian churches, a trend that began in the 1960s and 1970s and continues today, Christian churches recognized a need for a deeper level of spiritual practice. Instead of only Sunday morning church attendance, spiritual directors attempt to encourage further inner practices and a more in-depth spiritual development on an individual basis. However, this is still a relatively small movement within most Christian churches. While people in the practice of spiritual direction make it clear that spiritual direction is not psychotherapy, it bears a rudimentary resemblance to some forms of psychotherapy. This movement is further evidence that spiritual unrest exists and that a need for further guidance is increasing. This book would potentially be helpful to this movement.

INNER WORK FOR ATHEISTS AND AGNOSTICS

On the other hand, there are many people who are suspicious of religion due to negative encounters with churches or religious people. These people may seek counseling but want to feel assured that a therapist will not impose religious values in the process. However, these clients may have spiritual issues, such as fear of death, existential issues, or a need to understand inner experiences. In these cases help may be needed that is not delivered in religious terminology.

How might a book about spiritual transformation relate to atheists or agnostics? Some practices used within the belief system of religious adherents can be used effectively without the religious belief system. Scientific evidence has shown that many psychological, spiritual, and religious practices are beneficial procedures in themselves. For example, Herbert Benson, MD, selected elements from religious meditation practices and formed a type of meditation process that omitted all R/S aspects. He called it the relaxation response. After people were taught to use it, scientific studies took place to assess it. The results were very similar to outcomes produced in religious meditation practices. Adherents of these religions believe that it is their belief that makes these processes valuable. While belief can be a factor, it is also shown that psychospiritual procedures themselves can be valuable alone. If an atheist used a psychospiritual process like the relaxation response or a form of secular prayer, but attributed its value to something other than a deity, it may be that his or her belief itself aided the power of the process. This phenomenon is well known as the placebo response, in which a person's expectation of the benefit of a pill, for example, has been repeatedly shown in scientific research to be a potent factor in the relief of physical illness and injury recovery.

However, in many cases our beliefs, themselves, can also limit the possibility of certain benefits of psychospiritual processes. This is most often true if beliefs limit possible outcomes. For example, if one believes that an illness cannot be reversed, the likelihood of recovery is usually reduced.

DOES YOUR RELIGION OR SPIRITUALITY REALLY WORK?

An important general question must be asked: In times of stress, grief, and other life challenges are R/S beliefs functioning to provide relief. If, for example, religious resources do not help depression, it might be an indicator that R/S belief is not functional enough to provide coping mechanisms. If R/S beliefs are so flexible that they do not provide support or are too rigid to help during life changes, then R/S philosophy exploration might help expand spiritual resources. When unfair things happen or bad things happen, does the concept of God provide help to understand them?

One of the basic ways to evaluate a person's R/S beliefs is to question how they function in daily life:

- Are your R/S beliefs in conflict with your behaviors?
- Are your R/S experiences in conflict with your beliefs?
- Are your R/S concepts responsive enough to really help with life's challenges?
- Are your R/S concepts flexible enough to grow and mature with you?
- Are your R/S concepts rigid and not able to change or shift when it's in your best interest to change?
- Do your R/S ideas provide assistance in understanding the meaning and purpose of your life?
- Do your R/S ideas satisfy your feelings about death and dying?
- Do your prayers get answered?
- Have you had negative encounters in your past with R/S people or activities that still linger to disturb you?
- Have you had a near-death experience that has confused you or made you not want to live anymore?
- Do you have issues that you would rather not have your priest, rabbi, monk, or minister know about?
- Have you experienced tragedy or trauma that has disrupted your philosophy about life and religion?
- Have you had a spiritual experience that you have not told anyone about, and that you don't fully understand?
- Is your R/S experience in conflict with that of your spouse or partner?
- If you are an atheist, do you have a system of ultimate meaning that satisfies you?
- If you are agnostic, does your value system serve you in times of need?

Producing guilt about a person's shortcomings is not the purpose of the questions, although some people are all too ready to accept guilt for not being good enough in regard to beliefs about R/S. A periodic evaluation of many different life choices can be considered healthy, such as: Is your vehicle providing the benefits you bought it for? Are you holding onto friendships that are not in your best interest? Do you really use that item you thought would be helpful? So too, R/S choices should be accountable in regard to their appropriateness. It may be simply that a person is not participating in a religious faith in a manner that allows the religious institution to be beneficial.

On the other hand, a particular religion never really fit one's authentic belief but participation occurred because others wanted it. In some cases, a religion that was very meaningful in one phase of a person's life may not be an appropriate fit for the same person in a different life phase. Sometimes people can retain their R/S values but simply expand them to include other ideas that might help with current challenges. An alternative to the idea that a person's faith hasn't worked because it was not strong enough is that a person's faith has not worked because it is not internally congruent or that what has gone wrong may not be attributed to faith at all.

These questions and many others may often become issues that need to be addressed in psychotherapy by therapists who are equipped to help. While there are still therapists who are not updated about the use of psychotherapy for R/S issues, the separation of psychology and religion is largely dissolving.

ABIGAIL'S CASE

Another therapist referred Abigail to me because she was having some unusual experiences that could have been interpreted as medical or psychotic. Abigail reported symptoms of spontaneous body movements, perception of inner lights, and psychic awareness. She was from a Christian background but was currently very open about spiritual phenomena. Abigail was a twenty-year-old college student with a history of eating disorders. The symptom that was most problematic was a complete physical paralysis that occurred from time to time. These features are well known in many traditions, especially Hindu orientations, and are associated with spiritual awakening. However, Abigail possessed no knowledge of this type of spiritual awakening. Once I explained this to her and we worked through her symptoms, Abigail embraced her awakening.

In Abigail's case, her type of spiritual awakening was identified. Spiritual activity in many different faiths involves spontaneous body movements, but Abigail's church background did not include those features in a concept of spiritual awakening. The perception of inner light and visions are also universal spiritual phenomena, but they are seldom recognized as such in Protestant churches. All of these symptoms were described as a normal form of spiritual awakening in our session. This information substantially reduced Abigail's anxiety, and the ETT® process reduced the unpleasant aspects of her symptoms.

The experiences of Abigail, along with other types of spiritual awakenings, appear to be taking place more often. However, Western Christian thought rarely includes understanding of these universal phenomena. Psychotherapists knowledgeable of these experiences can guide people through these events without psychiatric drugs or medical interventions.

Some spiritual issues involve people who are either seeking, or have had, direct spiritual experiences for which neither conventional religion nor psychiatry has provided answers. At one time, I was a part of the "spiritual emergency network," which was originated by Stanislov and Christina Grof and concerned unusual spiritual experiences. These events were often treated as psychiatric or medical conditions by conventional methods to no avail, or in many cases made worse by these interventions. These events possessed a wide array of symptoms that appeared psychotic or as medical conditions that were unresponsive to treatment. These symptoms were so peculiar that if these people sought help in conventional churches, they were not validated as spiritual and were referred to doctors. The number of these cases has shown a steady increase recently.

While this increase can be attributed to several factors, one factor stands out. Various types of meditation have become popular and increasingly used. Most recently, mindfulness meditation has seen a substantial growth in numbers (Pickert, 2014). Although research has validated an array of positive psychological health benefits that are related to meditation, many people have experienced a range of peculiar spiritual experiences that are unexpected. Problems exist because these experiences (a) are not seen as linked to meditation, (b) do not fit a conventional understanding of spiritual experiences, and (c) tend to cause people to feel like something is wrong with them. Therefore, more and more people are bringing these unusual phenomena into counseling. Seeing visions and/or hearing voices are well documented in the history of most major religions, but they are also identified in dysfunctional psychological conditions. Differentiating pathology from authentic spiritual experiences is often needed.

SABRINA'S CASE

> I have been to almost every type of religion and tried several types of prayer and meditation but have never had a direct experience with God. I entered the Catholic convent as a teenager for a few years. I spent years in a spiritual community called the Self-Realization Fellowship founded by Yogananda where we meditated a lot. I explored several different Christian churches, Native American quests, and Buddhists retreats. While I heard about God in so many different ways, I have never felt the direct presence of God and I want that.

Sabrina was a sixty-year-old, divorced woman who touched me by her authentic spiritual quest. Through the ETT® process we worked on all her failed spiritual quests so that those feelings would not contaminate her present experience. We accessed possible psychological blockages until Sabrina felt less restless by the end of the session, but she did not have a direct spiritual experience during that time. However, the next day Sabrina called me and excitedly told me that she had experienced a direct contact with God as the result of our work. She said it happened when she watched the sunrise the next morning after our session. Sabrina felt transported and expanded, but mostly she felt a profound love unlike anything she had previously experienced as she watched the sunrise.

After all the spiritual activities in so many different religious formats, Sabrina finally felt the presence of God in a meaningful way as a consequence of removing her psychological blocks. This connection was not facilitated in a church, synagogue, or temple, but simply by working through her blocks in an ETT® session and ultimately with the light of the sun.

One category of people who may seek counseling for R/S issues are people who go to counseling for the purpose of assistance in a spiritual quest. This category may currently possess the smallest number of people but is possibly the fastest-growing category. This book may be most helpful to the people in this group. There are often psychological blocks that interfere with a person's spiritual quest. Some examples are as follows: (a) negative experiences with churches, (b) lack of worthiness to receive spiritual gifts, and (c) defense mechanisms like avoidance, rigidity, and dissociation.

The orientation of this book is to view the diverse array of religious, spiritual, and atheistic/agnostic views with respect. At the same time, there appear to be universal phenomena that occur across cultural and religious practices. Many of these practices, such as prayer, have now been scientifically studied. Therefore, these research outcomes will be acknowledged whenever they are appropriate to the issues. This work intends to show how to increase the capacity of psychospiritual approaches to produce functional outcomes such as the following:

- accessing spiritual resources during times of emotional challenge
- maximizing R/S fulfillment
- assisting the internal consistency of spiritual/behavioral/physical/ cognitive integration
- facilitating states of extreme wellbeing
- supporting authentic spiritual experiences that may not be supported by a person's peers, community, or churches
- facilitating authentic psychospiritual experiences
- facilitating a positive transformation of identity, functionality in life, and effective emotional regulation
- facilitating an awareness of the deep inner subjective experiences that produce meaningful value

The thrust of this book is to provide an impact on a client's spiritual growth that can extend beyond that which churches, books, or spiritual practices already provide. This is not based on an assumption that R/S practices are deficient, but rather that innovative ways to improve these practices have been developed and should always be welcomed. While this approach is designed to help with spiritual issues as needed, its greater goal is that of spiritual transformation. This transformation should have a deep, pervasive impact on spiritual growth to the extent that a radical elevation of spirituality takes place within a shorter time than previously thought to be possible.

CHAPTER 1 SUMMARY

This chapter began by noting the substantial change in identification with religion and spirituality that has occurred in the United States within the last twenty years. There is a general movement away from participation in religion and toward diverse forms of spirituality. Simultaneously, psychological counseling has seen an increase in the acknowledgment of spiritual issues. Mental health organizations have now developed qualifications for psychotherapists who conduct counseling on these issues, one of which was described. This approach adopts an acceptance of each client's R/S perspective and attempts to help them within this context. Then an introduction to ETT® is briefly described because it is a method uniquely able to implement psychological counseling on religious and spiritual issues.

Next, this chapter examined theory, research, and case studies regarding the most typical types of issues occurring in the context of religion and spirituality. Since perceived religious hypocrisy is the most common reason people give for not participating in religion, hypocrisy is explored. This is followed by an examination of people who have been wounded by churches or church authorities by rape, sexual abuse, shaming, or other means. Counseling for people who are atheists, agnostics, and apostates who have "spiritual" issues is explored. The unique issues that occur in families of the clergy are described. Then a case study of counseling with a priest is provided to show these unique issues. Next, two case studies of Christian fundamentalists, who are prone to oppose counseling with someone outside their faith, are provided to show how to manage the process with these clients.

In the section "Does your religion or spirituality really work?," an approach to challenging the functionality of one's faith by assessing the degree of a person's internal psychological consistency about their beliefs is provided. Another topic is illustrated in one case study in which a person was experiencing a spiritual experience whose nature was outside the range of understanding of conventional religion. Then a case study is used to describe a client whose search for an authentic spiritual experience had failed. In this case study, it was shown how ETT® facilitated a spiritual awakening. Finally, a list of the uses of ETT® regarding spiritual and religious issues is given.

Chapter Two

What Is ETT® and How Does It Work?

Sara said, "I am shocked, sad, angry, and guilty because I just found out that my best friend committed suicide. I love her so much (weeping). I was out of the country when she died. I feel guilty that I was not here with her when it happened. Jackie and I were so close.... I know she was having marital problems and her husband had had affairs, so I feel angry at him. I feel so sad and cry all the time. I am stunned."

The shock of the event was worked on first. Then emotions followed more freely and sadness was pursued. When I see an existential crisis of this type, I immediately know that the event has cracked a person's usual facade and psychological defense system and created a search for ultimate meaning. This often leaves a person open to a direct spiritual awakening, if the distress is transformed. As the sadness and shock eased in the first session, it gave way to intense anger at Jackie's husband. This took another session to process.

In the third session, Sara began to ask questions about the meaning of suicide. Why did she do it? She must have been in extreme pain to kill herself. How will my life be without her? Sara suffered most with the empathy for Jackie, assuming how painful it was. I told Sara that nobody actually knows what Jackie was feeling when she died, but many people report a sense of relief when they escape a painful situation. In fact, this movement toward escape is often attended by a sense of control and empowerment. Survivors of suicide attempts have reported feeling euphoria at the moment of making the decision to die. Sara resonated with this idea, and her worry lifted.

All of the aforementioned issues were processed by using the light device. Therefore, emotional distress that would normally take months or years to process was completed within a few sessions.

As soon as she processed her existential issues, Sara began to experience a blissful state. She described it as a tingling all over which she attributed to the presence of God. Whenever she felt this tingling, a peaceful smile dominated her countenance. I encouraged Sara to commune with her deceased friend in a letter. Sara wrote the following:

> These past two days, my body is experiencing a heavy weight being lifted, my mind and soul allowing a solace of peace and hope to envelope me. My anger and my rage are giving way to allow grieving and acknowledgment of my loss. The many questions that have gnawed incessantly are giving way to acceptance of never knowing the answers. God's unconditional love for you, Jackie, is also enveloping and comforting me now. I am feeling God's bright shining light and energy warm and wrap around me with a soft comfort, soothing and caressing me in gentle waves, an electric tingling.
>
> Now I can begin to move forward again, the frozen numbness that paralyses when death has shocked your entire being has loosened its grasp over me. My mind is no longer stuck in one place—reliving, questioning, and agonizing in repetitive cycles. God's peace, light, and warmth has thawed and dissolved the paralysis, allowing my mind freedom again.

While many people encounter grief from a traumatic loss, few process it so quickly and even fewer achieve a spiritual transformation as a result of this type of trauma. Using the Emotional Transformation Therapy® (ETT®) model, this type of transformation is frequent. Even today, five years later, Sara still feels the tingling presence of God almost daily. Sara has even become a qualified Unity minister, although that is not her occupation.

In order to understand the rest of this book, it is important to understand the basis of the ETT® approach to psychotherapy. This chapter summarizes this approach.

WHAT IS ETT®?

ETT® is an innovative form of psychotherapy that consistently facilitates cessation of current emotional distress within a few minutes. Within a brief series of sessions, ETT® also permanently resolves core emotional memory that is the source for current emotional symptom patterns. It uses an attachment-based interpersonal process whose outcomes are radically amplified by using precise elements of the client's visual ecology. This approach was developed to improve the impact of psychotherapy. In addition, ETT® can facilitate resolution of physical pain within minutes. Brain scans before and after ETT® sessions have verified that it facilitates a change of brain function which means brain chemistry has changed.

Why does speed of treatment matter? While there are many people who can't or don't feel their emotions, the majority of people experience distress that they cannot adequately quell. Humans have a vast array of defenses to keep unwanted emotions under control, such as avoidance, amnesia, somatization, and others. The fact that most people never seek counseling and go to their physicians for psychiatric medication suggests that people do not want to encounter unpleasant emotions. However, if a form of psychotherapy can extinguish emotional distress within seconds or minutes, the long, drawn-out emotional experience of conventional talk therapy is also largely omitted. While it is true that even in ETT® clients must face distressing emotions, they do so for only a minimal amount of time. Ultimately, these brief encounters are comforting because the dread of experiencing tormenting distress is lost. In most cases, relief occurs faster than what most medications can achieve, with the same or better outcomes. In addition, faster outcomes result in less costly psychotherapy and reduce the risk of dropout. There are many types of "exposure" therapies, like prolonged exposure therapy, desensitization, and eye movement desensitization and reprocessing (EMDR). The success of these therapies suggests that exposure to unpleasant emotions may be necessary; however, reducing the length of the process produces therapeutic results that are far more comfortable. Dropouts from therapy would be far fewer because ETT® is quick. Ultimately, therapy becomes more humane when it is faster.

ETT® therapists are trained to identify each client's attachment pattern and subsequently identify the client's pattern of emotional regulation. With this knowledge, the therapist can custom-tailor responses to each client, a process that increases client–therapist bonding. The bond created causes the client to feel supported and elicits trust that encourages disclosure. This interpersonal contact helps clients to be cared for while at the same time moving toward improvement of entrenched attachment disorders that are responsible for dysfunctional emotional regulation (Brisch, 2002).

ETT® offers new levels of effectiveness for treating a wide range of psychological disorders as well as physical pain syndromes. It has been used extensively with posttraumatic stress disorder (PTSD) because it changes the condition so fast and at such a depth that these changes are often permanent. If the symptoms which pharmaceuticals target are eliminated, the need for medication becomes obsolete. ETT® typically eliminates depression without the need for pharmaceuticals, or if clients are on pharmaceuticals, after ETT® sessions either the dosage is lessened or more often medications are eliminated altogether. Anxiety disorders are usually relieved in a single session, but permanent change often requires a brief series of sessions. The permanent elimination of addictive craving can take place within a single session, but more often permanent resolution for each addictive substance or addictive behavior usually occurs within a brief series of sessions. This achievement offers a new breakthrough in the treatment of addiction. ETT®

has also developed protocols for advanced treatment of obsessive-compulsive disorder, dissociative disorders, learning disabilities, brain injury, and others. However, its most frequent use is with complex trauma, which may include a combination of PTSD, addiction, relationship dysfunction, medical conditions, and an array of complicated issues.

Bipolar disorder is commonly held to be a permanent condition for the person who suffers from this disorder. Also, it is believed that the use of psychiatric medications is the only remedy that can correct the symptoms. Without the use of ETT®, this concept might largely be accurate. However, any psychological disorder that has emotional disturbance as its main symptomology is what ETT® treats best. Therefore, bipolar disorder is highly responsive to the use of ETT®. The essential difference in treatment approach is that pharmaceuticals tend to partially reduce the symptoms but not cure the condition, whereas ETT® rapidly reduces the symptoms, and then within a series of sessions usually eliminates the core emotional memory that causes the symptoms. This treatment usually results in permanent erasure of the condition.

ETT® possesses a high level of success in relieving chronic physical pain. So far, it has eliminated physical pain in migraine headaches, low back pain, temporomandibular joint syndrome, Morton's neuroma, rheumatoid and osteoarthritis pain, fibromyalgia, ankylosing spondylitis, and physical pain from accidents, injuries, and surgery. Typically, physical pain is markedly reduced or omitted during the first session. Then after a brief series of sessions, pain is usually relieved permanently. This is done without the use of medication, or if medication has been used, once ETT® has demonstrated relief, pain medication is appropriately discontinued. Through the ETT® addiction protocol, any addiction to pain medication can be eliminated. At this point one of the earliest uses of ETT® was with severe arthritis, and now sixteen years later one client has maintained relief from severe rheumatoid arthritis pain.

VISUAL BRAIN STIMULATION

During ETT® visual brain stimulation is used to amplify the interpersonal process to produce faster and more permanent outcomes. The concept that visual brain stimulation can be so potent that severe emotional distress can be alleviated within seconds is a puzzling phenomenon to most people. People often ask how looking at a light could possibly affect the brain that much when we live in a lighted environment all the time and it doesn't heal us. People living in northern climates who have seasonal affective disorder (SAD) can attest to the impact of less sunlight during the winter months. Many people have headaches and suffer other discomfort under fluorescent lighting. Therefore, it can be noted that the type and amount of lighting may have negative effects. What is less known is that precise forms of visual stimulation, used in conjunction with engaged psychological states, produce rapid positive changes of those distressing states.

The fundamental principles of ETT® include the following sequence of light-brain activity:

1. When light enters the eyes, photoreceptor cells in the retina convert light to biochemical processes and then into neural impulses.
2. These neural impulses travel through a vast array of pathways that can potentially reach almost every brain cell.
3. Many of these visual neural pathways allow us to see, but many others go directly to parts of the brain that control emotions, thoughts, and physical experiences.
4. Using precise wavelengths of light during a specific type of emotional experience, neural impulses can be directed to the parts of the brain responsible for that distress, which substantially aids in changing the distress.
5. When the brain mechanisms responsible for a certain symptom are changed, it occurs by means of the light stimulation resonating with emotions which alters brain chemistry.

What people most often do not know is that (1) the visual neural pathways can affect parts of the brain that are "non-image forming," or have little to do with the function of seeing, and (2) our eyes convert light into biochemical processes so that the brain chemistry is affected without having to take chemicals to do it. Once these points are understood, it is important to consider that these neural impulses of the brain can be directed and harnessed to rapidly change emotions, cognition, and physical experiences. If the interpersonal process has provided enough comfort to hold the targeted state engaged, the visual stimulation amplifies the entire experience.

To some people this approach is so completely different that people wonder what therapeutic model ETT® is based upon. In the 1960s, Barker developed what has come to be known as ecological psychology (1968). It is so fundamentally different from conventional psychology that ecological psychology differs even with regard to the conception of the nature of the brain. Instead of conceiving of the brain as existing only in the human head, it proposes that the brain and the environment are a single unit composed of interacting feedback loops between the physiological brain and the environment. This continuum between the brain and the environment forms the ecological brain. Supporting evidence is that the physical brain acts very differently when a person is in different environments. Gibson wrote an entire book specifically about visual perception and ecological psychology (1986). This is important because about eighty percent of our sensory intake from the environment is visual. Ecological psychology is primarily a theoretical discipline. However, ETT® has taken this concept to profound levels with powerful applications. Ultimately, ETT® utilizes the mutually interacting feedback loops via the visual elements to provide radically impactful therapeutic outcomes.

The ETT® method uses four basic modalities of light stimulation to acquire harnessing visual neural pathways to relieve symptoms. They are as follows:

- Multidimensional eye movement (MDEM), which uses precise eye movements and positions in conjunction with specific colors
- Spectral resonance technique (SRT), which uses a specialized spectral chart of maximally saturated color
- Peripheral eye stimulation (PES), which uses specialized goggles that control small beams of light entering specific angles of the periphery of the eyes
- The use of the Neuro Theralight, which is a light-emitting device

While all of these modalities are powerful natural means of precisely stimulating the brain during emotional processing, it is highly unlikely that these exact forms of stimulation would occur in the daily visual environment. Four different modalities of visual stimulation provide the ability to custom-tailor treatment to each therapeutic challenge because each modality helps in different ways.

MDEM

MDEM is different from EMDR in at least thirteen ways and looks entirely different as a process. MDEM is based on entirely different premises from EMDR. For example, EMDR relies heavily on bilateral brain stimulation activated by lateral eye movements. While this sometimes works, it is inaccurate to assume that all distress is associated with asymmetry of brain hemispheres. In most cases, MDEM eye movement is unilateral. However, the range of eye movements used is vast because they are individualized to each person. While MDEM bears greater similarity to the process of brainspotting, it possesses some significant differences. The main one is that MDEM uses specific wavelengths of light. This factor alone often facilitates healing regardless of eye movement. However, when eye movement is combined with precisely selected color, its impact is consistently powerful.

MDEM is best used when there is a consciously known trauma in which traumatic images are associated with a shocking event. In these cases, both the image and the trauma are often permanently deleted within minutes, to the complete surprise of most clients. However, the range of application for the modality extends far beyond this use. It can be used to transform any specific emotional distress, one emotion at a time. MDEM can be used to facilitate change of physical pain symptoms within minutes. Once a core emotional memory is accessed, MDEM can facilitate rapid change of these emotional memories.

MDEM bases its selection of eye movements, or more often eye positions, on the client's eye scanpath. When a particular disturbing emotion is retrieved and felt, at least eighty percent of people automatically move their eyes either in a distinct eye scanpath or eye position (Hollingworth, Williams, & Henderson, 2001). The eye scanpath or position is linked with an entire neural pathway from the eyes and throughout the brain. By slowly replicating this exact eye scanpath or position with a precisely selected visual target, the entire neural network possessing a distinct, disturbing experience becomes accessed and rapidly releases the disturbance permanently in most cases.

Imagine that you are seated with your client as the client describes a traumatic experience imprinted with an indelible image. This happened with Diane, who walked into the room after her brother committed suicide and saw his blood and brains splattered on the wall. Watching her eye movement during the telling of the experience, I noted her eye scanpath. Then I asked her to stay focused on that image, and I stood up and chose specific colored dowels. As I held the dowels in the exact same eye scanpath, about two or three feet away, I slowly moved the colored dowels. Within two minutes Diane reported that the visual image of the suicide room had faded and her emotions of shock and dismay had dissipated. When I asked her to repeat her initial story, she described it as devoid of emotion, and she could no longer recall the visual image. Her facial countenance had been transformed. It is stunning to watch this process as a therapist.

SRT

The SRT is an interactive process that involves the use of a specialized chart composed of colors that are so maximally saturated that it is far beyond what people are likely to see in their daily environment. The process primarily produces three therapeutic outcomes that are rarely accomplished by any other means. First, it spontaneously evokes retrieval of implicit memory and emotions when directed for that purpose. Second, it instantly identifies dissociation, which allows the therapist to reengage the client's attention. This ultimately leads to elimination of dissociation and facilitation of mindfulness. Third, SRT identifies escalation of emotion before it is consciously known to the client. This allows overwhelming distress to be averted, while optimal emotional engagement is harnessed for processing emotions to completion. These three processes drastically advance the therapeutic outcomes.

SRT uses naturally occurring visual feedback and distortions that have been scientifically documented to be related to brain functions (Barrick, Taylor, & Correa, 2002; Friberg, Bremer, & Dickenson, 2007; Vandewalle et al., 2010; Whitson & Galinsky, 2008).

Disengagement from emotion is a key defense mechanism that occurs spontaneously to protect a person from intolerable distress, but when it becomes habitual and out of awareness, it prevents the engagement necessary to resolve emotional distress. The ability to instantly identify relevant emotion and change it offers a new therapeutic capacity. However, the ability to identify and stop emotional escalation can completely avert intense, overwhelming emotion so that both the comfort and the productivity of emotional processing can be effective. Many people enter therapy in states of confusion and/or an inability to access the core emotional memory from which current symptoms are produced. If and when retrieval of relevant memory is appropriate, SRT can elicit that awareness. The Single Eye Technique with SRT can permanently delete unwanted emotional patterns within a session and is based on scientific research (Blake, 2001; Logothetis, 2002).

Imagine yourself as a therapist seated beside your client facing him/her while the client is facing a large chart with extremely bright and clear bands of color. You ask the client to talk about a disturbing issue that he/she wishes to understand and/or resolve. As one color is selected to view while the client talks, you can provide verbal support. As the client's emotions emerge, the color appears to disappear from the client's view. This surprises the client. Then the client—with eyes closed— is asked several present tense questions to bring attention into the here and now. Next the client is asked to open his/her eyes again. This time the color looks fully intact again. Through repeating this process, dissociation is detected, stopped, and the reengagement occurs. By maintaining this engagement of emotions, the disturbing emotions can be facilitated to progress to completion much faster and in more depth because the brain's spontaneous defense is identified, changed, and overcome. As a therapist you observe the client process the emotional disturbance to conclusion in most cases.

PES

The ETT® modality of PES usually concerns the use of specialized goggles that limit input of environmental light into the eyes to specific angles. By directing tiny beams of light at precise angles into the eyes, specific neural networks of emotional and physical symptoms are immediately accessed.

PES is usually the most rapidly impacting modality. Intense emotional or physical distress can often be changed instantly with this method. It is particularly valuable for people who are highly sensitive to light, sound, and stimulation in general because it largely blocks out most light. This makes it ideal for treating migraine headaches. However, PES has the unique capacity to rapidly diminish intense, overwhelming emotions or physical pain within minutes. It can also diminish intense psychotic states. Therefore, it is usually selected when a client enters a session already in overwhelm.

One of the unique attributes of PES is the capacity to literally segment specific states of consciousness and reorganize how it is configured and then delete distress. Retrieval of distinct implicit memory is also likely.

Picture yourself, as a therapist, sitting in front of a client who is overwhelmed by emotion to the extent that it produces extreme sensitivity to light and sound. You select the peripheral goggles and ask the client to put them on. The client is instructed to look only straight ahead while tiny beams of light from the external environment enter the periphery of the eyes. Then the client is asked to report the disturbance again. Typically, there is a reduction in intensity of emotion within seconds. As you change the angle of light exposure, an entirely different experience may occur in a range from more intense emotions to complete alleviation of distress as it varies from angle to angle. Eventually, within a few minutes, the initial distress is calmed and insight about the nature and contributing causes of distress tends to emerge. This process is one in which you simply systematically change the angle and ask the person to repeat the issue over each time while you provide attachment-based responses each time. Once the emotional distress falls to a lower intensity, other procedures can be used.

LIGHT-EMITTING DEVICE

The Rolls Royce of ETT® modalities is the light-emitting device called the Neuro Theralight. This technology has drastically improved over the years. As of this writing the light device, controlled by a laptop program used by the facilitator, emits monochromatic light chosen from hundreds of wavelengths and levels of saturation. It uses a red-green-blue system from which all colors can be selected. This is similar to technology used in television and computer monitors. It can be used to do almost all of the functions of other modalities but is most valuable when the session involves a complex array of emotions and physical states to process because it can adapt so quickly to attune to each state. When this takes place, each emotional distress can be changed within seconds.

The Neuro Theralight device possesses capacities that work best in conjunction with therapist interactive attunement to the client. In fact, the majority of impact is due to the interpersonal process, but it is a blend of therapist-technology synergy. This modality is the main one used to facilitate states of extreme wellbeing.

See yourself as an ETT® therapist and this is how the process might look. Picture your client seated in front of a light-emitting device facing a four-inch lens about two feet away from his/her face. The device is placed within a hood that blocks out all peripheral light. You cannot see the client's face, but verbal communication is unrestricted. You are facing a laptop or iPad that has a program for controlling the exact wavelengths—from among a range of hundreds of options, a brightness control, and a strobe rate control (optional) that produces what the client sees. As you listen to the client, a different wavelength of light is chosen according to the changing emotional states reported by the client while simultaneously providing verbal support and feedback. Typically, the visual stimulation and verbal support facilitates rapid transformation of emotional and physical states to either neutrality or wellbeing within minutes. However, as one emotion subsides, often another more underlying emotion emerges and insights frequently occur. Since light into the eyes tends to evoke attachment-based responses, even without a therapist, visual stimulation typically provokes awareness of buried emotion to emerge and then is used to relieve the distress.

ATTACHMENT-BASED INTERPERSONAL PROCESSES

Attachment patterns are originally formed by the manner in which an individual interacts with his/her parents or caretaker in early development. These patterns of interaction eventually internalize to become how a person interacts with other people. These interaction patterns form the basis for regulating emotions and brain biochemistry. While these patterns are usually firmly entrenched in adults and tend to be exhibited as a life-long pattern, they are changeable through specific types of relationship interaction. When these attachment patterns are dysfunctional, people develop unresolved emotional distress, which leads to conditions like depression, anxiety, and traumatic experiences. Since attachment pattern dysfunction is at the source of malfunctioning emotional regulation, identifying and changing these patterns is key to facilitating long-term change of emotional distress.

Characteristic attachment patterns arise when a crisis occurs in a person's life. This emergence tends to occur automatically without voluntary control. These patterns are typically out of the person's conscious awareness, yet they typically dictate how emotions will be managed. Psychological research has identified four basic attachment patterns. However, at least one researcher has identified several subtypes (Brisch, 2002).

If the interpersonal aspect of psychotherapy focused on identifying each client's attachment disorder and adjusted the therapist–client interactions to provide the exact response helpful to alter the person's attachment pattern, over time it could improve emotional processing. The most effective forms of therapy are those which are custom-tailored to each individual (Krebs, Norcross, & Prochaska, 2011). Therefore, an attachment-based interpersonal therapy provides a potent means to activate more in-depth and rapid changes. The challenge for ETT® therapists is to be able to alter their interactions in a way that adapts to each person's attachment pattern. Then, when visual brain stimulation is precisely used in conjunction with this interpersonal process, the impact is radically improved.

A more comprehensive description about how attachment-based responses are used in ETT® is described in a full chapter in a previous ETT® text (Vazquez, 2013, pp. 21–56). For the purpose of this work, it is important to note that attachment patterns are projected onto all relationships, including our relationship with the divine and other spiritual entities. Research has shown, for example, that atheists tend to have a greater tendency to possess avoidant attachment patterns. Therefore, identifying and correcting dysfunctional attachment patterns can have a direct bearing on either removing blockages to spiritual fulfillment or enhancing spirituality.

PERSONAL CARE VS. TECHNOLOGY

Initially, two diverse reactions tend to occur when presented with the use of visual modalities during the counseling process. One the one hand, many people would prefer a technology for psychotherapy in which the device does all the work and an interactive human being is not necessary. Some examples of this orientation are biofeedback, transcranial magnetic stimulation, Internet programs, and others. In contrast, counselors may initially object to ETT® on the basis that the visual modalities may interfere with the important relationship quality of the therapeutic process.

While some technologies can certainly be shown to be beneficial, most psychological disorders are derived from interpersonal dysfunction. If a technology can alleviate the current symptoms but must be repeated over and over, it lacks the ability to correct the core emotional issues which constitute the basic problem. For example, if emotional neglect is the source of loneliness, using technology alone as a remedy lacks an emotional responsivity and reinforces the emotional neglect, while the technology tinkers with the brain temporarily to correct the symptoms. In this case, the underlying dysfunction remains intact and continues to evoke the symptoms as the remedy may act only as a suppressant. Many people need human contact. For example, if the client's issue is not feeling heard, no amount of technology will resolve this. This requires a human response that communicates being heard.

Some counselors are concerned that a lack of face-to-face contact potentially impairs the therapeutic process. This might be true if the therapist focuses on the use of the ETT® modalities and reduces interpersonal responses. However, most ETT® modalities tend to activate the client's emotional awareness far beyond typical face-to-face interactions. This awareness and disclosure have the potential to enhance intimate bonding, if the therapist is appropriately verbally interactive. It has been found that in psychoanalysis in which face-to-face contact is used versus Jungian analysis, in which the client is not facing the therapist, better bonding takes place while the therapist and client are not facing each other (Perlman, 1999). Clients tend to feel safer and more comfortable when the therapist and client are not facing each other. This positioning is also supported by brain research with trauma clients. Because the superior colliculus of the brain is activated by direct eye contact, these clients react by cowering, withholding, and generally withdrawing. Nonetheless, therapists are accustomed to face-to-face contact, and there is an assumption that lack of face-to-face contact limits the bonding process.

The challenge for therapists is to acquire comfort with a triadic relationship composed of the therapist, the client, and the visual stimulation. Since modalities such as the spectral resonance technique tend to retrieve client emotions far faster and at a greater depth than face-to-face dialogue, a therapist's empathy, expressed in soothing, validating, and appropriate praising, can have an amplified effect in this context. Research has also shown that client body language is far more significant in communication than face-to-face verbalization. The optimal flow of such interactions might be that a therapist's verbal input fits into the client's verbalizations so seamlessly that at the end of a session, the client reports not even recalling the therapist's verbal input. Because the client was so immersed in his/her own verbal processing and the therapist's input was so in tune with it, the verbal input felt like a part of the flow rather than a distraction. This type of interaction is highly intimate and very personal. If the process is conducted in this manner, there is no loss of rapport between the therapist and client; in fact, rapport is enhanced.

Since some ETT® processes amplify emotions and sensitivity to the environment, every little verbal input by the therapist is actually amplified further than it would be with only face-to-face contact. When visual contact is shut off, the other senses may become more attuned to offset the deficit. However, if the therapist feels cut off by the use of a visual modality and interacts in a less personal manner, the therapist can make therapy a less personal process. Therefore, ETT® therapists are taught to use attachment-based interpersonal verbalization to enhance the impact of ETT®. This means that interpersonal responses are custom-tailored to each person's needs. Attachment-based responses to clients are healing in themselves.

PERMANENT ERASURE OF PSYCHOLOGICAL DISORDERS

What Is Core Emotional Memory?

> Underlying the diverse behaviors, moods, emotions and thoughts for which people seek therapy are "implicit" emotional learnings—learnings that are not in conscious awareness and that enter into memory during experiences involving strong emotion.... Implicit knowledge is often termed procedural knowledge.... Such knowledge consists of schemas (patterns, templates, or models) that have been abstracted and extracted from experience and stored in memory systems other than those that hold one's explicit, autobiographical, "episodic" knowledge of past events. (Ecker, Ticic, & Hully, 2012)

Furthermore, this core emotional memory is deeply entrenched. It is the source of most emotionally disturbing symptoms for which people go to therapy. Since these emotional memories exist out of awareness, they defy responsivity to most forms of face-to-face talk therapy and are not eliminated by known pharmaceuticals used in psychiatry. If it were possible to access and transform all the core emotional memory responsible for a psychological disorder, like PTSD, depression, bipolar disorder, panic attacks, and others, these conditions would cease to exist permanently.

Until 2004 only electroconvulsive therapy and drugs used in animal studies demonstrated that emotional memory could be permanently eradicated (Ecker, Ticic, & Hully, 2012, p. 14). Core emotional memory is usually implicit and is the source of current emotional distress. Since conventional cognitive talk therapy usually cannot elicit it nor eliminate it, new positive learning from talk therapy is simply added to entrenched disturbing emotional memory during psychotherapy. This positive addition may temporarily alleviate current transient distress and provide some benefit. However, this new emotional learning creates a competition with the old emotional learning, which leaves the person in a continuous struggle to overcome distressing old learning. An alternative concept is that of "transforming" old learning into new learning. This means that the old disturbing learning no longer exists to be overcome. Because this process is the essence of this method, the name Emotional Transformation Therapy® was selected.

From the biochemical perspective of psychiatrists, some forms of intense, enduring depression are referred to as "biologically based depression." These types of conditions tend to return over and over regardless of medications or conventional psychotherapy. In these cases, there are likely to be one or more core emotional memories at the base of the condition that have not been accessed or processed to completion. Since these psychiatrists usually do not know how to access or transform the core emotional memory through psychotherapy, they usually assume that the depression or other psychological conditions are genetically produced and are unchangeable without psychiatric medications. In a pharmaceutically dominated society, a person who has never observed accessing and transforming core emotional memories would consider this to be a reasonable assumption. What is not reasonable is a lack of openness to different ways to help resolve these conditions when it is clear that medications only partially alleviate the problem and foster a long-term dependency.

Many psychotherapy methods involve regressive techniques and claim to discharge the distress that has been retrieved. What I have observed is that (1) many times regression may access memory but not necessarily access core emotional memory; (2) when core emotional memory is accessed, the cathartic "discharge" often does not eliminate the core emotional memory; and (3) if it does eliminate the core emotional memory, there may be nothing to replace it with, if it was not "transformed." One woman who underwent years of Bioenergetic therapy repeatedly stated after ETT® sessions, "I am surprised that I never found all these underlying causes after so much Bioenergetic therapy." In another case, a woman who had been through sixteen years of psychoanalysis and believed she was aware, still had no idea why she had physical pain after all medical evaluations proved inconclusive. In the first ETT® session, she became aware of chronic dissociation and the source of her pain. Generally speaking, psychotherapy methods that involve retrieval work take a long time, and insurance companies prefer not to pay for such lengthy, in-depth methods. Therefore, a method like ETT® that is both in-depth and brief is generally assumed to be impossible.

ETT® is used to permanently transform core emotional memory by creating a mismatch, or cognitive dissonance, that is carefully facilitated. This mismatch pairs a core emotional memory arousal with either a contradictory current experience or a stimulus that can eradicate the arousal. In psychotherapy, this mismatch is carefully elicited. However, it can, though rarely, occur in specific natural circumstances. The following example of a rare natural occurrence with impeccable timing is of the type that often leads to an attribution of divine intervention.

As I sat across the table from Don and his wife at a restaurant, Don gave me the details of an extraordinary experience that I will never forget:

> I had reached a low point in my life and decided to commit suicide. I felt determined to do it that day. So I was climbing a mountain and was planning to jump off a certain cliff that I knew would mean a swift and certain death. As I was getting near the top, I heard someone calling out for help. I immediately went to where I heard the noise. I saw a man who had been a rock climber dangling from a rope when I looked down from the cliff. I called out to him that I could help and began pulling him up with great care. My suicidal thoughts left the second I spontaneously sought to help him. My heart was pounding, adrenalin rushing, and I was compelled to save him. Once I pulled him to safety the grateful look on his face and his kind words made me feel very good.
>
> The oddest thing was that my suicidal thoughts evaporated. I no longer wanted to escape my life, and it is now about ten years since that experience. The timing of my suicidal intention and his need for rescue was so exactly right that I felt like it was a life-affirming message to me. I still had unresolved issues, but everything looked different after that.

This unusual pairing of circumstances forced a psychological change to occur. Don's obsession to commit suicide was matched with a circumstance that elicited Don's care-taking, life-saving inner inclinations at the same time. This combination transformed his suicidal intention into a life-affirming one. Because the strong, life-affirming feelings interrupted and abated the suicidal feelings, the suicidal arousal was transformed. Therapists using ETT® purposely access positive inner resources to transform unwanted core emotional memory.

The sequence of processing that involves the transformation of core emotional memory includes several factors. First, an understanding of the client's psychological history and current symptoms is explored during the first half hour of the first session while rapport is being established. If enough safety is built, there is an attempt to identify the most current disturbing symptom and reduce or change it by the end of the first session. Other current symptoms are pursued and relieved in a second session. It is possible that trauma, depression, or anxiety might be completely relieved in the first session if the client's readiness and awareness of the issue is clear. However, if there are multiple traumas and issues and the client is highly defended, it will take longer. ETT® can facilitate transformation with radical swiftness, but a client's readiness is a factor affecting the speed at which change can take place. One of the unique issues with the use of ETT® is the possible disorientation that clients tend to feel when a lifelong issue is transformed rapidly. However, there are built-in ETT® processes to accommodate this issue. In these cases, ETT® treatment can focus on readiness issues to increase the speed, or it can focus on integrating rapid changes if necessary after a major transformation.

IS SPIRITUAL AWAKENING PRACTICAL?

Although many people have had profound spiritual experiences, they are often unable to access these spiritual resources when they are in great need. Their lives are in shambles while intermittently having great spiritual experiences. While some people dissociate and then have spiritual experiences, others have a mature spiritual development that is simply not available to them during times of great distress. Only recently has scientific brain research with people having spiritual experiences revealed that spiritual experiences actually take place in different brain circuits than other experiences. Newberg & Waldman (2009), citing Kandel, provided the following technical explanation:

> The striatum plays an essential role in creating contentment and a sense of safety in the brain. Our brain-scan study showed increased striatal dopamine release during meditation, which helps explain the sense of relaxation, happiness, and peacefulness meditators experience. The striatum sends this information on to many parts of the brain, including the thalamus, which orchestrates our senses about the outside world. The brain perceives this as an internal sense of reality….
>
> The claustrum is heavily interconnected with most of the cortex, *with the exception of the thalamus*…. The thalamus creates a holistic sense of reality, but obviously this sense of reality is disconnected from the sense of reality created by the striatum…. There are two reality maps created by the brain, one conscious, the other subconscious, and they process incoming data about the world in very different ways…. When you add to this model the discovery we've made that advanced meditators have unusual asymmetric activity in the thalamus, we are drawn to the conclusion that spiritual practices may create independent realms of separate realities, or they may help to unify separate realities that coexist in the brain. (p. 260)

This research suggests that while spiritual experiences may be wonderful, their integration into daily life is unlikely without an integration process of some type. However, some spiritual awakenings may unify the brain. Even when this unification is very beneficial, it may still require adjustment, especially when the change is rapid. There are several ETT® processes that can help integrate independent realities and several ways to assist adaption to a new sense of wholeness.

DAN'S CASE

Dan was plagued by continuous anxiety most of his life. Dan was a forty-eight-year married man with two children. He was a devout Christian who was active in his church. Dan reported having an underlying fear. He said that he believed there was always something to fear, but on the other hand he believed in a loving God. The Spectral Resonance Technique was selected to use in a process that accesses the right and left brain hemisphere activity alternatively while viewing each color one at a time.

As the procedure took place Dan would express his inner conflict at each position and exhibit first the emotion of fear and then the thought of God's love. As this process was repeated his fear gradually diminished and his sense of feeling loved increased. On orange he reported his ears getting warm when his right hemisphere was stimulated, and his solar plexus felt tense when his left hemisphere was activated. As the right side perception was visually superimposed onto the left, symptoms reduced and his throat felt tense. Blue stimulation alleviated his throat tension. With yellow stimulation, both sides of his issue integrated and Dan reported feeling better.

This procedure facilitated the integration of Dan's spiritual resources and his fear. Many people experience this inner disparity and possess no strategy to unify the discrepancy. People can often build their spiritual resources, but without a means to integrate them into functional emotional experiences, these strengths become very limited.

Almost all major religions include a long history of the use of color in visual environments for specific spiritual purposes. Color often enhances direct contact with the divine. For example, in the Christian Bible it is written in Exodus 26-35 that God told Moses to use very specific colors for the interior of the first church (Nave, 1962, p. 213). This type of specific direction in the use of visual stimulation strongly suggests that color offers a vehicle to access the divine.

DISCOVERY OF TRANSCENDENCE WITH ETT®

After developing the ETT® method and training hundreds of other professionals to use it, I began to notice more and more frequent experiences of extreme wellbeing that occurred during the process. While some of these transpersonal experiences occurred during private individual sessions, many of them took place in front of large group demonstrations with people I had just met. These profound events typically occurred spontaneously without any discussion about spiritual experiences. Here are some examples:

- On the first day of an introductory workshop during the first demonstration using the light device, the volunteer exclaimed as she was brought to tears that she felt an overwhelming experience of love and oneness with everything. She was of the Sufi faith and lived in a Sufi community where she had meditated daily for years, but she had never experienced "oneness" before. She said, "I have meditated for years and then the first time you put me on this light machine, I have the experience I have been seeking all my life."
- In another ETT® training session, a woman volunteered to work on an intensely disturbing issue of conflict with her boyfriend. As I was using the peripheral goggles, little response took place until we got to the 12 o'clock angle of light entering her eyes. At that point she suddenly described herself expanding and expanding until she became as big as the universe. During this expanding she reported more and more peace and awe. When she was asked about the original issue, she reported that it was no longer of consequence. Months later when I asked her to recall the visual experience with the goggles, she reentered the expanded state again.
- During another training session, a man requested that he enters a state of bliss. Using MDEM, he soon reported the bliss state he had been seeking.
- After the use of the spectral resonance technique one person described a profound state of "wholeness" unlike any he had ever felt before.

Alan Watts captures what so many people describe in different ways when they have experiences of extreme wellbeing during ETT® sessions:

> Existence.... ceases to be a problem; the mind is so wonder struck at the self-evident and self-sufficient fitness of things as they are, including what would ordinarily be thought the very worst, that it cannot find any word strong enough to express the perfection and beauty of the experience. Its clarity sometimes gives the sensation that the world has become transparent or luminous. (1984, pp. 14–15)

However, these states of extreme wellbeing tend to occur most frequently during the use of the light device. They tend to occur immediately after the complete release of a traumatic event, sometimes referred to as posttraumatic growth. I recognized that many of the ETT® experiences facilitated a type of spiritual awakening classically categorized as a Kundalini awakening. Many of these experiences served as gateway events to further spiritual events or awakenings to the development of spiritual "gifts."

After observing dozens of these experiences with people of all types of spiritual orientations, I sought ways that would consistently produce these states of extreme wellbeing. My success in developing and understanding these states of extreme wellbeing has led to the techniques that are the focus of this book.

At the time this book was written there were four research projects that were either planned or in progress on various aspects of ETT®. The outcomes of these research projects can be found using the information in Appendix C of this book.

Many people who are highly developed spiritually still possess a number of unresolved psychological wounds. However, there are many people who have worked through their psychological issues but have not developed their spiritual potential. Psychotherapy addresses one set of issues while spiritual practices address other issues, and both approaches can address many symptoms. For example, while it is well documented that meditation and prayer can lower stress, psychotherapy can also lower stress by facilitating relief of trauma, depression, and anxiety. Psychotherapy is particularly valuable in processing relationship issues which may create a foundation for the development of a relationship with God or whatever one's ultimate conception may be. This marriage between Western psychotherapy and spiritual meditation is a relatively new synthesis. It has been described as spiritual practices aiding in "waking up" and psychotherapy as "growing up" (Welwood, 2000, p. xviii). However, with the development of ETT®, psychotherapy is amplified to entirely new levels of proficiency and spiritual awakening can now occur so quickly and consistently that the radical experience of "waking up" requires psychotherapy of a high level to adjust to this type of spiritual change. However, psychotherapy at this amplified level often provokes spiritual awakenings as a by-product.

While this relationship between psychotherapy and spirituality may seem confusing, one of the purposes of this book is to show how the two domains can be addressed congruently. The primary focus is on the use of "psychotherapy" for religious and spiritual issues. However, in the case of ETT®, psychotherapy itself grew up to advance spiritual practices when appropriate. In the case of ETT®, the marriage of psychotherapy and inner spiritual practices flows so confluently that they usually operate as one system.

CHAPTER 2 SUMMARY

This chapter reviews the nature and scope of the method of ETT®—a psychotherapy method by which spiritual and religious issues are optimally processed. An initial case study showed how transformation of the shock of a friend's suicide changed into a spiritual awakening. A definition of ETT® was provided along with a characterization of its typical outcomes for PTSD, depression, anxiety disorders, addictions, as well as chronic physical pain. Then technical descriptions about how visual stimulation can be harnessed to affect specific brain mechanisms were given. Finally, the theoretical basis upon which ETT® rests was described as principles from ecology psychology.

There are four visual modalities used by the ETT® method: MDEM, spectral resonance technique, peripheral eye stimulation, and a specialized light-emission device. The theory and research that provide the base for ETT® is given along with a functional description of each modality. Then a brief description about how and why the interpersonal portion of the ETT® process uses attachment-based procedures is reviewed.

Next, issues about controversies regarding the ETT® method are explored. On the one hand, counselors tend to oppose the use of technology and props because it can be seen as an obstacle to the valuable interpersonal portion of psychotherapy. On the other hand, some people want the technology to implement psychological change through methods such as electroconvulsive therapy, transcranial magnetic stimulation, deep brain stimulation, and other technological means. ETT® offers a new hybrid that enhances the interpersonal portion while using appropriate technology to advance the healing process.

The next portion of the chapter describes how and why ETT® can facilitate permanent changes of psychological conditions. This is based on research concerning memory reconsolidation in which core emotional memories are retrieved and extinguished. Then the chapter included how facilitation of spiritual issues can be integrated into daily life functioning. Finally, there are descriptions of the spontaneous spiritual experiences that eventually led this author to pursue ways to use ETT® to purposely facilitate transcendent experiences.

Chapter Three

Facilitating Authentic Forgiveness

> In my first marriage my friends let me know about several affairs my husband had had. At first I didn't believe it. Gradually, it was confirmed. It was a total shock! As his betrayal was revealed, it devastated me. Then as divorce was sought, he brought our children into it and told them all types of lies about me. They believed him. That broke my heart! He was a millionaire and he managed to keep almost all the money. Today, twenty years later, he flaunts his money at every event of our grandchildren and is loud and obnoxious. I hate him. He makes me so mad every time I see him! I will probably always resent him.

Sandra was about as bitter as one could get, even twenty years after the divorce. After a few sessions in which she expressed a painful array of emotions, she began to feel better, but her resentment was deeply entrenched. I asked her if she would like to let go of her resentment permanently. She said, "Yes." Then I conducted a single-eye technique that is conducted within the spectral resonance technique (SRT). It took only a few minutes and resulted in the complete elimination of the resentment toward her ex-husband! This stunning and rapid change of long-term hatred is a revolutionary achievement. We tested its completeness by having her talk about all the emotions regarding resentment. Sandra was stunned to realize that her resentment became completely absent. She was unable to retrieve it. It never returned. Then, forgiveness was easy.

Forgiveness is a valued process in all major religions. In all the Christian denominations forgiveness is a central concept. The Jewish perspective includes the view that we must forgive others as God forgives us. If the transgressor has repented, forgiveness can be received. Jews are more likely to believe that some sins are unforgivable (Cohen, Malka, Rozin, &

Cherfas, 2006; Rye et al., 2000). Muhammad provided an example of forgiveness for all who follow Islam (Rye et al., 2000). Buddhism offers the value of compassion which is similar to forgiveness (Higgins, 2001). In Hinduism, forgiveness is advocated in the context of providing good karma (Klostermaier, 1994). The emphasis on forgiveness and rituals to assist it might make one think that religious people can forgive better than nonreligious people.

The history of religion is replete with violent wars and revenge. The Crusades put thousands of people to death for the sake of "Christian" values. In Ireland the Catholic–Protestant conflict has been a grudge conflict. The grudge between the Sunni and Shiite Muslim sects began soon after the death of Mohammed in the year 632 and continues to the present day. The Jews and Palestinians continue to hate each other. In short, the sum total of revenge and resentment that exists in the name of religion is massive. While forgiveness exists in the doctrines of these faiths, there is little evidence for success in the implementation of forgiveness.

However, there are extraordinary examples of forgiveness among certain religious groups. Gandhi, Martin Luther King, Jr., Desmond Tutu, and Caesar Chavez are leaders who sought nonviolence and compassion toward perpetrators. McCullough cites an example of the Amish in the following:

> A gunman entered a one-room Amish schoolhouse in Nickel Mines, Pennsylvania.... The police arrived on the scene, but before they could disarm the man, he shot and killed five girls, wounded the remaining five, and then killed himself.
>
> Within hours of the Nickel Mines shooting, people from the Amish community in Lancaster County were assuring the reporters who flocked to the scene that the Amish would find it in their hearts to forgive the killer. Indeed within days they were reaching out to the killer's family with the expression of love and concern. (2008, p. 205)

Historically and cross-culturally, religion has been involved in both the most atrocious revenge violence known to humankind and the most extraordinary displays of forgiveness. Understandably, the average person feels confused by the demonstrations of both extreme violence and forgiveness. When religious people give lip service to forgiveness but display behavior based on grudges, the entire issue becomes confusing to many people.

Scientific studies in the United States measuring people's forgiveness of specific events found that there is usually no difference between religious people and nonreligious people (McCullough & Worthington, 1994). Another study showed that people who conceived of a vengeful God had lower forgiveness scores (Tsang, McCullough, & Hoyt, 2005). The evidence of conflict, hostility, and the physical consequences of stress and resentment strongly suggests that forgiveness is not well understood and not effectively implemented (Witvliet, Ludwig, & Vander Laan, 2001). The following is a list of consequences produced by a lack of forgiveness that various clients have exhibited:

- emotional discomfort that hurts the recipient of a transgression but not the transgressor
- chronic physical pain
- discomfort about others that interferes with the ability to establish or maintain a fulfilling affectionate relationship
- feeling resentment toward a parent or parents
- unresolved resentment toward another person that contributes to obsessive ruminating about that person
- inability to trust others
- irritation about certain categories of people like men, women, authority figures, children, teachers, and others
- revenge or hate motives toward others
- recurrent nightmares about being hurt or violated
- unresolved emotions toward others that interfere with one's relationship to God or one's spiritual fulfillment

Of course, there are also other symptoms whose roots lie in issues of resentment. The matter can become more difficult when these unresolved emotions are buried only to reemerge when interpersonal triggers bring forth a disproportionate response. In these cases, a person may have no awareness that unresolved emotions even continue to exist. However, it is often the aforementioned symptoms that suggest the possibility of unresolved resentment. In addition to the unresolved resentment toward a transgressor, there are several symptoms that suggest unresolved self-forgiveness in the following list:

- continuing to feel bad about mistakes made long ago
- guilt about parenting errors
- hating or disliking one's physical body
- continuing to feel incompetent even when the facts do not warrant it
- selecting destructive partners or friends
- feeling guilt or shame
- feeling unworthy, inferior, and inadequate
- not believing one deserves forgiveness

These symptoms are pervasive in counseling clientele. Generally, people do not enter psychotherapy identifying forgiveness or self-forgiveness as their objective. Instead, clients simply describe symptoms they want to be resolved. The aforementioned symptoms are the types of issues that often ultimately achieve resolution through forgiveness or self-forgiveness. Since the actual meaning of forgiveness is often disputed, first for review will be a consideration of what forgiveness is *not*, followed by a move toward the concept of "true" forgiveness.

WHAT FORGIVENESS IS *NOT*

Forgiveness is not excusing a transgression. In order for the forgiveness process to proceed, it is first necessary to acknowledge that a transgression has occurred, instead of avoiding its existence. For example, if parents claim, "We did the best we could," it may serve to imply that their transgression should not be acknowledged. If this justification is interpreted by the child of these parents as a reason to excuse the parents from any reactions to the parents' acts, the child may be left with unresolved emotions. Even if parents believe they have very good reasons for abusing or neglecting children, the emotional reactions to this behavior may still exist within the child, and the outlet for resolution may be blocked by excusing the existence of these emotions as valid. To deny these feelings is to falsify experiences. This lack of resolution may contribute to everything from depression to chronic pain. However, once these emotions are recognized and expressed, true forgiveness is a possibility. Excusing a transgression is not the same as forgiveness. Once true forgiveness is accomplished, the transgression no longer matters, but this perspective is born only after the emotions have been processed to completion.

Authentic forgiveness is not the same as condoning a transgression. If a husband beats his wife and the wife chooses to forgive him after working through her emotions, this does not mean that the wife approves of the beating. While true forgiveness can neutralize the response to a transgression, it does not change an ethical or moral value. In other words, one may continue to hold the value that spouses should not physically hurt each other, even though the transgression has been neutralized by forgiveness. Sometimes, however, there might actually be an error in judging an action as malicious. In the case of a perceived wife beating, if a man accidentally tripped and hit his wife as a consequence, an entirely different understanding could change the meaning of the perceived hitting. However, far too often we are willing to change perspectives in order to avoid having to face working through emotional responses in reaction to a transgression. Unfortunately, this avoidance only serves to perpetuate the discomfort while deceiving oneself. A transgression needs to be acknowledged as an offensive act that is not condoned. However, when true forgiveness is achieved, compassion towards the transgressor often naturally occurs during Emotional Transformation Therapy® (ETT®) sessions, but this response is not the same as condoning the transgressor.

The familiar commonplace, "I can forgive, but I cannot forget," is widely affirmed. When this is stated in an angry tone, it does not indicate the type of authentic forgiveness indicated in this work. The type of "forgiveness" indicated by this statement may be an intellectual statement of forgiveness without the elimination of the emotional component. "Remembering" an offense as indicated in this statement often serves as a protective emotional scar retained to prevent future pain. Also, it serves the purpose of holding the transgressor accountable for the offending deed while retaining resentment. This approach to forgiveness bears no similarity to true forgiveness.

Authentic forgiveness and justice are not the same and are often confused. Those suffering from injustice should be encouraged to identify and express their reactions. For example, immediately after a woman has been raped, shock, fear, rage, and shame about the injustice should be expressed as it is being felt. At those times it is usually premature and inappropriate for forgiveness to take place. However, after these emotions have been explored and any relevant learning has taken place, forgiveness of the transgressor may be an option that can permanently alleviate the emotions. When this does not happen, the trauma tends to imprint on the brain in such a way that a trauma reenactment is likely. The fact is that when a woman is assaulted, she becomes four times more likely to be assaulted again compared to other women (Resnick et al., 1993). Therefore, evidence suggests that authentic forgiveness can actually be protective. Forgiveness extends beyond the concept of justice to an emotional transformative position.

The U.S. justice system has begun the movement toward forgiveness through methods of "restorative justice." This method advocates a face-to-face meeting between victims and offenders. Crime victims typically experience posttraumatic stress disorder, and criminals who have been imprisoned tend to commit more crimes when they get out of prison. However, participants who have experienced restorative justice have been shown to have less posttraumatic stress disorder (PTSD), and criminals who participated have lower recidivism rates (Angel, 2003, 2005).

Authentic forgiveness is not the same as absolution. Absolution may be understood as absolving the transgressor of all responsibility of his/her transgressive deeds. If this means pardoning people from imprisonment for acts that were illegal, this is not necessarily the same as true forgiveness. Absolution may or may not be a part of true forgiveness. One can forgive a transgressor for the commission of a criminal act but still choose to reject absolving the transgressor of the consequences of prison time when it would serve to protect oneself and others. True forgiveness of the transgressor would serve to free a person of the torment of hating the transgressor.

One of the greatest misuses of the term forgiveness, especially among religious people, is the "spiritual bypass." This form of "forgiveness" is usually an attempt to avoid acknowledging and expressing emotions that are seen as unpleasant and not in synchrony with one's image. The spiritual bypass is often pursued with positive intentions and attempts to move beyond all the "lower level" emotional reactions as though one is operating at a "higher level." In this case the speed and comfort of resolution is sought without due regard to the thoroughness of the process (Cashwell, Glosoff, & Hammond, 2010). In 1984, the phrase "spiritual bypassing" was coined by John Welwood to mean "a tendency to use spiritual practice to try to rise above our emotional and personal issues—all those messy, unresolved matters that weigh us down" (2000, pp. 11–12). This tends to mean that people infuse their dialogue with a spiritual context, but in fact, religion is being used as a defense to avoid all the authentic emotional processing necessary to actually accomplish true forgiveness.

WHAT IS FORGIVENESS?

Many people tend to view forgiveness as a form of giving in, admitting defeat, or sacrificing. From the perspective of a scorned or betrayed lover, the idea of forgiveness may be seen as weakness. To "forgive" at the time of rejection suggests exposing vulnerable emotions at a time when one may need temporary protection. If one can experience healing from the pain of a transgression, the next step might be to pursue authentic forgiveness so that the distress will not linger on into perpetuity. It requires courage to face one's most painful emotions, which is a different way of viewing strength. Forgiveness is a form of overcoming, not giving in.

There are three main ways in which regulation of emotions can become dysfunctional. First, emotional states can become maximally intense. This means that anger can result in violence or explosive rage expression, sadness can produce overwhelming crying, and shame can become pervasive. Second, people can disengage from emotions to the degree that they are amnesic or numb, or they intellectualize the situation and the emotions remain intact but buried. Third, emotional states can be actively aroused and endure unabated for months, years, or a lifetime without resolution. In this case, people do not have the ability or awareness to actually bring emotional distress to complete closure and are continually emotionally aroused. Closure would mean that it is no longer possible to actually feel the emotion from an incident, at all, on a permanent basis. While the first two dysfunctions are a part of the defenses that prevent forgiveness, the lack of closure is the central emotional dysfunction that authentic forgiveness cures. Since most people are unaware of closure, they are oblivious to the fact that all emotions are potentially transient states.

In my experience, two groups of people commonly believe that the permanent elimination of emotional distress is impossible. War veterans believe their trauma "never goes away," and a parent whose child has died will say, "I'll never get over it." Fortunately, I have witnessed many times the permanent emotional completion of distress in both of these cases. Therefore, the possibility of completely overcoming these traumas does exist, at least through ETT®.

Resentment is the main emotional target for forgiveness. Anger can be seen as a current event and resentment can be seen as the retention of anger over an extended period of time. Anger is part of the fight or flight response built into all of us. Since it is part of a survival mechanism, anger tends to be automatically retained unless a concerted, well-directed effort is used to rescind it. First, it needs to be accessed because it is either buried or the avoidance defense keeps people from pursuing it. Second, it often needs to be expressed in order to begin to free it. This can be done verbally or in writing or otherwise expressed. In most cases a caring listener is required for the best benefit. Third, it needs to be relinquished. While many forms of psychotherapy include the expressive step, fewer forms of counseling effectively retrieve buried emotion, and even fewer accomplish permanent relinquishment. While authentic forgiveness involves all three steps, the third step of relinquishing emotion is best known as forgiveness. However, a fourth step typically occurs in ETT® sessions in which a spontaneous shift in perspective occurs when compassion for the transgressor emerges.

At the most basic level, forgiveness simply means to pardon or cease to demand penalty for a transgression. However, the concept of forgiveness in this work far exceeds the gesture of merely saying, "I forgive you." In psychospiritual work authentic forgiveness is an entire transformation process that may move a person from intense resentment through sadness, shock, shame, etc. and finally arrive at permanent emotional neutrality, extending into compassion toward the transgressor (McCullough, 2001). When this type of transformative process takes place, the physical body changes, cognition shifts, emotions are reversed, night dreams radically shift, and the impact on one's relationships, in general, may change substantially (McCullough & Witvliet, 2002). All of these changes rest on the capacity to progress through intense emotions toward completion and beyond. This type of in-depth emotional shift is rarely achieved by most people, and religious rituals have demonstrated only minimal success for most people. Transforming unresolved emotions is the central strength of ETT®. Therefore, ETT® offers one of the most in-depth and consistent methods to facilitate authentic forgiveness.

JOANNE'S CASE

Joanne, a fifty-eight-year old remarried woman, was the mother of three adult children. She was the victim of severe childhood emotional neglect and abuse. This abuse was corroborated by her two sisters who also suffered from severe psychological dysfunction as adults. As a consequence of emotional neglect, a younger Joanne craved touch so much that she did not resist numerous experiences of sexual abuse by boys. She also experienced rape several times in her history. Joanne had been in over a dozen psychiatric hospitals and had been on numerous psychiatric medications for over forty years. She survived several stranglings—first by her mother and then by a man who was jailed for the offense. Joanne endured over forty rounds of electroconvulsive shock treatments. She lived as a street person for several years. Joanne's diagnoses were extensive—depression, bipolar disorder, complex trauma, PTSD, anorexia nervosa, bulimia, borderline personality disorder, and numerous other conditions. However, after years of psychotherapy, it became clear that at the foundation of a lifetime of severe psychological challenges were both the pervasive childhood neglect and abuse by her mother. Joanne possessed intense hatred toward her mother.

The string of severe negative consequences gave Joanne every possible reason to hate her mother. Even though her mother was now deceased, the buildup of resentment was enormous. Dozens of sessions involved dealing with the consequences of the horrendous abuse. However, after much retrieval of various traumas and massive amounts of cathartic expression, the distress mercifully came to an end.

While the idea of forgiveness finally emerged as an option, Joanne feared that forgiveness would weaken her and condone her mother's behavior. When it was brought to Joann's attention that her mother was dead and that Joanne was the only one suffering by the retention of resentment, she recognized the potential value of forgiveness. As Joanne uttered forgiveness, compassion for her mother emerged for the first time. This occurred while she was viewing yellow wavelengths of light stimulation to hasten the process. All the hard work of forgiveness was done in years of therapy. The final stage of forgiveness arrived with her decision. Joanne reported a physical lightness in her body as if a burden had been lifted.

WHY DON'T PEOPLE FORGIVE?

First, people don't forgive because they are afraid of facing the painful emotions involved in the process of forgiving. Avoidance is often preferable to processing emotions. However, many people simply do not understand the value of forgiveness, especially if it has never been experienced before. Many people rationalize that there is no need to forgive because doing so will not really change the pain. While the past cannot be changed, the emotions felt in the present that have emerged from the past can be changed. These unresolved emotions from the past are really the only components of a disturbing experience that contaminate our present experiences. Some people suppress the expression of current emotions but feel them, while others block them out to the extent that they are no longer conscious of them. In other instances people are simply not yet ready to pursue forgiveness.

Because most people are under the illusion that retaining unresolved emotions will protect them from future transgressions, they do not forgive. Withholding forgiveness creates a definition of us as good and the transgressor as bad. When one has been victimized by a transgressor, the retention of anger may foster the temporary self-perception of being powerful as a means to compensate for powerlessness. Although this is often an illusion of actual power, it is a choice some people make. To protect, to define oneself as good, and to create a temporary sense of empowerment are very significant motives that lead people to abstain from forgiving a transgressor. Therefore, it is not surprising that these psychological defenses are selected over forgiveness. Nonetheless, these are defenses, not resolutions, and unfortunately these defenses tend to be used over and over, resulting in overwhelming symptoms caused by unresolved grudges which form barriers to interpersonal comfort in general.

Clients who deny the need to forgive have displayed the following behaviors:

- a tendency to detach from their emotions
- a dismissal of the connection between their current disturbance and past experience
- an unwillingness to talk about certain people or events in their past
- a minimizing of unresolved emotions
- lying about the truth of their past
- the recurrent experience of unwanted emotions for no known reason
- the failure to remember significant times in their lives
- the defensive rejection of repeated feedback from others about certain topics
- a physical numbness caused by being unaware of body symptoms related to unresolved distress
- a rationalization that it is not valuable to face unresolved emotions from the past
- a tendency to escape discomfort through drugs, work, computers, or other means

Before forgiveness is advocated too strongly, it is important to note the reasons people do not pursue forgiveness. These psychological defenses make it imperative that strategies be developed to overcome these defenses before the possibility of forgiveness can be entertained. Psychological defenses are primarily enacted for the purpose of attempting to avoid or manage disturbing emotions. Therefore, strategies within ETT® are ideally suited to penetrate defenses, access awareness of emotional disturbance, and then rapidly process them to completion. Authentic forgiveness may be one of the most frequent outcomes of ETT®.

One important forgiveness issue occurs when people get angry at God and cannot or will not release this resentment. One study showed that sixty-three percent of the American population report being angry at God at some point in their lives (Exline, Yali, & Lobel, 1999). This resentment is dependent on how a person conceives of God and God's role as an active force in his or her life. If, for example, God's attributes include being all-powerful and a force for "good," this concept sets up disappointment when something tragic occurs. If people project attributes of parental authorities onto the divine, then the same characteristics of parental figures limit the conception of God. Anger at unfair or neglectful parents is likely to be directed at one's version of God. An inability to let go of resentment at human figures is likely to be the same inability in relating to God. Nonetheless, to forgive God is challenging for many people. A small or narrow version of who and what God is can make people vulnerable to anger at God. This resentment presents a challenge as big as any other inability to forgive. The same principles used in psychotherapy for other forgiveness issues can be applied in this issue.

SELF-FORGIVENESS

Forgiving oneself may be the most difficult type of forgiveness. All people make mistakes that they regret. This creates a need to resolve these regretful behaviors. If attachment deficits exist, a person's ability to process emotions is likely to be comprised, leaving regrets unresolved. Therefore, one regret after another may exist unresolved and may be stored as implicit memory. This accumulation of negative emotions directed toward the self can contribute to the belief that one is unworthy, ashamed, incompetent, inferior, or deserving of self-hated, among others. Over time these negative self-perceptions often become viewed as "facts."

One of the unique difficulties of forgiving oneself is that if one feels unworthy, there is often not enough sense of deserving to even consider self-forgiveness. Therefore, the pursuit of self-forgiveness is thwarted by the negative self-perception itself. For example, if one views oneself as "damaged goods," this perceived "fact" compromises motivation to even believe it is possible to correct this negative self-perception. In most cases it is the experience of debilitating symptoms that finally motivates people to enter psychotherapy, and self-forgiveness is only recognized as an issue during this therapy. Unfortunately, most people needlessly experience pervasive shame, guilt, regret, or self-hated without knowing there is a path out of their misery. Even though some people seek help to relieve their self-torture, many of these meet with unsuccessful therapeutic or religious experiences and either give up or perpetually go through rituals attempting to find relief. One of the central tenets of Christianity is that one's "sins" can be forgiven by God. While forgiveness procedures do take place, research suggests that far too many people never acquire relief. Therefore, many people conclude that no real answers exist for them.

Negative self-perception, including that existing outside of conscious awareness, appears to contribute to autoimmune medical conditions. There is significant research to support this concept as well as its effect on health in general (Vincent et al., 2014; Toussaint, Shields, Dorn & Slavich, 2014; Webb, Toussaint & Conway-Williams, 2012). The common factor in autoimmune conditions is that the patient's own immune system attacks itself. In my view the immune system is not malfunctioning when it attacks one's own body. Instead, the immune system may simply be carrying out the brain's directive by attacking the perceived enemy, which in this case is oneself. Self-hatred or shame or a lost sense of self may cause the brain to identify oneself as the enemy, against which the immune system attempts to direct its "protection." Autoimmune conditions include arthritis, multiple sclerosis, Hashimoto's disease, fibromyalgia, and many others. Shame, guilt and self-hatred are believed to be deserving of self-punishment. There is no more exacting form of self-punishment than physical pain, especially chronic physical pain which is an aspect of most autoimmune diseases. I have repeatedly observed that by accessing self-denigrating thoughts and emotions and processing them to conclusion, physical pain and other symptoms can be reduced or concluded in autoimmune conditions.

TREATING RESENTMENT AND GRUDGES

Since the entire idea of forgiveness is best known in its religious context, many people are unaware that certain forms of psychotherapy can facilitate the process for forgiveness efficiently.

Fortunately, I have discovered a particular band of wavelengths of light that profoundly affect self-perception when interpersonal dialogue arouses the emotional aspects of various negative self-perceptions. While an entire range of wavelengths are ultimately necessary to facilitate the process, the key wavelengths of light that impact self-perception involve what appears as some degree of the color orange. Brain research has shown that when people view pictures of themselves, the right prefrontal cortex is activated (Fink et al., 1996; Romanski, 2007). I combined the thousands of observations of orange wavelengths that activated self-perception issues with the brain research about the right prefrontal cortex to target self-perception issues while people are talking about negative self-perception. What occurs consistently and fairly quickly in the process is the change from negative self-perception to positive self-perception. However, there may be traumatic incidents, unresolved core emotional memory, or issues with parental role models that must be processed for the orange visual stimulation to facilitate a long-term change. When aspects of negative self-perception are targeted, a change in self-perception can make possible the steps to self-forgiveness.

The usual resentment possessed by people who have not forgiven others or themselves is typically alleviated by orange or yellow wavelengths of visual stimulation during relevant expression. However, underlying this resentment is often sadness and a wounded self-perception. Green wavelengths affect sadness, and orange helps to relieve negative self-perception. These processes can be facilitated by the use of the spectral chart and the Single Eye Technique for a complete deletion of intense emotions. The advantage of using SRT is the recognition and elimination of dissociation. The Neuro Theralight can also eliminate distressing affect. Multidimensional eye movement (MDEM) can relieve distress from a specific event quickly and efficiently. Peripheral eye stimulation via specialized goggles is a valuable means to rapidly reduce intense current distress. The entire array of ETT® tools and processes are distinctly designed to transform unwanted emotions, which makes ETT® ideal for facilitating forgiveness.

Different forms of prayer and meditation are used to relieve distress of various types. Scientific research has revealed that people who meditate have a greater tendency to forgive others and themselves as compared to people who do not meditate (Oman et al., 2008). This and other evidence strongly suggest that appropriate and consistent attentional skills in meditation encourage less intense reactivity to environmental stressors as well as a capacity to reduce arousal after an unpleasant challenge. To actually forgive is very difficult for most people, and evidence suggests that most people are unable to achieve authentic forgiveness on their own. However, contemplative prayer or meditation can be a very helpful tool. In the case of ETT®, assistance is provided plus inner attentional strategies are used.

One type of meditation that has been found to most directly affect the potential for forgiveness is the Buddhist loving-kindness meditation. This type of meditation involves activating the feeling of loving-kindness and then directing it toward (1) oneself, (2) close friends or relatives, (3) other people one knows, and (4) people one dislikes. This form of meditation has been shown to enhance relationships and even improve low back pain (Carson et al., 2005; Salzberg, 1995).

A case can be made that all forgiveness is self-forgiveness. When one holds resentment toward a transgressor, the holder of the resentment feels the distress, not necessarily the transgressor. It has been said that not forgiving is like taking poison and expecting it to harm the other person. Of course, the one with resentment experiences the torture. When authentic forgiveness occurs, one sheds the distress, thus benefitting the forgiver. This act of self-care can be construed as self-forgiveness.

WHAT GOOD DOES IT DO TO FORGIVE?

How forgiveness fits into such a variety of different religious orientations is interesting. It may be that the transformation from resentment to compassion moves a person closer to a transcendent state. The moral concept of forgiveness is in keeping with several religious perspectives. A third idea is that the act of authentic forgiveness may evoke an alignment with the divine. In Hindu philosophy, forgiveness eliminates bad karma.

The benefits of authentic forgiveness are so vast that is seems irrational not to forgive. However, most people cannot envision the outcome of forgiveness. Therefore, it is important to help people imagine these benefits, especially if they have never experienced them before. Substantial scientific research exists verifying the benefits of forgiveness (Bono, McCullough, & Root, 2007; Karremans et al., 2003; Lawler et al., 2003; Lawler-Row, 2010; Sandage & Janowski, 2010). The following is a list of beneficial outcomes I have observed when authentic forgiveness takes place:

- relief of physical pain
- elimination of obsessive thinking
- the ability to trust and relax more easily
- cessation of nightmares
- spiritual awakening
- ecstasy, joy, or euphoria

Benefits of self-forgiveness may include the following:

- elimination of guilt
- elimination of shame or unworthiness
- comfort with one's body

- improved self-esteem
- confidence
- a greater ability to give and receive love
- self-compassion, self-love
- elimination of physical pain

Several factors contribute to the capacity and choice to forgive. This ability is in part learned through role models. The tendency to forgive is largely influenced by the manner in which people learn to regulate emotions. There is substantial research that patterns of emotional regulation are dictated by attachment patterns formed in early life by the nature of the bond with caregivers. Attachment disorders tend to result in a dysregulation of emotions that is largely characterized by an inability to bring emotional distress to closure. Forgiveness is a means to bring emotional distress to closure. For this reason most people lack the skill of emotional closure and more often repress distress. Therefore, the focus on forgiveness in all major religions around the world is well placed on a fundamental deficiency that is a pervasive problem.

BEING FORGIVEN

In addition to forgiving others and forgiving oneself, the issue of being forgiven can be an issue for many people. Being forgiven is highly related to self-forgiveness. If one cannot forgive oneself, being forgiven by others or by God may not be effective. The concept of being forgiven by God is a central principle of Christian traditions. Since most people have made mistakes which they regret, there is often a need for resolution, even though many people attempt to block or deny the distress.

On many occasions people possess a longing to actually hear words of forgiveness from the one who suffered the offense. It has been shown that receiving forgiveness directly from the victim of one's deeds is not necessary for many people. This is known because I have witnessed people working through unforgiveness when the other person has been deceased. However, some people firmly believe they need to hear "I forgive you" from the person they have harmed in order to let go of the remorse. When this actually takes place, sometimes it works to relieve the regret, but sometimes it does not relieve it. When another's forgiveness does not bring relief, we often discover that a lack of self-forgiveness is the more challenging problem. Then self-forgiveness is therapeutically pursued. The same process also occurs when people have a need to be forgiven by God. Sometimes a ritual of receiving forgiveness by God brings relief and at other times it does not accomplish completion. There is a risk that the spiritual bypass may occur. The spiritual characterization of being forgiven deludes one into believing forgiveness has been received, but the lack of authentic self-forgiveness blocks complete resolution. In this case self-forgiveness is then pursued.

Recognizing how a person conceptualizes the need to be forgiven is important, and the therapist must operate within the person's frame of reference. Sometimes psychotherapy can prepare clients to become aware of their authentic emotions so that when they do partake in religious rituals to be forgiven, these rituals have a higher possibility of achieving their aim.

The process of "making amends" often involves seeking another person's forgiveness for an act that is regretted. Seeking others forgiveness is often valuable in and of itself, regardless of whether the other person agrees to issue forgiveness. However, not receiving forgiveness from others when it is sought can further disturb people who seek forgiveness. Making amends is a risk. Other people need to work through their own victimization when they are ready and in a manner that works for them. While the exercise of making amends can be valuable for the transgressor, further therapeutic work may be necessary to complete the distress resolution. Ultimately, the transformation of emotional distress is highly successful through a variety of ETT® techniques.

WHAT IF FORGIVENESS REALLY WORKED?

Since every major religion sees the need to forgive and be forgiven as a major issue, it suggests that far too many people are living with hate, anger, and distress without a method of consistent relief. Scientific evidence has shown the success rate of forgiveness for those in a religious setting, in general, does not show any better success rate than for those outside of religion (McCullough & Worthington, 1994). While the target of forgiveness is well placed, the actual skill, while well-intentioned, has not generally yielded the outcome sought. This is not to denigrate religion or religious beliefs in any way; it simply highlights the need for better outcomes. ETT® produces a high percentage of successful outcomes in transforming anger into peace, hate into love, and resentment into forgiveness.

Imagine a world in which the skill of forgiveness prevailed. Hypothetically, violence would be drastically reduced. Autoimmune conditions of chronic physical pain would be largely wiped out. People would no longer live being weighed down by grudges. In place of these conditions, there would be a pervasive ethos of compassion for others and for oneself. All of this could be accomplished by mastering one skill—forgiveness.

CHAPTER 3 SUMMARY

This chapter began with a case study that illustrated how ETT® resolved an intense resentment within a single session. Then the universality of the concept of forgiveness in all major religions was shown. Simultaneously, the existence of resentment and violence occurring in history and currently among religious people was noted. Consequences for the lack of forgiveness were listed. This chapter cites research on forgiveness throughout.

A detailed examination of several controversies and ideas of the concept of forgiveness occupied much of this chapter. First, an identification of several ideas takes place because these ideas are disputed to actually be forgiveness, but some people do see them as attributes of forgiveness. It was briefly noted how forgiveness can take place in the justice system through the principle of restorative justice. Then a careful discussion takes place that defines and explains what the nature of forgiveness is according to this author. A case study in which a woman had every reason to resent her mother showed how forgiveness could be facilitated.

Next a close exploration of why people do not forgive took place. A long list of defense mechanisms that are used to cope instead of using forgiveness was provided. How to overcome these defenses is one of the strengths of ETT®. Then the concept of self-forgiveness was examined because self-forgiveness may be the greatest challenge in the psychotherapy of forgiveness.

Resentment and grudges are often the central obstacles to forgiveness. Specific ETT® approaches to resolving resentment and grudges were described. The role of prayer and meditation in forgiveness was described. Then the question "What Good Does It Do to Forgive?" was addressed. Many positive benefits for forgiveness were identified and explained. The issue of being forgiven was explored. Finally, the chapter looked at the possible implications for society if authentic forgiveness really worked.

Chapter Four

Facilitating Extreme Wellbeing

The Emotional Transformation Therapy® (ETT®) samadhi process is one of the most rapid and powerful processes used in psychotherapy or spiritual practices. In various forms of Buddhism and Hinduism, samadhi is viewed as "a state of consciousness that lies beyond waking, dreaming and deep sleep in which mental activity ceases" (Schuhmacher &Woerner, 1994, p. 296). This state is the goal of many forms of meditation, and a similar concept is the goal of Christian centering prayer. To Hindus, samadhi refers to "a super conscious state where there is complete absorption of the intellect into the object of meditation" (Grimes, 1996, p. 296). To Mahayana Buddhists, samadhi could be experienced as the void, "shunyata," total unity, or "dharmakaya." This result can occur when one's consciousness merges with one's sensory experience, such as with sight. A similar Christian concept to samadhi is the "still-point," which is believed to be the interface between the individual soul and the divine. People spend months, years, or a lifetime in spiritual practices to attain these ultimate states. A version of samadhi has been developed through the new method of ETT® that attains this state with maximum speed. This clinically assisted state of samadhi can also facilitate radical improvements for people who may not view it as spiritual and who are not interested in spiritual matters. While aspects of the samadhi process have been developed in various spiritual practices, its basic principles appear to be universal.

Samadhi has been discovered to occur in ETT®, and its facilitation can now take place fairly consistently. The Hindu term samadhi comes closest to capturing this phenomenon, so this term was chosen. One does not need to adopt the Hindu philosophy in order to use it or benefit from it. The consequences of activating this state are usually profound. In-depth improvements, far beyond the scope of known psychotherapy, tend to occur on a consistent basis, and the changes wrought may last weeks, months, or even permanently.

This samadhi states that psychologists might call "pure consciousness" is not just a temporary escape, but an immersion into the roots of being that potentially evokes changes at a fundamental level.

In the shamanic traditions of the Indians of northern Mexico, a similar state to samadhi is referred to as "inner silence," described in the following:

> A peculiar state of being in which thoughts were canceled out and one could function from a level other than that of daily awareness … inner silence meant the suspension of the inner dialogue…
>
> The desired result is what the old sorcerers called "stopping the world," the moment when everything around us ceases to be what it's always been…
>
> It is the moment when man the slave becomes man the free being, capable of feats of perception that defy our linear imagination. (Casteneda, 1998, pp. 103–104)

At the time this book was written, a research project on the brain activity during the ETT® samadhi process was planned to take place. To find the outcome of this research, please check the contact information in Appendix C in the back of this book.

Two different people can have the same experience and describe it using different philosophical concepts. For example, an atheist may have an extremely uplifting experience and call it a "high," but a Pentecostal Christian may have a similar experience and describe it as "God touching me through the Holy Spirit." In fact, Abraham Maslow, one of the founders of humanistic psychology, was an atheist who studied exceptional people—those living highly fulfilled lives—to find out what separated them from others. His research resulted in discovering that these people more often experienced unusual states of well-being. Since Maslow was an atheist, he chose not to use religious or spiritual terms. He created the term "peak experiences" to characterize them. However, the description often bore a resemblance to what many people have described as religious or spiritual experiences. Religious or spiritual labels often confuse or alienate people, but strictly scientific terms may also alienate people with a religious orientation. Since this technique and its outcomes work with agnostics and atheists, I searched for a term to describe the outcomes that encompassed both the religious and nonreligious. I selected the phrase "extreme well-being" because almost all those who have experienced it characterized it as well-being. However, it is a form of well-being that is typically more extreme than most people have ever felt. Therefore, the result of the ETT® samadhi process is one of a variety of forms of extreme well-being that are possible.

There is currently a burgeoning field within psychology called positive psychology (Cooperrider, Whinney, & Stavos, 2003; Orem, Binkert, & Clancy, 2007; Seligman, 2002). This approach suggests that too much emphasis has been placed on problem-focused therapy in the field of psychology and not enough on building strengths and accentuating positive aspects of the client's psychology. While focusing on positive psychological attributes has merit, the methods used to achieve positive states are superficial by comparison and tend to lack the magnitude of positivity that the ETT® samadhi process achieves. Conventional positive psychology uses methods that try to add new emotional learning without transforming old negative emotional learning. This creates a continual competition between old disturbing learning and new positive learning. This leaves the person struggling to overcome psychological disturbance. Instead, ETT® eliminates and transforms old emotional learning into new learning that is effortless to maintain. The focus of facilitating states of extreme well-being without the use of substances is relatively unknown outside of certain psychospiritual practices. Those practices often take so long that most Americans do not sustain these practices consistently or long enough to reach states of extreme well-being. The facilitation of states of extreme well-being advances the idea of positive psychology to entirely different levels of positive experience.

DEVELOPMENT OF THE ETT® SAMADHI PROCESS

From time to time as I was conducting various ETT® procedures using the light device, clients reported the occurrence of spontaneous transcendent experiences. These incidents often took place without bringing up religious or spiritual issues of any kind. After observing this phenomenon repeatedly, a search was conducted to understand why it worked so that these beneficial events could be purposefully produced. Because of the diverse variety and extraordinary quality of these transcendent manifestations, they became referred to as states of extreme well-being. Immediately preceding or during these events clients reported that the light appeared three-dimensional and its beauty was perceived as extraordinary. I noted that when these visual perceptions occurred, people appeared to enter a different state of consciousness and would (1) experience a state of awe and wonder, (2) experience a self-reflective state of observance beyond ego-based emotions, and (3) experience perception of a euphoric state of seeing beauty. I eventually recognized that these visual experiences were indicators of depth awareness or transcendence. Several people who had these experiences eventually had Kundalini awakenings. It was noted that preceding and during these awakenings clients often entered a state of mind in which they experienced a complete stoppage of thoughts. At these points I became curious about how these cessation experiences led to states of extreme well-being.

In Goswami's (1980) book, *Layayoga*, ancient concepts were translated from Sanskrit into English. He states,

> When the functions of the senses, sense-mind and intelligence completely stop ..., super conscious knowledge arises from the calm and one-pointed consciousness.... The highest stage of one-pointedness of consciousness is Samadhi—superconcentration. In this state of prana (power principle), functioning in relation to mind becomes concentrated and, as a result, mind is transformed into supermind. (p. 78)

He goes on to say that this state provides a fertile ground for the supreme union of Shiva (divine masculine) and Shakti (divine feminine). I determined that complete brain entrainment by use of light, strobe, and interpersonal guidance achieved this cessation point (one-pointnessness) much faster and more easily than did months of meditation effort. I was aware of the impact of breathwork through yoga, Rebirthing, and Radix. I hypothesized that limiting a specialized form of breathwork to five minutes would be all that was necessary, since it was combined with visual stimulation. This combination could yield a more precisely directed process with enormous impact (supermind). Finally, I added the assertion of the client's verbalized wish in order to target an outcome. The result of this synthesis yielded consistent and radically powerful outcomes.

The ETT® samadhi process draws from ancient wisdom and current technology and is designed to facilitate transcendent states along with appropriate stabilization that often provides

1. contact with a person's deepest inner self
2. an experience of living in the present moment to a profound degree
3. profound relief of distress
4. direct spiritual experiences
5. an experience of states of extreme well-being that may last for weeks or even permanently
6. relief of physical pain and other physical symptoms.

PURPOSE OF THE ETT® SAMADHI PROCESS

The ETT® samadhi process can be used for a wide variety of objectives. While the process can be largely directed toward targeted outcomes, results may occur beyond the objectives if the targeted outcomes are vaguely described. Results may be "surprises," moving a person toward a greater good. In one case, the client asked for the vague goal of resolving any spiritual blocks.

This request resulted in the surprise healing of a forty-year-old ruptured ear drum. This complete healing was verified by her physician. In another case, a woman who underwent the samadhi process reported synesthesia—the concomitant experience of one sense being experienced by another sense, such as hearing color or tasting sound. In her case, she heard the sound of sights. This woman had never even heard of synesthesia, let alone asked for it. More commonly when people seek peace or relief from anxiety, the omission of fear is so unlike anything they previously experienced that it is sometimes interpreted as feeling "dazed." Overall, the samadhi process possesses a profound capacity to interrupt long-term dysfunctional thinking patterns and shift perspectives.

Clients have used the samadhi process for the following purposes:

- to facilitate a direct experience with the divine if desired
- to facilitate living in the moment
- to relinquish fear
- to relinquish chronic grief
- to relinquish existential crises of lack of meaning and purpose in life
- to facilitate awakening of emotional experience
- to facilitate love
- to facilitate change from obsessive thinking
- to facilitate a variety of possible mystical experiences
- to facilitate peace
- to facilitate joy
- to facilitate relief of physical symptoms

The ETT® samadhi process often yields a profound transcendent experience while simultaneously allowing people to make direct contact with their deepest authentic selves. There are many theories that attempt to describe this innermost self. Carl Jung calls it the "Self." Almaas (1984) describes it as "essence." While there are theoretical differences in these concepts, for now I will simply describe it as the "authentic self." People going through the process often say it feels like "coming home." This authentic self is often ineffable and exists beyond all defenses, memories, thoughts, and learnings. As a consequence of making contact with this authentic self, people often recognize their purpose and direction in life, and sometimes they report getting back on their natural spiritual pathway.

> H. Almaas described "essence" as that which is most intimately ourselves. It is most deeply our nature, and it is the most precious and most beautiful center of us. It is what moves our hearts, illuminates our minds, fulfills our lives.... It is the reality of us, the truth of us. (Almaas, 1986, p. 81)

However, Almaas makes it clear that this essence is typically not conscious and is obscured by our personality, our defenses, and a lifetime of trying to be who others think we should be. Therefore, it usually requires extraordinary processes in order to make direct contact with this deep inner self.

OUTCOMES OF THE ETT® SAMADHI PROCESS

The following list of outcomes were produced within twenty minutes and occurred during each person's first experience of the ETT® samadhi process. The first two cases were facilitated by me, but all the other cases were facilitated by therapists who were taught to use it for the first time:

- In a live demonstration in front of an ETT® class, Lilly, a fifty-year-old married woman, went into a spontaneous state of ecstasy during the samadhi process. Her response was characterized by laughing, crying, and laughing. She later described it as overwhelming love and joy. She had been completely without sexual desire for months before the process. Two days after the process, without any touch, a spontaneous orgasm occurred while she was alone watching the news on TV. One month later she reported feeling "open, bolder, speaking up more, great energy, and feeling very alive."
- In the case of Emma, a thirty-year-old woman with stage IV breast cancer, the ETT® samadhi process allowed her to experience the presence of the God she had believed in but had never experienced directly. In a second ETT® samadhi session, Emma saw a cross and an angel praying in the light. A few days after this session, her brain scan showed a substantial reduction of cancer in her brain. While no one knows for sure if it was the cause of the change, the timing suggests it was.
- Macy, a sixty-five-year-old woman, asked for any spiritual blockages to be alleviated. She experienced brief ear pain after the process. She had had a collapsed eardrum for forty years. Medical examination two days later showed a completely normal eardrum.
- Leslie, a thirty-nine-year-old woman who was an extreme caretaker, was discovering an inner inclination to music. She had an experience of contact with her deceased father and with God. They both encouraged her, through verbal messages, to let go of taking care of them and others. The samadhi process yielded an experience of synesthesia in which color was perceived as music and other sights communicated sounds to her. However, she continued to be able to function normally. Her synesthesia continued long after the process (eight weeks at the time of this writing).

- Serena, an emotionally intense and anxious forty-year-old woman, experienced contact with her deceased grandmother during the samadhi process. It was a nurturing and soothing experience. Subsequent to the process, she felt "dazed," but realized later that it was a deep relaxation that lasted for weeks.
- Andrea, a sixty-five-year-old woman with chronic low energy and frequent stress, initially felt very "happy" after the process. She later described it as peace and reported a steady increase in the amount of her daily energy.
- Sharon, a sixty-year-old woman, initially felt conflict and excessive distress. During and after the samadhi process she reported an excited ecstasy but was still able to function well on a daily basis.

Alan Watts describes a variety of self perceptions that may parallel experiences in ETT® sessions following spiritual awakening in the following:

> One person may say that he has found the whole answer to the whole mystery of life, but somehow cannot put it into words. Another will say that there never was a mystery, and thus no answer to it, for what the experience made clear to him was the irrelevance and artificiality of all our questions. One declares himself convinced that there is no death, his true self being as eternal as the universe. Another states that death has simply ceased to matter, because the present moment is so complete that it requires no future.... One will get the sense that his ego or self has expanded to become the entire universe, whereas another will feel that he has lost himself altogether and that what he called his ego was never anything but an abstraction.... (1984, p. 16)

In most cases, a client undergoing the ETT® samadhi process has profound experiences during or immediately afterward. However, in some cases the effect is more subtle, and the most strongly felt impact occurs hours or days later. Because of this delayed effect, it may be difficult for the client to link the process with the outcome. For example, one complex client with whom I had worked for four years exhibited a unique form of dissociation in which extreme sleepiness took over each time emotionally charged issues emerged, a response which prohibited psychological progress. He finally recalled that as a child his uncle would lure him into sexual abuse, and afterward he felt so guilty that he would escape by taking a nap and then awaken as though nothing took place. The pattern became so conditioned that it did not allow him to participate in the emotional aspects of psychotherapy. We finally broke the pattern by first using spectral resonance technique (SRT) to reduce the dissociation. In the next session, the ETT® samadhi process was used in which he participated without sleepiness. Next, profound emotional memories arose, but this time he was able to participate in psychotherapy in such a way that he progressed through intense affect and had life-changing insights. His major symptoms were gone for the first time.

In this case, psychotherapy had been limited for four years because he would immediately fall asleep whenever significant emotions arose. The extreme slowing down of therapeutic processes was complicated by a huge array of unresolved emotions from a severely dysfunctional family of origin. It was necessary to get beyond this automatic sleep reaction before he could even participate in the ETT® samadhi process. Then the ETT® samadhi process was used, and while it felt good immediately afterward, it was not particularly transcendent. However, his response to psychotherapy concerning intense emotion was markedly different from that experienced during the previous four years of therapy. He, in fact, stated that more change had taken place in those four sessions than in the previous four years!

The following describes the experience of a nonreligious person who underwent the ETT® samadhi process:

> As an atheist, my experience with the samadhi process was similar to other times in my life where I had experienced a change of consciousness, only there was more of a sense of wholeness and clarity. The feeling was that of floating, of disconnecting from the material world. I was connected to my body and I had an awareness of having a body, but I was not "feeling" my body. The feeling was as if I were a traveler in space with nothingness all around me. This "nothingness" carried no judgment with it. It was not good, not bad, it just was. It was a consciousness of "being," just being, not being anyone, or anything, just being. It was a state of being in which the nothingness was growing inside me and expanding me, not in an excited or joyful or happy way, just expanding. I was aware that there was a world around me, but suddenly it didn't matter, nothing mattered, only the "nothingness" mattered. I would say this was euphoric, but not in a sense of a drug-induced euphoria, more of a euphoria that resulted from being in the universe. My thoughts were clear, they just were not important. Being was all that mattered.
>
> Afterwards, the physical sensation of floating remained, as did the feeling of being separate or apart from the world, and it was ok. I could not think about anything, I didn't want to think about anything, I just wanted to enjoy being.
>
> My experience was as a part of learning the samadhi process so I could use it with my clients, but I had to wait until a week later to find out how to do it. I was the first volunteer in my class, and after I achieved that state of consciousness, I couldn't focus on the procedural aspect. I really didn't want to. I just wanted to "be" and to enjoy that feeling of being. Objects appeared closer and larger and colors more brilliant, and I just didn't care about anything.
>
> Having that experience has opened the door for me to practice recognizing what is really important in my day-to-day life. It has helped me realize that "being" is the most important thing we can do and to recognize when the world gets in the way of my ability to just "be."

Many therapists assert that facilitating "presence" is a high goal in counseling (Stern, 2004). This procedure routinely facilitates a perception of a more profound presence.

Cross-culturally, dialogue with deceased people is very common, although in the United States and Europe it is generally considered very peculiar (see Chapter 9 for more about this). In one ETT® course in which the ETT® samadhi process was taught, several therapists facilitated and experienced the process. In the six sessions conducted, three of these healthy participants experienced dialogue with deceased relatives and one person reported hearing a message from God. None of these people have had these experiences previously, nor did they seek them. In all cases, the messages were positive and helpful. Dialogue with deceased friends and relatives is a common experience in people with near-death experiences.

POTENTIAL OBSTACLES AND RISKS

The overall ETT® samadhi experience consists of a sequence of three phases: (1) preparation for readiness, (2) samadhi process, and (3) adjustment to aftereffects. The key to readiness is that the client must have enough trust in the facilitator and the method to fully relax into the process. This may require one session or many, depending on the individual's bond with the facilitator. Sometimes it is necessary for the person to first work through issues of control and hypervigilance in order to be able to surrender to the process. For example, obsessive thinking would be an obstacle to overcome. Dissociation also prohibits success of the samadhi process. Clients are asked to identify anything they wish to let go of and anything they wish to move toward, so that this intention can be incorporated in the process.

The risk of potential seizures exists when a strobic light is being used. Less than one percent of the general population has epileptic seizures. Less than one percent of epileptic seizures are photosensitive seizures, seizures initiated by flickering light (Breiling, 1996, p. xix). In actual experience I have conducted ETT® with a strobing light on thousands of people in eight different countries, and only one person had a seizure. The possibility of having a seizure is averted by simply asking each client if they have a history of seizures. All ETT® therapists are trained about what to do if a client has a seizure. If clients have had seizures, the strobic portion of light stimulation is then not used. However, it should be noted that certain medications such as antidepressants increase the risk of seizures. In one case, a woman reported to have had photosensitive seizures when she was on an older antidepressant, Ludiamil. However, once she got off that medication, all seizures disappeared. Since we did not know if the medication had long-term seizure effects, initially the mutual decision was made to avoid the strobe function. However, she later chose to use it, and there were no seizure effects. In the vast majority of cases, even though antidepressants lower the seizure threshold, it is extremely rare for a seizure to occur. While the risk of provoking seizures hypothetically exists, it is an infinitesimally small risk.

While the treatment of addiction can be aided significantly by the ETT® samadhi process, it is not an addiction treatment procedure by itself. The use of alcohol, marijuana, cocaine, and other drugs before a session can limit its impact. An entirely separate and complete addiction treatment process used within ETT®—a breakthrough in addiction treatment—is available.

When people possess significant repressed psychological material, the ETT® samadhi process may produce awareness of emotions that were not conscious. This can be interpreted as a negative emotional outcome if the participant is unaware that the surfacing of unresolved emotions is potentially constructive. Of course, when this happens these emotions should be processed to completion to prevent ongoing discomfort. This function of the ETT® samadhi process occurs less frequently, but potentially serves to relieve the person from symptoms associated with repressed emotions, which potentially leads to states of extreme well-being.

One important observation I have made is that people may ask for certain outcomes, but the fact that they have never experienced these outcomes means they cannot actually know that they want these results. For example, one person considered herself to have a Buddhist perspective. She asked to let go of her massive amount of fear and to live fully in the moment. After the samadhi process she was highly disoriented and reported that she couldn't think. The next day she was asked if she felt any fear. She said no. When she was asked if she was living in the moment, she said yes. To actually eliminate focus on one's past or on the future and be totally immersed in the present is more of a radical change than one might imagine before having the experience. Basically, some people have difficulty accurately imagining what it would be like if their fondest wishes came true. Therefore, client-initiated objectives should be pursued with appropriate caution in regard to the outcomes.

Even when a person has had a very positive experience and change due to the ETT® samadhi process, the people closest to the recipient may have difficulty adjusting to the change. In the case of Sharon, mentioned earlier, her change was so radical that her loved ones thought something was wrong with her after the process. In fact, her chronic anxiety changed to peace. In other cases if the participant in the process became more independent, but the partner had become accustomed to his/her dependency, the change might be perceived as intimidating, distancing, or strange. All of these perceptions could result in distress for the partner, friend, or colleague. The magnitude of the transformation from the process could change an individual's self-perception so substantially that when other people continue to view the participant in the same way they did before the ETT® samadhi process, the mismatch of self-perception with other's perceptions could result in distress. The difference between the old self and the new self must be talked about and reconciled for the best long-term outcome to be maintained by the person who went through the process.

ELEMENTS OF THE ETT® SAMADHI PROCESS

The ETT® samadhi process combines three elements, all of which possess therapeutic powers when used separately. When combined in the prescribed manner, this synthesis elevates all three modalities. The modalities include interpersonal support, precise visual brain stimulation, and specific breathwork. These elements are uniquely combined to elevate the nature and power of the impact while simultaneously eliciting stabilization.

In the realm of spiritual practices, there are a variety of breathing procedures that have been used in yoga and other Eastern methods. These approaches conceive of breath as spirit itself, or in Eastern terms, "prana." Prana, considered to be universal energy, is harnessed in yoga and meditation. The practice of specific forms of breathwork for spiritual purposes is called pranayama.

Powerful forms of breathwork have long been used in certain forms of psychotherapy, particularly for their capacity to enhance relevant retrieval of implicit memory. The neo-Reichian method of Radix uses breathwork to enhance its body-oriented form of psychotherapy (Kelly, 2004). The method of Rebirthing has as its central focus, intensive breathwork (Orr & Ray, 1977). Stan Grof, M.D., developed holotropic breathwork as a means to access implicit memory and transcendent states (Eyerman, 2013; Holmes et al., 1996; Rhinewine & Williams, 2007). While these methods are certainly impactful for retrieval, it is questionable in many cases if these methods actually accomplish long-term change of emotional memory.

Although breath, spirit, and/or prana refer to a universal force, accessing the subjective experience of this universal force often requires specific ways of using breath and consciousness. I have seen many people who had recently undergone holotropic breathwork (shallow, rapid breathing for extended periods with a guide). While they all retrieved unconscious psychological material, they also had not integrated the experience. I could see that long intense breathwork was powerful, but I could also see that a cathartic experience was often temporary relief. Therefore, the use of a short-term intensive breathing regimen (five minutes) to activate access to this universal force was selected while simultaneously using specific wavelengths of viewed light. This facilitates a more rapid access to implicit memory and transcendent states while simultaneously grounding and guiding the person.

This brief form of breathwork allows clients to suspend their defenses, resulting in an elevated impact of viewing the light and hearing the facilitator's input. This process of using breath with sight is more likely to rapidly infuse perception with spiritual phenomena than the use of breathing techniques alone. Transpersonal events become more palpable when one's visual experience is dominated with specific wavelengths of light known to activate specific brain mechanisms. However, the far red wavelengths tend to activate the brain's insula, causing a sense of embodiment which renders stability as transcendence occurs. The ETT® samadhi process begins and ends with far red wavelengths of light to elicit a stable context for transcendence to occur.

The ETT® samadhi process involves an interpersonal facilitator. This is important for several reasons. First, a trusting bond with a personal facilitator increases the client's ability to surrender to the process because the participant knows someone is present to make adjustments, provide encouragement and support, and to demonstrate compassion. Second, the samadhi process often brings about an inability to think and make decisions because a central component of the process is to yield control, which often results in focusing on experience not thoughts. Third, the ETT® samadhi process magnifies sensitivity to many aspects of the present experience, including an awareness of the facilitator's voice and intonation. This means that if the facilitator is caring, the participant's experience of comfort is elevated. Of course, the opposite is also true. Therefore, a facilitator must be aware that his/her state of mind and verbal communication should be optimal. A trusting bond between the facilitator and participant can magnify the effects of the ETT® samadhi process to profound levels of benefit.

Samadhi occurs when one's sensory experience merges with one's consciousness (Goswami, 1980). Of all the five senses, our visual sense accounts for eighty percent of our sensory intake. The visual neural networks of the brain account for the majority of brain cells that access directly or indirectly almost all parts of the brain.

Immediately after the breathwork on far red, embodiment is established. Then other wavelengths of light are used in a careful sequence throughout the process. Since a rhythmic flickering light elicits brainwave entrainment within seconds or minutes, the rhythmic flickering light is used to capture mental attention consistently and easily. Therefore, when the flicker rate of the light is slowly elevated, the client is asked to report at which point his/her attention feels absorbed by viewing the light. At that point consciousness and vision merge. Whenever visual stimuli dominate attention in certain ways, visual perception merges with the subjective sense of consciousness, yielding a state of pure consciousness. If the person can verbalize during the process, he/she often describes the feeling as being one with the light.

The visual stimulation component of the ETT® samadhi process is the key element that transforms normal waking consciousness into samadhi.

A sequence of precise wavelengths of light has an amplified impact when it is used immediately after the intense five minutes of breathwork. At the key point in the process, the client reports that he/she experiences complete absorption into the visual stimulus. Just after this occurs the client is encouraged to verbally make requests. Then the procedure involves surrender into the process. The facilitator provides support, direction, and often silence as the client experiences samadhi.

INTEGRATION OF SAMADHI EFFECTS

1. One of the outstanding effects of the ETT® samadhi process that occurs almost one hundred percent of the time concerns a shift in the intensity of sensory experience. This is also well known to occur after meditation. Since this approach involves visual stimulation, it particularly affects the experience of visual perception. Things appear brighter, clearer, and have more depth. People use terms like high definition in comparing their sight to television. However, people often describe their visual perception as three-dimensional. Sights, sounds, and touch appear to be awakened in a new way as if the immediate environment appears new, more intense, and more "alive." Clients often report a fascination with their sensory perception of certain things around them. It is helpful to inquire about participant's perception so that they may express it and be validated. They often recognize that something is distinctly different but cannot pinpoint what it is until they verbalize it. The change is often so significant that body movement causes a brief disorientation and the need for readjustment.
2. For safety purposes clients are asked to sit for a few minutes until they feel stable and competent to drive a vehicle.
3. A follow-up on the client the next day is highly recommended. Most clients experience disorientation because the experience is likely to be so different from anything they have previously experienced.
   A. Many people say they wondered if they were going crazy.
   B. Peculiar physical changes may cause people to have medical fears.
   C. Absence of usual cognition makes some people report feeling "dazed."
   D. Positive euphoria makes people wonder if others perceive them as strange.
   E. Unusual spiritual experiences may occur, leaving those who are unprepared with no way to make sense of it.

In general, the ETT® samadhi process facilitates states of extreme wellbeing. However, one person diagnosed with bipolar disorder experienced a more embodied, emotionally quiescent experience with this process, which was perceived as a form of comfort more than well-being in the usual sense. Since the samadhi process dominates one's experience so profoundly, normal cognitive skills made it appear as if the person cannot think normally for a period of time. Upon further exploration, it was discovered that one's usual capacity of intellectualization tends to be suspended during and immediately after the process but resumes later. In fact, cognitive capacity is ultimately usually enhanced when such issues as fear, anger, and sadness are released because these emotions no longer interfere with cognition. However, some people initially mislabel "different" as "bad":

4. Even though outcomes are almost always ultimately positive, the impact of radical changes often requires support, explanations, and normalization.
5. Adjustment is particularly challenging when contact with one's essence challenges one's ego perception. Not knowing who one is can be disturbing and requires help for resolution.
6. If the participant has been participating in spiritual practices, such as meditation or Christian centering prayer, and is acquainted with the possibilities attainable through these practices, the adjustment may be easier. Many people with these backgrounds reach new heights through the ETT® samadhi process.

It is a risk to drink alcohol, smoke marijuana, or use significant mind-altering substances soon after the ETT® samadhi experience. One woman experienced the ETT® samadhi process in the late afternoon and that night proceeded to drink two glasses of wine with her dinner, which had never been a problem before then. However, this evening the wine made her profoundly dizzy, disoriented, and it was as if she were severely drunk. Her sensitivity level was completely different after the samadhi process.

It should be noted that all of these disorienting aftereffects occurred in earlier cases. Further development of the ETT® samadhi process includes incorporation of the phrase "I ask that my adjustment to the changes I wish will be quick and easy." This wish is incorporated into the process to enhance a smooth transition. This request has eased the degree of disorientation.

THE ETT® SAMADHI PROCESS AND PSYCHOPATHOLOGY

Accessing one's innermost authentic self may be the most depth aspect in all of psychotherapy. Since the ETT® samadhi process penetrates beneath the personality and the defenses with which people have identified, contact with it can be very challenging. In fact, A.H. Almaas recommends against it for people with severe psychological diagnoses because people with severe disorders are seen as too unstable to manage the effects. While it is appropriate to recognize that penetrating personal defenses can make people feel vulnerable in a way that they have never felt before, it can also bring them in contact with the authenticity they have often searched for all their lives.

My experience with people who have severe psychological pathology has been that the ETT® samadhi process can be used effectively with these clients under certain circumstances of use. The following types of severe psychopathology have been treated:

- borderline personality disorder
- bipolar disorder
- dissociative identity disorder
- severe major depression

In the cases of borderline personality and bipolar disorders, if the interpersonal bond had been carefully built over time and the clients achieved a good level of trust in the process, the ETT® samadhi process helped, but not without substantial support of adjustment. In the dissociative identity disorder case, if a single alter personality could remain engaged during the process, the ETT® samadhi process could be used with one personality at a time. In this Dissociative Identity Disorder (DID) case, the impact was significant, but not life-changing, until it took place several times with each separate personality. In cases of severe depression and/or trauma, a single session of the ETT® samadhi process was radically transformative. The ETT® samadhi process can be used to amplify progress in severe psychopathology if more preparation before and more adjustment support afterwards is custom-tailored to the client's unique features.

There is a striking similarity between what people in various spiritual practices have observed and described and what has been observed with the ETT® samadhi process. For example, Welwood's (2000) description of spiritual awakenings parallels what has been seen in the ETT® samadhi process:

> As awareness starts to move beyond the boundaries of the conditioned personality structure, this expansion inevitably challenges that structure, flushing out old, subconscious, reactive patterns that often emerge with a vengeance. Traditional religions used to describe these obstacles and attacks along the path in terms of demons or devils. But from a modern perspective, they can also be understood and worked with psychologically—as subconscious aspects of one's conditional personality structure that often break through into consciousness only when that structure is thoroughly challenged by the process of awakening to one's larger nature. If these psychological issues are not addressed, they often cause

> distortions in people's spiritual development. So it is not enough just to have spiritual realizations. It is also essential to deconstruct the subconscious emotional and mental patterns that are held in the body and the mind that prevent people from fully embodying a larger way of being in their lives. (pp. xvii–xviii)

CASEY'S EXPERIENCE

Casey was an attractive, bright, fifty-year-old divorced female who had been in weekly therapy for many years. She had issues that were consistent with borderline personality disorder and had a history of pervasive dysfunction in her family of origin. Although Casey had progressed in therapy, it was a long and difficult struggle involving an enormous amount of emotional distress with pervasive fear. Casey described her early childhood as dominated by fear of her father. She recalled him as being unpredictable, ready to explode in anger at anytime, and highly abusive to the entire family. Her mother was always sweet and beaten down by him. Casey believed her father might literally kill her if she did the wrong thing. This fear of her father was internalized as continuous fear throughout her life, even though her father had now been deceased for many years. In all the cases in which I have used the ETT® samadhi process, this one showed the most disorientation.

I decided to offer the ETT® samadhi process to Casey. I carefully explained that it is a powerful process that could end all or much of her fear, but that it would only take a few minutes. I explained that it might facilitate changes that were so strong that she might feel disoriented. However, Casey was so exhausted from struggling with intense emotions that she was willing to take the risk. When I asked what her goals might be, she said, "I want to let go of my fear and I want to live in the moment." Then the ETT® samadhi process was conducted in fifteen minutes.

After the ETT® samadhi process, Casey appeared highly disoriented and was encouraged to sit in the waiting room for a while before she drove her vehicle. However, she refused to stay and left. I talked to Casey by telephone later that day, and she was very angry at me for conducting that procedure. She reported that she couldn't think and that I had not adequately prepared her for the consequence.

I spoke with Casey again the next day and she was even angrier at me for her disorientation. This time I asked her if she was living in the moment, and she said "Yes." Then I asked her if she felt any fear and she said "No." However, she continued to be angry at me. I strongly encouraged her to come in for another session to alleviate the disorientation.

When she entered the next session, I encouraged her to express her distress and anger at me. After providing support and empathy as she expressed herself, we began to explore what took place. She reported that the fear from the relationship with her father was her central emotion and all other emotions could only be identified in relation to that fear. Without that fear she could not label her emotions. Without these emotions she became unclear even about who she was.

This perspective was a radical departure from how Casey felt and thought throughout the three years I had seen her. While Casey was an atheist, much of what she said could be seen within the framework of spiritual wisdom. Regardless of what philosophical framework one chooses to use, this was a profound transformation of emotions and identity.

Subsequent to this dialogue, Casey reported total surprise at what she felt and said in the position of the "emergent self." This was a completely new orientation of confidence, strength, and clarity. We conducted two more sessions in a similar manner. By the end of the third session, Casey spontaneously felt the prior self merge into the emergent self. This process occurred as if the emerging self was how she would be without incorporating any of her childhood fear. It appeared that the samadhi experience penetrated beneath all her defenses and personality structure to an authentic secure essence, and then brought resources forth into conscious awareness. While this emergence left her initially disoriented, with appropriate integration work, the new resources were implemented into her consciousness.

SAMADHI COMPARED TO PRAYER

The ETT® samadhi process can incorporate a wish fulfillment function that yields consistent outcomes which could be compared to some aspects of intercessory prayer. Currently, there is a massive amount of research dealing with the efficacy of prayer (Ai et al., 2010; Astin, Harkness, & Ernst, 2000; Byrd, 1988; Curtis & Robertson, 2009; Hodge, 2007). However, many people continue to report that their prayers remain unanswered. The ETT® samadhi process includes (1) perception of direct contact with pure consciousness, the divine, or ultimate reality, (2) asserting an intention in the form of a request, and (3) surrendering the need to control the outcome. While most forms of prayer bear a similar sequence, the direct experience of oneness does not often occur during typical prayer to the extent it does through the ETT® samadhi process. By virtue of achieving this transcendent state, a different state of consciousness is brought into play so that the request is more likely to achieve desired outcomes. Due to this key factor, the ETT® samadhi process consistently yields profound pragmatic positive effects.

The comparison of the ETT® samadhi process to intercessory prayer is intriguing because not only do people's requests for themselves manifest consistently, but requests concerning other people have been known to occur. For example, a sixty-six-year-old woman had an ex-son-in-law who appeared to be on the verge of committing a violent action against her daughter. This man did not believe in psychotherapy and had refused counseling many times. As this woman was undergoing the ETT® samadhi process, she requested that he seek treatment. She was stunned to report to me later that the ex son-in-law voluntarily entered a psychiatric hospital the next day after her samadhi experience. Events like this appear to occur at a rate beyond chance possibilities with the ETT® samadhi process.

THE FRUITS OF CONTEMPLATION

Certain types of inward attention characterized by mental stillness focus on experience in the moment. These practices are variously called meditation, contemplative prayer, or other terms. These practices exist in different variations in almost all religions. While these practices are most central to Hinduism and Buddhism, they are essentially a universal phenomenon. It may be that people using contemplative practices in different religions may have more in common with each other than with people within their own religion who do not participate in contemplative practices. There is a risk of offending people in many religions by this perspective because adherents to each religion tend to deem their beliefs as the right and only way, and the idea that there is a commonality among contemplative methods may be discounted. Certain consistent phenomena appear to occur in contemplative practices that activate spiritual, psychological, and physical potentials to extraordinary levels over time. People in different religions who have had the most profound experiences have often credited contemplative practices to be the most significant factor in their growth. In fact, research on various types of meditation verifies most of these claims today (Lindberg, 2005; Shapiro & Walsh, 2003; Wolf & Abell, 2003). The ETT® samadhi process shows strong evidence for achieving the same benefits as most contemplative practices; however, it is a rapid, direct path to these same benefits while requiring less diligent perseverance and self-discipline. It may be that benefits are not from the ability to endure, but in the fruits of the state of consciousness acquired.

IS IT GOOD TO FEEL GOOD?

Just because something makes people feel good does not mean it is necessarily healthy, constructive, or in the best interests of the person. People claim that illegal drugs, prescription drugs, or addictive behaviors like sex addiction, gambling, or shopaholism makes them feel good. However, if these means for happiness produce addiction, they foster dependency, loss of control, and obsessive-compulsive drives.

There is a distinct difference in the effect of addictive drugs, whether legally prescribed or illicit, and contemplative states in that addictive drugs tend to facilitate blockage from psychological distress resulting in states of perceived wellbeing. However, contemplative states, psychedelic drugs, and plant medicine tend to provoke unpleasant or buried emotional distress to conscious awareness on the path to states of extreme wellbeing. This second route often necessitates a cleansing or purification in order to achieve extreme wellbeing. If a person has not processed unwanted or buried emotional distress, psychedelic drugs, plant medicine, and contemplative practices will likely cause the distress to surface that already exists. Psychedelics like lysergic acid diethylamide can often produce bad experiences because they are unconscious amplifiers. Not only does one re-experience unresolved trauma but the experience is amplified to a higher intensity. While both categories of activators can produce states of extreme wellbeing, one is at high risk to pursue spiritual experiences through psychedelics or plant medicine if clearing unresolved distress has not been done. Therefore, the quest to feel good is not the same with addictive drug use versus contemplative approaches like the ETT® samadhi process.

It can be pointed out that some eating disorders, the runner's high, and some sexual addictions do activate internal resources for pleasure in an addictive way. People can get addicted to their own inner biochemistry. Is there a possibility that ETT®'s samadhi process could also be addictive? Almost anything can produce addiction. However, the ETT® samadhi process itself possesses built-in mechanisms to identify and eliminate addictions by incorporating the issue into the ETT® samadhi process. The ETT® samadhi protocol for addictive craving elimination is a separate process that can be used for a permanent change. The ETT® samadhi process is not focused only on getting high for the sake of getting high. In fact, research on people in substance abuse programs who have spiritual transcendent experiences found that these people have better outcomes than those who did not experience transcendence (Piedmont, 2004). By virtue of contact with the person's essence, euphoric experiences are instead a natural by-product of discovering one's authentic awareness.

NATURAL WELLBEING

Two of the most common means for coping under crisis conditions are the use of pharmaceuticals, both prescription and illicit, and the use of support through religion and spiritual practices. While these approaches can be helpful, both of these means are fraught with risks and ineffectiveness. While the ETT® samadhi process can literally replace most drug remedies and acquire more productive long-lasting benefits without drug side-effects, it can also amplify the religious/spiritual benefits to more profound levels. In the list of previous case study outcomes, Lilly had a profound euphoric state of extreme love and joy which paralleled the states acquired by the drug ecstasy, except that it was produced in twenty minutes, lasted over two months, had no drug side-effects, and left her able to function.

One person in six who underwent the ETT® samadhi process in an ETT® training course developed synesthesia from it. Synesthesia has long been the topic of significant controversy, ranging from conceiving of it as a serious pathology to a higher skill (Dann, 1998). Synesthesia has been the subject of numerous scientific studies for decades (Cytowic & Engleman, 2011; Saenz & Koch, 2008; Ward, Huckstep, & Tsakanikos, 2006). It is now understood how it occurs in the brain and that it is a fairly uncommon phenomenon. The fact that synesthesia occurred as a consequence of the ETT® samadhi process parallels research findings that a much higher percentage of meditators experience synesthesia than the general population (Walsh, 2005). It is perceived to be related to creativity, and its value may be related to how it is accepted and used.

Another outcome of the use of the ETT® samadhi process is a phenomenon that is sometimes referred to as "transcendent sex." However, this term can be misleading because it may occur before, during, or after a sexual encounter that may or may not involve actual sexual intercourse. While transcendent sex is not the purpose of the ETT® samadhi process, nor is it likely, it has taken place and is a possibility. Dr. Jenny Wade has conducted scientific research on this phenomenon and interviewed ninety-one people who have reported this experience. Dr. Wade (2004) characterizes transcendent sex as follows:

- the sense of transcending (going beyond or breaking through) the usual constraints of space, time, or self that constitute normal, waking consciousness
- a pervasive sense that these events participate in, or come from, a supernatural force, which people usually associate with Spirit, however understood
- involves relationship (Wade, 2004, pp. 11–12)

However, the samadhi process is not a sexual technique designed for the purpose such as Tantric methods. Religion and sexuality have had a very tenuous relationship in almost all major religions. However, research suggests that sexual experiences may be the most common trigger for transcendent experiences, but over eighty percent of people who experience it do not tell their partners (Wade, 2004, p. 18).

Dr. Wade's research has found six basic principles that describe transcendent sex, all of which might topple the expectations of ordinary people. They include the following:

1. Transcendent episodes have little or nothing to do with sexual mechanics or technique…
2. Transcendent sex is not related to physiological differences associated with male or female arousal…
3. Orgasm is not a casual factor…
4. Sexual abuse is not a casual factor…
5. Transcendent sex isn't limited to certain relationships. It can happen … even after years with the same person or during a one-night stand…
6. Transcendent states produced have no discernible relationship to a person's spiritual beliefs or practices…. (Wade, 2009, pp. 11–15)

These experiences can be so profound that they may leave the person feeling scared, confused, or disoriented. Therefore, it is helpful for therapists using the ETT® samadhi process to be aware of these possibilities. One person described it as unlike anything she had ever experienced and tried to make it happen again but was unable to replicate it.

DOES IT LAST?

Several factors determine whether the ETT® samadhi process facilitates a temporary change or a permanent change. If the distress targeted is trauma of learnings from earlier in life that no longer currently have a function, the release of this distress is usually permanent. For example, unresolved grief is usually relinquished permanently. In one case, all of the childhood fear regarding a client's father was eliminated and never returned. In the case of Macy, whose ruptured ear drum was healed, the symptom never returned. However, if one achieves a current state of peace, for example, various traumas or distractions can reactivate defenses and thus distress. It should be noted that in these cases a follow-up session using the process can more easily reactivate peace than any experience previous to the use of the process. Generally speaking, when euphoric states, love states, or transcendent states are activated by the process, the length of retention is about eight weeks, unless extreme circumstances disrupt it. Another excursion into the innermost self two or three times typically has a very long-term effect. This is particularly true if it is nurtured and followed up by appropriate meditation or other activities that reinforce this gain.

In one case, a thirty-five-year-old woman named Wanda flew to see me for a week of treatment in which the ETT® samadhi process was used. She reported continual daily high anxiety, frustration, perfectionism, and as a result she was depressed and unhappy. It seemed to her like everything bothered her. Wanda had undergone this experience for at least ten years on a daily basis. After initial sessions that allowed her to express her feelings and clarify her issues, the ETT® samadhi process was used. The following email was received from her one week later:

> It's been a little over a week since I finished the sessions at your offices and wanted to give you an overview of how I've been. Despite having a bad case of the flu and a sick child during the week, I feel great. I have noticed a big difference in my thinking and actions when there is stress that would have historically sent me into a downward spiral. I'm conscious and aware of the emotional triggers, but things just don't seem to escalate for me anymore. I've been tested this last week and letting things go is simply easier, and challenges that come up seemingly go smoother. I'm very aware of the changes and really feel like things are different and will last.
>
> The interesting thing is that my husband doesn't seem to notice the differences, and any changes he does see are very subtle in his perception. I realize most of the down spiral thinking was internal for me and maybe it didn't escalate enough externally for him to notice a pattern of behavior. I find it a little disappointing that he doesn't notice what I feel like are monumental changes!
>
> Overall, I'm happier and feel calmer. Maybe the changes are subtle to the outside world, but I feel like I've moved mountains. Thank you again for facilitating these changes in my life. I'm so grateful.

A NEW BEGINNING

The ETT® samadhi experience can initiate a person into an entirely new venue of spiritual experiences. Its effects can be long-term in that it could start a new spiritual path in realms beyond anything experienced before. In traditional Hindu culture, a samadhi experience is considered a foundational step toward a Kundalini awaking. If this takes place, the awakening process could take place for several months, and it is best to have a spiritual guide to go through it effectively. The samadhi experience can initiate a variety of experiences roughly known as "psychic openings," which can dramatically change one's entire spiritual direction and experience in life.

People have long extolled the virtues of contemplative or meditative approaches in a wide array of religions. The accolades primarily come from those who have participated in them, while nonparticipants have difficulty imagining how inward focus could possibly be so beneficial. The growing number of people participating in meditative practice suggests that there must be something significant about it. Now a considerable amount of scientific research exists that verifies a variety of psychological, physical, and spiritual benefits. The problem has been that these magnificent processes are slow, tedious, and take a considerable amount of time in general. In addition, the American inclination is to think in terms of pharmaceuticals to remedy distress, and most Christians are not aware of the contemplative tradition within their own religion, so it can be seen as a threat. The ETT® samadhi process meets all of these issues. It works more quickly than pharmaceuticals, lasts longer than drugs, takes place in a fraction of the time of traditional meditation, and can function in a way that operates within most people's frame of reference. Research is currently being conducted to produce empirical evidence for the efficacy of ETT—successful results which have been noted anecdotally for the past decade by psychologists using ETT. Soon we can imagine a future where mankind has the means to change brain chemistry without taking chemicals, acquire extraordinary benefits matching those previously achieved by everything from psychedelic drugs to prayer and meditation, and at the same time bring an individual's authentic inner self to the light of day.

CHAPTER 4 SUMMARY

This chapter begins by defining the term samadhi—the essential process that facilitates states of extreme wellbeing produced by ETT®. This concept has parallels to procedures produced in many cultures in various religions. It was also viewed in the context of the field of positive psychology. Then the basic features of the ETT® samadhi process were listed as well as the purpose of it. The concepts of the "Self" or "essence" were identified as features of samadhi. The origin and development of this procedure was described.

The experience of the ETT® samadhi process was illustrated through descriptions of seven different brief case examples. Then the relevance of the ETT® samadhi process to psychotherapy was explained. Further outcomes of this procedure were clarified with more in-depth case illustrations. Then potential obstacles and risks for using the ETT® samadhi process were enumerated.

Next the essential elements that compose the ETT® samadhi process were explained. The role of interpersonal support is the first component described. The second element is the use of a particular form of breathwork. The third component is the unique way in way in which visual brain entrainment is used in conjunction with the first two elements.

Since the aftereffects of the ETT® process tend to be so strong, the need to integrate these effects can become vital. Some of the typical psychological aftereffects were listed, and then ways to assist their integration were suggested. Then an exploration of the pros and cons of applying this procedure to different types of psychopathology took place. A case study illustrated this application.

Since the ETT® samadhi process is a contemplative experience, it was briefly compared to prayer and meditation. Then the benefits of contemplative approaches were described in the form of natural wellbeing. The unique phenomenon of transcendence in conjunction with sex was examined as one outcome of the process. Then the question, "Does It Last?" was answered. Finally, the overall potential impact of the ETT® samadhi process on society was explored.

Chapter Five

Meditation at the Speed of Light

Although there are several ways to achieve samadhi, it was through meditation that samadhi states were first discovered and understood, and the techniques to facilitate these states have been honed over the centuries. The Emotional Transformation Therapy® (ETT®) samadhi process is a discovery that substantially complements the historical development of the samadhi experience. The relationship between prayer, hypnosis, and brainwave biofeedback with samadhi is clear—all these methods report the occurrence of transcendent experiences. A comparison of the ETT® samadhi process with older methods reveals the superiority of the new approach. Another revealing comparison can be made between samadhi and near-death experiences (NDEs). Finally, this chapter will explore the nature of psychological absorption, along with many other issues concerning the nature of samadhi.

BIOFEEDBACK

Brainwave biofeedback or neurofeedback (neurotherapy) is a modality that has documented the capacity to facilitate transcendent states. The basic premise of neurofeedback for spiritual states is that neurofeedback can train a person's brain to access specific brainwave states. If it is known which brainwave states are associated with spiritual states, then those states can be learned, and spiritual events will occur when those brainwave states are activated. While this occurrence has been documented to take place, there are several limitations to neurofeedback with regard to facilitating samadhi:

- The transcendent states do not always occur when these brainwave states are learned.
- Brainwave states do not fully account for these phenomena, although they are a part of it.
- Even if transcendent states are achieved, they may or most often may not be the samadhi state.
- Interacting with technology alone, can dehumanize the process for some people. In many cases, interpersonal contact during the pursuit of transcendence is a predecessor to direct contact with the divine.
- Neurofeedback typically requires many sessions before a brainwave state is learned (at least many weeks).
- The opportunity to select the variety of specific states of extreme wellbeing that are available in the ETT® samadhi process is limited in neurofeedback.

There are some well-known deficits in using neurofeedback. One neurotherapy specialist of many years' experience described the relationship between learning brainwaves and their effects on targeted symptoms as follows:

> Sometimes our assessment of people's brainwaves after neurotherapy will not show correction, but the client's symptoms will have improved. At other times the client's brainwaves will have been corrected, but their symptoms remain. Apparently there are other factors in the brain that contribute to the targeted symptoms than their brainwaves. However, after conducting a quantitative EEG to assess brainwaves after ETT® treatment of one of your brain injured clients, both the brainwaves and the client's symptoms were corrected. (Walker, 1999)

Although it is possible that samadhi states may be acquired by means of neurotherapy, it is unlikely. Neurofeedback primarily uses theta brainwave training to facilitate transpersonal states. While brainwave states are a significant component in these transpersonal aspects, they are not the only factor. During the ETT® samadhi process, a rhythmic flashing light is used to entrain specific brainwave states almost instantly. Therefore, the ETT® process tends to instantly elicit results that require numerous sessions to achieve in most forms of neurofeedback—a technique that provides a hit-or-miss possibility for access to samadhi states. Specifically, to acquire samadhi, ETT® rapidly facilitates the point at which consciousness and one's sensory experience merge. This may occur in any number of specific brainwave states and is custom-tailored to each individual. Samadhi is not consistently associated with one specific brainwave state for everyone.

HYPNOSIS

Although various forms of hypnosis have been identified, a few basic features define hypnosis regardless of the type. Hypnosis includes the following four steps:

- An induction technique is used.
- A client enters into a hypnotic trance.
- Suggestions are made.
- An interpersonal process takes place.

Some people are hypnotizable and others are not. The success of hypnosis is largely dependent on the client entering an altered state of consciousness in which it is believed that the client becomes suggestible. More recent forms of hypnosis are naturalistic, meaning inductions are custom-tailored to the client's individual style. This technique results in a higher percentage of people being hypnotizable. A vast number of scientific studies have verified the outcomes of hypnosis for a wide variety of outcomes. However, hypnotic methods possess numerous individual styles. By observing a hypnotic session, it is apparent that hypnosis does not look like the ETT® samadhi process, although there are some commonalities.

Unfounded stereotypes of hypnosis exist primarily because of "stage hypnotists" who use aspects of hypnosis for entertainment, an experience distinctly different from therapeutic hypnosis. It is important to clarify what hypnosis is not as well as what it is, in order to discuss it without false assumptions. For example, one of the mistaken beliefs about hypnosis is that it can make a person say and do things against that person's will. In any interpersonal situation, one person can influence another, but persuasion cannot be accounted for by hypnosis alone.

There are many types of hypnotic induction techniques. While most of these methods can induce hypnotic trances, few of them engage the senses in a way that is necessary to produce samadhi. However, some ancient or seldom-used methods of hypnosis do engage visual attention. I had to explore induction techniques as far back as the late 1800s before I found inductions that roughly resembled the ETT® processes. Dr. Luys of the Charity Hospital in Paris developed a device described as "consisting of two mirrors rapidly revolving in opposite directions, and by gazing at this for a short time, the sight becomes tired and dazzled and hypnosis is easily produced." (Young, 1899, p. 109) The word "tired" may refer to relaxation, and the term "dazzled" might be what we would call absorbed attention and awe. However, since this method does not adjust its rate of motion to each person's responsivity, it probably does not individualize its effect. Therefore, it would result in a hit-or-miss capacity to achieve samadhi, but through this induction technique, samadhi might be possible. However, it might place the recipient at risk, if neither the facilitator nor the client recognizes or/understands the magnitude of potential for this samadhi state. The commonality between hypnotic trance and the samadhi state is the experience of absorption of attention. The difference between the states in part concerns whether the absorption of attention accesses one's inner essential self or not. Since most hypnotherapy is not intended to discover the innermost authentic self, nor is it intended to access divine contact, at best hypnotic procedures may accidentally stumble onto samadhi. Without proper conceptualization of the nature of samadhi, the parties involved would likely be surprised or confused by its impact as I was initially.

My dissertation in 1981 was partly about Ericksonian hypnosis. It is possible that the samadhi state has been accessed by people in hypnosis. However, most hypnotherapists cannot distinguish the samadhi state from a hypnotic trance. While these experiences may appear to be similar, there is usually a vast difference between hypnotic trance and samadhi. The samadhi state has far more depth and its potential for benefit is more substantial.

MEDITATION

Whereas hypnosis may accidentally access samadhi, many forms of meditation are intended to achieve samadhi. A vast number of meditative and prayer practices come from every major religion in the world as well as nonreligious meditative practice (Wacholtz & Pargament, 2005). These contemplative practices share certain common functions and some people have attempted to integrate them all into a contemplative approach (Oman, 2010). However, few have attempted to identify the deepest inner states commonly shared among all these practices. Nor has anyone developed a nondrug practice that will cut through the typically arduous meditative path to a rapid and direct contemplative path that produces the same ultimate states of consciousness achieved by long-term meditation. While plenty of scientific research now documents the psychological and health benefits of meditation and prayer, there are few studies on ultimate states of consciousness and even fewer studies on facilitating rapid access to profound states of consciousness, other than those derived from pharmaceutical substances (Wachholtz & Pargament, 2008). Pharmaceutical approaches are plagued by drug side-effects.

Some scholars have found that the original purpose of meditation in Judaism, Christianity, and Islam was to provide an experience of the creation of the universe. The concept is that entering a state of quiet stillness allows a person to re-enter the state of consciousness that existed before the universe began. Then as one reawakens from this state a person may recreate his/her life again from a fresh start. Passages from Genesis, the Hebrew scriptures, and the Quran have been cited from their original interpretation that indicate meditation was intended to contact the divine by contact with the stillpoint of pure consciousness (Douglas-Klotz, 2003).

The ETT® samadhi process is a facilitated procedure that can prepare a person for a profound inner stillness or ecstatic elevation. Furthermore, it can be adapted to each person's spiritual orientation as well as therapeutic goals. However, the impact can be so swift and strong that careful follow up is often necessary in order to integrate the experience into people's lives.

The most detailed conceptualization of samadhi occurs in Indian philosophy. There are numerous types of meditation, but they fall into two categories—active and passive. The active forms have the participant focus on one point, such as a mantra, a visual image, or a thought. Whereas the passive approach, as in "vipassna," or mindfulness meditation, primarily has participants observe emerging thoughts, feelings, images, or body/sensations instead of focusing on a single thing. Neither of these brief summations does justice to the full explanation of these forms of meditation. For purposes of comparative clarity, I will primarily focus on three types of meditation as well as Christian centering prayer, which bears a strong resemblance to Eastern forms of meditation. These three are as follows: (1) "vipassna," or mindfulness meditation, which is a passive form, (2) transcendental meditation, which is a more or less active form of meditation, and (3) Kirtan Kriya, which is an active form of meditation.

In most forms of meditation derived from Eastern concepts, some version of enlightenment is the ultimate goal. "Enlightenment," although a generic term, is usually accessed by first entering samadhi. Samadhi is achieved through weeks, months, or years of meditation. The Dali Lama himself said that he meditates four hours a day, and if there were a faster way on the meditation path, he would prefer to use it. While each step on the meditation path may provide incremental growth experiences, the process tends to take so long that most Americans do not have the discipline to maintain daily meditation. Most people do not sustain the practice long enough to gain the experience of samadhi. Since the majority of participants drop out before the ultimate outcome can be achieved, the development of a more rapid means to achieve this outcome would be an extraordinary benefit. The ETT® samadhi process represents a radically faster meditative process.

AN AMPLIFIED FORM OF MINDFULNESS

A second ETT® process offers a drastically amplified form of mindfulness. The spectral resonance technique (SRT), a sub-modality of ETT®, significantly advances mindfulness outcomes through an entirely different means. For example, during mindfulness meditation an attempt is made to observe one's inner activities for days, weeks, or months, while continually struggling to observe experiences vs. being immersed in thoughts and feelings. In SRT, however, the client receives immediate visual feedback from a specialized chart, whose color consistently disappears at the moment dissociation occurs or expands when emotional escalation is about to take place. This awareness allows the participant to depart from being immersed in emotions or dissociation and shift to a perspective in the present moment. This feedback in SRT allows a client to recognize more quickly when the observer orientation is being lost, so that voluntary control can reinstate attention to the observer state of mind. In terms of brain activity in SRT, one can reinstate participation of the dorsal medial prefrontal cortex that is associated with self-reflection. However, in SRT the nature of the visual feedback is specifically about affective states associated with cognitive and somatic experiences that change when affect is shifted. This primacy of affect produces a different emphasis from that in traditional mindfulness approaches that also leads to a deeper inner self-awareness. Nonetheless, the facilitation of increased mindfulness awareness is achieved in SRT in just one to three sessions, instead of the lengthy excursions into the mind that traditional mindfulness meditation would require.

Instead of the long random search for mental direction during conventional mindfulness, the visual feedback in SRT allows participants to recognize a lack of engagement in the present moment. When this occurs, participants are interrupted and rapidly led back on course by directing them to refocus to the present moment. Another difference between conventional mindfulness and SRT is that SRT requires a facilitator, at least at first, until the participant can manage the process alone. By responding to the visual feedback, participants are brought back into the present moment as well as into a self-reflective mode. Over time, self-reflection and emotional distress become integrated, giving the person the ability to simultaneously experience an emotional state and automatically be self-reflective. This capacity, occurring spontaneously outside of sessions, places clients in a position to choose how they wish to direct their emotional states rather than being swept away by them. In other words, they become mindful.

A comparison of the ETT® samadhi process to conventional mindfulness proves the speed of change is drastically faster with ETT®. The ETT® samadhi process tends to achieve an awareness of a person's authentic sense of "I-ness" or self that underlies emotions in twenty minutes. This rate contrasts with mindfulness meditation that usually takes weeks, months, or years to access the authentic inner self.

FORMS OF MEDITATION

During the 1970s, followers of the Indian guru Maharishi brought Transcendental Meditation™ to the West. At that time Christian contemplative methods had been largely lost in favor of a more cognitive approach, except for priests who continued to practice it in monasteries. Transcendental Meditation™ caught on for several reasons. Instead of devoting several hours a day to meditating, which was the norm among traditional meditation, it required only twenty minutes twice a day. This fit into the Western lifestyle. Also, scientific research that supported its effectiveness was compelling to the American consumer. This allowed it to be packaged and sold easily. Millions of people have learned this method since then. I was one of them.

The forms of meditation I am describing developed over hundreds or even thousands of years. These meditation techniques have been honed and passed down through generations by religious adepts. With new ways to measure the activity of the brain through technology, we now have a better idea of how these methods work and can verify that substantial brain changes, in fact, do occur.

One of the interesting scientific findings about meditation concerns the type of meditation called Kirtan Kriya. To the average person Kirtan Kriya has been largely unknown. When it was put to the scientific test, it was found to yield an unusual capacity to enhance human memory. This form of meditation developed during the sixteenth century in Northern India. It is different from other forms of meditation in that it integrates breathing, sound, and movement. I have found that when people do not have the patience for mindfulness meditation and cannot stay focused to do a form of one-pointedness meditation, they often can do Kirtan Kriya meditation. While Kirtan Kriya meditation does yield benefits, it takes a very long time to attain samadhi through this method.

We are all deeply indebted to the men and women who pioneered these meditation approaches over the centuries. Just as these methods were revolutionary in their time, all methods may eventually need to give way to new leaps in the development of methods to achieve samadhi. The ETT® samadhi process represents a radical new advance in meditation.

Scientific research reveals that many different types of meditation have shown a capacity to evoke a variety of outcomes. Transcendental meditation has been shown to increase practical intelligence (Canter & Ernst, 2003; Cranson et al., 1991), field independence, creativity, speed of processing information, as well as decreased anxiety (So & Orne-Johnson, 2001). The Brahma Vihara practice of Loving Kindness meditation involves four different meditations that have been found to produce compassion, love, equanimity, and empathetic joy (Carson et al., 2005). Research has also shown that improved self-perception can be achieved through certain forms of meditation (Haimerl & Valentine, 2001). Recently, mindfulness meditation or Vipassna has become popular and inspired research (Carson, Cranson, & Baucom, in press). One study showed that meditation can increase empathy (Shapiro, 2003). Of course, research also shows that meditation enhances transpersonal or spiritual experiences (Shapiro, Schwartz, & Bonner, 1998). Therefore, scientific research on different forms of meditation has shown distinctly different benefits. Each form of meditation is focused on particular outcomes depending on its philosophical orientation.

The ETT® samadhi process can be characterized as an amplified meditation because its effects are often the same as most forms of meditation, but its speed and depth set it in contrast to conventional meditation. The ETT® samadhi process is so flexible that it can be focused on different outcomes within different philosophical orientations. All of the aforementioned scientific outcomes found through meditation practices have been observed in the ETT® samadhi process, yet it differs in the following ways:

- drastically amplified speed of the process
- amplified subjective impact
- long-term aftereffects
- flexibility of targeted outcomes
- flexibility of philosophical orientation that can be incorporated in the process

Since the ETT® samadhi process requires a facilitator; it is less portable than other forms of meditation. However, with another person guiding the procedure, the client can surrender to the process more easily, since there is no need to maintain control to direct it. A facilitated process also has the advantage of incorporating a human bond as the foundation for launching into transcendent experiences. The interactive process of visual environment and brain activity keeps attention focused so that the tendency of mental attentional wandering is drastically reduced, thus allowing consciousness to descend into absorptive states efficiently.

PRAYER

Prayer is a universal aspect of religion. In recent years, there have been many scientific research studies on the impact of prayer. However, findings are mixed. There are different types of prayer. The results of one study in Akron,

Ohio, showed that there are four basic types of prayer used by the general population (Poloma & Pendleton, 1991):

1. petitionary prayer—asking God to meet material needs for oneself and others
2. colloquial prayer—a conversational petition to God that is less concrete and specific than petitionary prayer
3. ritual prayer—prepared prayers from books that might be memorized
4. meditative prayer—involving a relationship and intimacy with God that communicates, adores, or reflects

Research findings have shown different benefits for each type prayer. Only meditative prayer demonstrated a significant beneficial relationship with existential wellbeing and religious satisfaction; colloquial prayer was the only type of prayer to relate to happiness…; and ritual prayer demonstrated a relationship with negative emotions such as sadness, loneliness, tension, and fear. Beyond the types of prayer … the subjective experiences of the individuals praying were the most consistent predictors of wellbeing. That is, persons who during their prayers felt like they were experiencing an interaction with God or had feelings of increased peace were also the ones more likely to report greater levels of wellbeing (Plante & Thoresen, 2007, pp. 13–14).

These findings show that people pray in diverse ways, and different types of prayer yield different benefits. One Lutheran minister stated that "the effects of prayer are very different, depending on who is doing the praying" (B. Dasch, personal communication, October 2, 2008). The research suggests that the sense of subjective connection to the divine, regardless of religious orientation improves the impact. These issues complicate prayer research. Although "meditative prayer" was found, it is notable that Christian centering prayer may not have been represented at all in the study. This demonstrates the paucity of true contemplative approaches in the general U.S. Christian population. However, it is a growing movement among Christians.

Adherents of several different religions believe that prayer affects the health of others and changes events. Now there is scientific verification of this belief (Astin, Harkness, & Ernst, 2000). Across the board, the effect of prayer has shown a small but significant degree of effectiveness in several scientific studies (Harris et al., 2010). The ETT® samadhi process has shown benefits by virtue of procedures that bear a resemblance to some elements of prayer. However, initial findings with the ETT® samadhi process have shown a substantially higher rate of effectiveness for achieving the intended outcome. Christian centering prayer is a form of prayer that reports outcomes that are most similar to samadhi. However, it does not tend to seek a targeted outcome other than union with the divine, so it tends to lack the intercessory portion found in conventional prayer. The ETT® samadhi process targets specific outcomes like conventional intercessory prayer but also tends to access direct contact with ultimate states like those described in Christian centering prayer.

Centering prayer could be described as a method of Christian meditation or contemplative prayer in which there is a strong emphasis on inner silence. The history of this approach dates back many centuries to the desert fathers and the writing of St. Teresa of Avila, St. John of the Cross, and then to the more modern writings of Thomas Merton, Thomas Keating, and Basil Pennington. One version of centering prayer emphasizes intention rather than focusing on a thought or mantra (Merton, 1996). The intention is to seek the presence of God. In other Christian methods, the presence of God is sought by focusing on scriptures or Jesus and even visualizing these while simultaneously rejecting other thoughts. In other approaches, the "stillpoint" of direct contact of the soul with God is the ultimate goal. A long time of consistent daily prayer is required to eventually achieve this union with the divine, just as meditation requires for a similar goal. By contrast, what the ETT® samadhi process has to offer is a radically faster means to achieve the same goal.

When people believe that it is important to operate within a Christian frame of reference, the Christian centering prayer and stillpoint concepts offer that option within the ETT® samadhi process. Most religious traditions possess some type of contemplative prayer concept within which the ETT® samadhi process can be used without sacrificing the client's belief system. However, believing in God vs. experiencing direct contact with God may be radically different for the believer. In fact, it might not even be recognizable at first. Divine presence during silence and stillness is often difficult to put into words.

In many cases, meditation or Christian centering prayer is recommended, if it is appropriate, as a follow-up to the ETT® samadhi process. Clients who had already been using these disciplines before experiencing the ETT® samadhi process usually find that the quality of their experiences during meditation or contemplation advances substantially. Clients unfamiliar with these disciplines could be encouraged to use them to reinforce the ETT® samadhi process. This often results in sustaining the duration of the effect of the ETT® samadhi process.

SAMADHI AND NDES

The ETT® samadhi process yields most of the experiences found in NDEs. Studies on hundreds of NDEs have generated a list of common phenomena that tend to occur consistently. While the ETT® samadhi process does not produce all of these phenomena together in a single experience, neither do most NDEs. According to Greyson's scale, derived from hundreds of NDEs, ETT® samadhi outcome produced the following characteristics of NDEs (1983):

- altered sense of time
- sudden understanding
- feeling of peace
- surrounded by light
- feeling joy
- feeling cosmic unity/oneness
- out of physical body
- senses more vivid than usual
- extrasensory perception (ESP)
- visions of the future
- encountering beings
- mystical being

These same experiences have been reported in the ETT® samadhi experience. The only exception to this list is that the samadhi process has not included a "life review," which does happen with NDEs. While it is not known for sure what all the implications of this comparison may mean, it at least suggests that some of the benefits in NDEs can be acquired while one is still alive. It also suggests that the ETT® samadhi process can access universal transcendent phenomena. Many people who have had NDEs have difficulty wanting to continue living because their NDE was so wonderful. This process provides another option than choosing to die for those people who want to re-experience these events.

CHARACTERISTICS OF SAMADHI

The contrast between quantum physics and Newtonian physics offers a framework in which to understand some aspects of samadhi. Newtonian time is linear and separate from space, consciousness, matter, and energy. Whereas time in quantum physics is one continuous flow that incorporates the past, the present, and the future. Additionally, in quantum physics reality, space, time, matter, energy, and consciousness are all a part of each other. It is this concept of the impact of consciousness on time, space, matter, and energy that suggest a perspective for why emersion into quantum time has the capacity to alter reality. Essentially, changes in consciousness can alter perception of these other aspects of reality. However, since the Newtonian way of thinking tends to predominate in most people's mental activity, it requires special processes to awaken into the perspective of quantum reality where new possibilities exist. The ETT® samadhi process is a special means to facilitate entrance into a reality that bears a similarity to quantum reality.

TIME

One of the key features of the ETT® samadhi process is the complete cessation of thoughts and the experience of emersion into the present moment. This may sound either simple enough or so obscure that one may wonder what is so special about it. We all experience subjective time when we are doing something we do not like and it seems to linger on. When we are enjoying something, it often seems to occur within a short length of time. If we were to watch a clock while feeling impatient, our subjective experience is that time is moving slowly. The same is true with subjective experiences of the present moment. Its perceptual quality is different. The Greeks viewed "chronos" as objective linear time in which the present instant is a moving point of time on the way to the future. From this perspective, there is not actually a present moment because of the constant movement. However, the Greek term "Kairos" is a subjective experience of time, characterized by Daniel Stern (2004) as

> the passing moment in which something happens as time unfolds. It is the coming into being of a new state of things, and it happens in a moment of awareness. It has its own boundaries and escapes or transcends the passage of linear time. Yet it also contains the past. Kairos is a moment of opportunity....
>
> It is a small window of becoming and opportunity. (p. 7)

Fully immersed in the subjective experience of the present moment, a person can enter the void left by the cessation of thoughts, feelings, defenses, and personality. At this point, a person's core essence can be discovered. It often feels paradoxical that when "nothing" is happening, one may experience a depth of fullness that something enormous is happening. The alteration of subjective time is a key feature that allows this paradox to be experienced. In Christian circles attaining this "stillpoint" is a key experience. In Hindu and Buddhist philosophy, objective time is considered to be part of the illusion of reality, and subjective time is seen as reality.

SPACE

During the samadhi experience, perception of space may be altered. As one is viewing the light during ETT®, the light often appears to be moving beyond its boundaries. For example, it may appear to be jumping outside the edge of the lens or acquiring a three-dimensional aspect. At other times it may appear to be extending outward toward the person or even be perceived as totally engulfing the person viewing this light. However, the greatest indicator of samadhi occurs when the observer can speak enough to say, "I feel one with this light!" These visual alterations of perceived space can occur when a person is immersed in emotional distress or in the samadhi process, but the subjective report of distress vs. stillness or euphoria makes it obvious whether distress or wellbeing is occurring. In either case, there is a subjective emersion into the experience.

In addition to the visual, spatial perception of the light altering, sometimes the person himself/herself may experience aspects of changing or expanding. When self-esteem is elevated, participants frequently perceive of themselves as taller during or after the interactive lightwork. Sometimes people experience themselves as expanding into the universe among the stars in empty space. At other times, some participants may sense a connection with the objects, people, and plants around them, which may be felt as though these things are literally an extension of themselves. Research on meditators clearly shows that the part of the brain responsible for differentiating oneself from others is altered when an experience of oneness occurs. Specifically, the brain's temperoparietal juncture in connection with the prefrontal cortex and right brain hemisphere is known to be altered during these events. Therefore, there is a clear correlation between deep meditative events and the ETT® samadhi process even though the ETT® samadhi process is generally more visual.

The unique spatial alterations suggest that changes in states of consciousness influence how specific spatial perceptions occur. For example, it's not an accident that the light shifts from two-dimensional to three-dimensional during the ETT® samadhi process. This typically occurs when the client is undergoing a change of attention into an absorptive state. The very definition of samadhi concerns the merging of consciousness with one's sensory experience. Therefore, perceiving oneself as one with the light is often a feature of entrance into samadhi.

According to quantum physicists, empty space is not actually empty. Research has shown that matter and energy emerge from a total vacuum. For example, the light from the sun is literally invisible on its journey to the earth. Light appears to be absent while it is in empty space and only shows up when it reaches an object such as the earth. This empty space is called the zero point field in quantum physics, shunyata in Buddhism, and the Void in Hindu theology. When people undergo the ETT® samadhi process, they often reach a point of stillness and a sense of the zero point field, which gives them a feeling of being grounded in a universal source.

ENERGY

When someone enters the samadhi state via ETT® there is a characteristic change in his/her sense of mental and bodily energy. This shift in energy is usually clearly observable, but sometimes can only be known by the participant's report. One of the most common changes is from an agitated, physically fidgety state, to complete physical stillness. Of course, this is often reported as a movement from anxiety to complete calmness. However, many people who lack energy, even though they appear physically still during the ETT® samadhi process, report a significant elevation of their energy level.

In addition to calming and/or escalation of energy, there are other ways that energy shifts. Many of these changes concern mental energy. People report that "a weight has been lifted" off their minds or lightheadedness has changed into feeling solid or secure. When cognitive ability changes to clarity and ease of thinking, a person's perceived sense of energy often feels more efficient and flows in such a way that his or her energy feels lighter.

SYNESTHESIA

One of the outcomes of the ETT® samadhi process has been the spontaneous development of the condition of synesthesia. Synesthesia involves experiencing sensations in one sense modality when a second sense modality is activated. For example, music could be experienced not only as sound but also as a visual sight at the same time. Scientific research has identified over sixty different types of synesthesia. Brain scans have shown that this experience is not just an active imagination but operates across modal brain activation. Its occurrence has been found to be as rare as with one person in every two hundred to five hundred people (Baron-Cohen et al., 2013) Two factors have been found to induce synesthesia temporarily—psychedelic drugs like lysergic acid diethylamide (LSD) and N,N-Dimethyltryptamine (DMT) or severe psychopathology (Cytowic, 1998; Grof, 2001; Walsh & Glob, 2005; Cytowic, 2002). Roger Walsh conducted a research study in which he found that the incidence of synesthesia among long-term mediators was four to ten times higher than in that of the general population. The only other group that showed a significantly higher incidence (twenty-three percent) was people in the arts (Domino, 1980). While genetic inheritance could be the basis of some synesthetes, increased sensitivity via meditation or increased activation by psychedelic drugs may account for others.

There is a long history of interest in synesthesia. Evidence exists that synesthesia occurred in ancient China (Wong, 1997). Buddhist history clearly shows descriptions of synesthesia many centuries ago (Sessa, 2010).

Synesthesia was the topic of much debate in the 1800s in Europe. Only very recently has research in synesthesia become active again.

In a recent ETT® course, one in six people who experienced the ETT® samadhi process developed long-term synesthesia. This fact suggests several possibilities. First, the ETT® samadhi process parallels the activation of the same state of consciousness achieved in meditation. Because mediation and psychedelic drugs, which both activate the same neural receptors, have been found to induce synesthesia, there is a likely connection to the occurrence of synesthesia in the ETT® samadhi process. Synesthesia can be cultivated along with the heightening of the senses that occurs in almost every trial of the ETT® samadhi process.

In the case of one ETT® participant in the ETT® training, a sight-sound synesthesia was evoked. During the session that preceded this experience, auditory hallucinations of the voice of her deceased father and God's voice took place to her functional benefit. Specifically, her type of synesthesia is one in which organic colors projected sound, while plants and animals seemed to communicate with her. These experiences parallel the effects of psychedelic drug use without drug side-effects. Her initial response was that she was going crazy. After explaining synesthesia to her, she relaxed and enjoyed it. Therapists using the ETT® samadhi process should be familiar with synesthesia in order to normalize the experience for participants.

The fact that synesthesia is induced by meditation and psychedelic drugs, and is reported more frequently among people in the arts, suggests possible benefits and uses for the ETT® samadhi process such as enhancing creativity. Since meditation has been well documented to provide a wide variety of benefits, evidence suggests that these same benefits might be acquired through the ETT® samadhi process, except faster and more consistently.

LEVELS OF STATES OF CONSCIOUSNESS

Psychologist and Buddhist practitioner, Welwood (2000) describes three levels of states of consciousness, the last two of which can be entered by meditation. These states are the following:

1. At the surface level, mind uses the tools of focal attention and concept to fix its sights on one object after another. The surface conceptual mind perceives solid forms, thinks definite mind, thinks definite thoughts, and registers familiar emotions. This is the level of mind where ego operates—This is the level of mind where ego, through forming self-concepts, sets up a basic division between self and other which helps to master functional activities in life.

2. Underneath the conceptual mind is a wider kind of body-mind sensing/knowing that operates at a subtler, background way. This subtle body-mind contains both personal and transpersonal elements.... We can recognize this level of body-mind through a diffuse type of attention that can tune into subtle feeling and intuition, energy flow, and a sense of interrelatedness with all creation (p. 6).
3. At the deepest level, meditation practice reveals mind to be an open, nonconceptual awareness, which is the ultimate source of all our particular experiences.... This nameless, formless presence—in, around, behind, and between all our particular thoughts and experiences—is what the great spiritual traditions regard as our true nature (p. 7).

PSYCHOLOGICAL ABSORPTION

The ability to become psychologically absorbed in an activity or thought is a key element in the pursuit of samadhi. Psychological absorption is an experience of pronounced engagement with objects of attention. Examples occur when "we're 'immersed' in activities, 'captured' by feelings, 'absorbed' in imagery and dreams." (Wild, Kuiken, & Schopfocher, 1995) Absorption does not necessarily mean that the experience is pleasurable. For example, one could be absorbed in a tragic movie or play. Absorption has also been found to be related to an "openness to experience cognitive and emotional alterations." (Roche & McConkey, 1990) This openness to experience may be the most significant readiness characteristic, but it can be influenced strongly by the therapeutic bond. Absorption has been identified as a trait that is one of several characteristics in personality assessment (Roche & McConkey, 1990; Tellegen, 1974). It has been suggested that the characteristic of absorption may be due to genetics. Research has shown that absorption can be related to the experience of hypnotic trance (Nadon et al., 1991). However, evidence of numerous trials of the ETT® samadhi process demonstrates that the capacity for absorption can be experienced consistently, even with people who have not experienced it before.

Meditation and hypnosis tend to increase the capacity to experience absorption. The ETT® samadhi process drastically elevates this ability to eighty to ninety percent of the time in which the process is used. Psychological absorption appears to be a key element of the process necessary to facilitate the highest states of consciousness and/or ultimate spiritual union. However, there are many types and degrees of absorption, and not all of them facilitate these higher states. A continuum of different attentional states of consciousness can identify nonabsorption vs. absorption levels. It is hypothesized that there are five levels of absorption:

VAZQUEZ ABSORPTION CONTINUUM

1. Dissociation: This phenomenon represents numerous degrees and types of disengagement, such as amnesia, shock, and regressive states. This prohibits the whole person from absorption.
2. Conscious engagement: This is the "normal" daily focus of attention necessary for practical tasks on a daily basis. During these states a person is awake and alert, but his/her conscious attention is not "absorbed" in anything. There is no recognition of unconscious activity during this state.
3. Psychological absorption: This is the initial level of absorption, as exemplified by immersion into the arts, hypnotic trances, or intuitive moments. However, a sense of separate identity is still present.
4. Nonordinary states of absorption: At this level of absorption transpersonal phenomena like psychic experiences, astral travel, and energy healing can occur, but self-perception is usually still present.
5. Profound absorption: At this level people access awareness of the innermost self, samadhi, or essence, which in turn makes it possible to experience God, the "void," and states of unity, depending in part on the client's belief system. This level is characterized by mental stillness, no thought, but a timelessness of expanded awareness. At this level self-perception ceases to exist in the usual sense, and the experience itself is often difficult to put into words.

When people, even briefly, experience level five, it tends to impact the other levels. For example, after contact with level five, abilities in levels three and/or four may awaken, and one's philosophy and functioning based on awareness limited by level two may become initially disorganized.

At the first level, the person is at least partially disengaged from himself/herself. There are numerous types of dissociation that exhibit different degrees of disengagement from oneself and others. Common levels of dissociation are disconnection from one's body awareness, disengagement from one's emotions, and loss of memory. More intense levels include shock, regressive states, and amnesia. More severe levels incorporate identity distortion and/or separate identities. It is possible that during dissociative episodes, one part of the person may experience significant absorption at the same time dissociation occurs. However, generally speaking, dissociation is the opposite of absorption because absorption requires the involvement of one's entire consciousness.

At the second level, conscious engagement is neither disengagement nor absorption. This level of attention provides our ability to function in the outer world. It is awake, aware, and logical. Although one may possess religious beliefs and intellectually recognize unconscious events, direct experience of these events is lacking. This level of consciousness is the most acceptable in Western society and is considered to be the normal waking state.

The third level of attention in consciousness is psychological absorption. At the third level of consciousness one's attention becomes immersed in an experience to an extended degree. Experiences such as immersion in the arts, intuitive moments, feeling connected to nature, or romantic encounters exemplify these states. Psychological absorption occupies one's attention in ways described by Csikszentmihalyi in his concept of "flow." It can occur during sporting experiences, yoga, or other physical activities. Psychological absorption is generally a brief departure from normal conscious engagement but is generally not a spiritual awakening, although it may provoke confusion or curiosity that conflicts with logic. Hypnotic trance primarily occurs at this level.

At the fourth level of absorption, experience of attention reaches an even deeper level, one considered "nonordinary" by conventional society. Experiences such as psychic phenomena, contact with deceased entities, astral travel, and contact with spirit guides are reported to occur at this level of experience. In Western society, suspicion and a lack of acceptance is the typical response. Events at this level tend to be so impactful that people who develop these abilities often think they have reached ultimate spiritual reality. However, the ego is still present in conjunction with this level of absorption, which risks contamination by human desires, foibles, and the need for power. This level of absorption can significantly disrupt the preceding three levels to the extent that it may cause people to feel disoriented and reappraise beliefs in the first three levels.

The fifth level of attentional consciousness is profound absorption. At this level of absorption, described as samadhi, it is possible to have direct experiences with the divine, the void, or whatever one conceives as ultimate reality. It is experienced as timeless, expansive, yet ineffable. Characterized by stillness and a sense of unity, it lies beyond one's perceived sense of self. People who have had only had a brief encounter with this state of absorption find that contact can disrupt all previous understandings based on experience at levels one through four. This level of absorption is considered to be among the highest states of consciousness.

Watts (1984) describes not only the experience of level five absorption, but also the significance of its aftereffects and value in the following:

> The central core of the experience seems to be the conviction, or insight, that the immediate now, whatever its nature is, is the fulfillment of all living. Surrounding and flowing from this insight is an emotional ecstasy, a sense of intense relief, freedom, and lightness, and often of almost unbearable love for the world, which is, however, secondary. Often the pleasure of the experience

> is confused with the insight lost in the ecstasy, so that in trying to retain the secondary effects of the experience, the individual misses the point—that the immediate now is complete even when it is not ecstatic. For ecstasy is a necessarily impermanent contrast in the constant fluctuation of our feelings. But insight, when clear enough, persists; having once understood a particular skill, the facility tends to remain. (p. 15)

In the Eastern faiths of Hinduism, Buddhism, Jainism, Sikhism, and yogic schools, samadhi is known but is characterized slightly differently in each system. In the Christian tradition, variations of experiences occurring in Christian centering prayer bear a very strong similarity to samadhi. Essentially, the contemplative aspects of all these major religions produce very similar experiences. With due respect to all of these religious traditions, I will be using this common theme among these orientations when referring to samadhi. The phenomenon of absorption is a central characteristic in common with contemplative spiritual disciplines from different religious orientations. Therefore, the ETT® samadhi process is a way to achieve absorption faster and more consistently and increases the probability of achieving the aims of these contemplative efforts, while maintaining one's spiritual philosophy.

There has been much discussion among both psychologists and religious authorities about the nature of our deepest self. It is generally agreed that it exists beneath our conscious awareness, which makes it difficult to describe and define. Psychiatrist Carl Jung refers to it as the "Self" that interfaces with the collective unconscious. Many Christians would call it the soul. Almaas refers to this aspect of ourselves as "essence" and describes it in great detail (1986). Most Hindu traditions call it "atman," which is "the real immortal self of human beings known in the West as the soul." However, most Buddhist views deny the existence of atman. The experience of samadhi allows direct access to this innermost self. Absorption is a characteristic of the samadhi process that makes it possible to achieve awareness of this deepest self.

Several religious traditions identify the evolution of various degrees of "samadhi" once the initial samadhi state is experienced. Roberts (1991) described six levels of experience toward the movement of the "no self" state that is reached by some people in Christian centering prayer. There are other descriptions of the degrees of samadhi, for example according to Pantanjili, from the Hindu tradition, samadhi is the last and highest of the eight limbs of yoga (Gentz, 1986, p. 923).

One perspective of samadhi in the process toward spiritual fulfillment is that it occurs in a three-step sequence. The first step is purgation, in which one is purified from unresolved emotional and physical issues. The second phase is illumination, in which one experiences various positive states of extreme wellbeing. The third phase is an experience of unity with the divine. This is the ultimate state of consciousness for many people, but Bernadette Roberts views these states as only the beginning of six further subdivisions of level 5 absorption.

Roberts, who uses Christian Centering Prayer as her mode of contemplation, describes the six phases of spiritual growth after unity contact as:

1. Entrance into the Dark Night of Spirit in which a painful loss of self-control and egoic helplessness gives way to the soul.
2. Remaining passive and peaceful as one experiences the stillpoint of the interface between the soul and the divine.
3. This is the peak of the fullness of the contemplative unified state of interior silence.
4. This is the final death of the inner self in which numerous exterior trials and potential suffering are met with the soul finding its refuge in God.
5. This phase is "the finest blossoming of the unitive life" in which we go out to help others with an open mind.
6. This phase is the end of the inner-self which dissolves into the divine, a point of divine stillness. (1993, pp. 9–14)

One of the reasons ETT® can produce absorption at such a high rate is that within the repertoire of ETT® techniques is the capacity to identify tendencies to disengage and correct them. Specifically, dissociation from engagement and escalation into overwhelming emotions are immediately identified and corrected before the ETT® samadhi process is used. This insures full conscious engagement during the ETT® samadhi process that is elevated into rapid absorption.

THE POWER OF OUR INTERNAL DRUGS FOR ALTERED STATES

Plant medicine has long been an adjunct to spiritual journeys among indigenous people. Some Native American tribes have used psilocybin mushrooms and peyote cactus in their religious rituals. In fact, I once placed a Native American medicine woman on the light device, and she immediately likened the experience to their ritual with fireplaces. She said they used fire not only for cooking and keeping warm but also for seeking visions. South American natives have long used ayahuasca to facilitate visionary experiences. While these experiences have been discredited by some critics, based on the idea that hallucinogenic substances produce artificial illusions of spirituality; in fact, they do work because humans naturally possess neural receptors for these substances. When I was in Peru, I had my light device with me. As I placed a native Peruvian on the light, his immediate response was "ayahuasca!" He explained that he recognized the light stimulation to be just like his ayahuasca (DMT) experience. In the case of the ETT® samadhi process, it appears that potentials are activated for mystical experiences that are similar to plant medicine.

When biochemists were trying to understand why drugs such as morphine have a pain-killing effect on humans, it was found that the effect was possible because humans possess neural receptors for these drugs. Why would humans have receptors for drugs that range from morphine to heroin to hallucinogens, ecstasy, or many others? These receptors exist because our bodies naturally possess the capacity to activate these receptors through our own biochemistry. In other words, we possess our own morphine to plug into these receptors, and we even have neuropeptides that possess pain-killing capacity 200 times more powerful than morphine. Therefore, we possess the capacity to have this wide range of extraordinary experiences within ourselves. However, it is not generally known how to activate these receptors without drugs, except for the placebo effect.

The placebo affect has been demonstrated to eliminate physical pain and virtually almost every type of illness. In fact, drugs must surpass the placebo effect in at least two scientific studies in order to be Food and Drug Administration (FDA) approved. While pharmaceuticals have achieved these standards, in most cases it took numerous trials in order to acquire two trials in which placebos were exceeded. For example, it took eight trials for Prozac to exceed the placebo in two of them. In reality, these scientific studies have demonstrated that the placebo effect may be one of the most powerful healing mechanisms available. Therefore, it would make more sense to activate the mechanisms used in the placebo that exist in our natural systems than to devote the time, money, and effort to find drug remedies for all our issues. Evidence suggests that the ETT® samadhi process and other ETT® techniques tap into this vast reservoir of resources for healing because the same effects that are achieved by the placebo effect and by many drugs are acquired with this ETT® approach.

Using an array of consciousness-altering, psychospiritual processes, often found in the East, powerful states of mind can be produced. By using these psychospiritual mechanisms via the ETT® samadhi process, various states of extreme wellbeing can be accessed. Through this means various neural receptors can be selectively activated to achieve peace (similar to heroin), physical pain control (similar to morphine), emersion into the present moment (similar to marijuana), elevated self-esteem (similar to cocaine), hallucinatory experiences (similar to psilocybin, LSD, or DMT), or ecstatic love (similar to ecstasy or MDMA). However, when these states of consciousness are accessed naturally, there are no drug side effects, legal risks, or short-term effects. These states can last weeks, months, or even permanently. Furthermore, there is no need to take drugs to escape intolerable distress because ETT® can eliminate distress so efficiently.

Taking an external substance by ingestion may activate similar receptors, but it also has side-effects that are a function of the drug that do not occur when our own biochemistry activates these receptors. For example, ecstasy, which is actually referred to as MDMA or methylenedioxymethamphetamine to biochemists, has significant side-effects. Although researchers have suggested that a class of compounds called entactogens in MDMA allow the person deeper contact with the true self, and others found it helpful for depression and schizophrenia, there are substantial negative effects (Parrott, 2007). These negative effects include but are not limited to the following:

- acute psychological distress (Cohen, 1998; Parrot et al., 2001)
- neurochemical depletion leading to tiredness, irritability, depression (Curran et al., 2004; Greer & Tolbert, 1986)
- acute metabolic/psychobiological distress (Baylen & Rosenberg, 2006; Darvish & Gudelsky, 2005)
- long-term loss of verbal memory (Schilt, 2008)

These risks have not been found in ETT® samadhi sessions, but the benefits have been found.

One might wonder why hallucinatory experiences would be considered desirable and not pathological. LSD is generally viewed by the public as a dangerous hallucinogen. While there is evidence that LSD use has risks when it is improperly used, historically LSD was initially used in the 1950s to aid psychotherapy, and, in fact, produced beneficial effects. However, once LSD became randomly used in the 1960s by the public, its consequences became more dangerous. This led to LSD becoming illegal. Recently, psychedelic substances like LSD have become legal to use under strict scientific guidelines for research. Entire professional journals have emerged that focus on exploring the use of psychedelic substances and psychedelic drugs that have again shown beneficial results (Sessa, 2012). The ETT® samadhi process is a nonpharmaceutical means that may acquire some positive hallucinations without drug risks. For example, in three of six people who underwent the ETT® samadhi process during a training session, auditory hallucinations took place. These experiences all turned out to be functionally beneficial. The fact that our brain–body system possesses neural receptors for positive hallucinations suggests that it is a human potential that exists for a purpose. Apparently, these experiences are part of the states of extreme wellbeing that mystics have described for centuries. Julia's case illustrates the constructive use of positive psychedelic hallucination via the ETT® samadhi process.

JULIA'S CASE

Julia was a fifty-five-year-old woman who struggled with trying to lose weight for years. Her intention for the process was to let go of the excuses and embrace herself in a fit and healthy body. The following was her ETT® samadhi experience:

> I saw the most detailed stone mosaic that rivaled the ancient Volubilis depictions of royal life. This mosaic was alive, undulating in waves with twists and turns that became so brilliant in color that it seemed to transform into stained glass!
>
> It was captivating … it felt as though I was being invited to go into it somehow … which I yearned to do but was hesitant. Within a blink of an eye I acknowledged my desire, and then I was whisked into the swirling kaleidoscope of diamonds … translucent technocolors opening a doorway to another dimension that moved both at the speed of light and in slow motion simultaneously! I was physically embraced in a sensation of wholeness … of safety and security which was exhilarating to the point of tears.
>
> As I was in it, I was approached by what seemed like a pod of dolphins that surrounded me. We soared here and there, twisting and turning and jumping and diving in what seemed to be perhaps the ocean. With each twisting jump breaking through the water it seemed as though I was now soaring in the sky, through storms, when light emerged, I would dive into the waves … it seemed as though I was diving deep into what appeared like space with the Milky Way with stars everywhere, then in a blink it was as though I was encompassed by the brilliance of Northern Lights that lit the pathway into the ocean again where I was joined by the pod. I could not resist the playful twisting, turning, somersaults and racing deep and back to the surface again…. I could see the curls of enormous waves on both sides of me, yet felt the warmth of being blanketed in tropical sun while diving and soaring through clouds … unsure if it was sky or ocean, as I know longer had form familiar to me…. I was a mermaid….
>
> I had a freedom of now knowing that I can celebrate the body I have! I can embrace the process of restoring my body to healthy and fit, because I have experienced me in a fit and healthy body before.

After her experience Julia confessed that she had used a lot of recreational drugs in her younger years, but she had never had any experience as profound as this three-dimensional, multisensory event. In fact, Julia reported that it was the best experience of her life.

The ETT® samadhi process often functions as a spiritual gateway experience in which a vast array of other experiences may occur. Much of the rest of this book is devoted to an understanding of these experiences. Among the transpersonal experiences that may occur subsequent to a samadhi experience is a profound type of awakening that is known by different names in different cultures and different religious orientations. Among its characteristics in common is a profound physiological experience of the divine that is often mistaken for a medical malady or a psychological disorder. In Christian circles it might be described as rapture by the Holy Spirit, but in Hindu culture a similar experience is known as Kundalini. In my second book I describe the Kundalini experience in great detail (Vazquez, 2013, pp. 207–212). It is important to note this type of awakening so that it will be recognized by facilitators and appropriately guided. Two of the best recent descriptions of the Kundalini type of spiritual awakenings have been written by Bonnie Greenwell—*The Inward Journey* and *The Awakening Guide* in 2014.

The synthesis of ancient wisdom about meditative processes and current-day technology can provide a new means to achieve profound states of inner experiences. Since this new synthesis achieves the same experience, it has become accessible to more people who operate in today's lifestyle. While this represents an extraordinary burst into higher states of consciousness, it also requires preparation and follow-up assistance so that disorientation can be minimized and accommodation to this change can be maximized. This potential disruption of one's religious philosophy can occur if direct experience or contact with the void or the divine fosters an incongruity between experience and intellectual concepts. However, it is the nature of true spiritual transformation or rebirth that a radical change occurs. On the other hand, this level of change may fulfill one's grandest dreams as contact with one's deepest authentic self is achieved.

CHAPTER 5 SUMMARY

This chapter surveys various methods for achieving samadhi and the various benefits that can occur due to it. First, an exploration of the use of biofeedback for the purpose of achieving transcendent states takes place. Then the specific limitations of this method for this purpose are described. Next, hypnosis is examined as a means for producing samadhi and compared to the ETT® samadhi process. While these approaches can and do achieve samadhi for some people they are rarely intended for this purpose and are inconsistent for producing samadhi.

Various forms of meditation have long achieved samadhi and have been developed over the centuries for this purpose and more. However, since there are several forms of meditation three well-researched types of meditation were to chosen to explore—mindfulness meditation, transcendental meditation, and Kirtan Kriya. Most of the most powerful benefits form meditation, such as samadhi, occur when it is used for a length of time, daily over a long period of time. This type of devotion does not often fit in American cultural patterns. Whereas the ETT® samadhi process works as though it were an amplified form of meditation that occurs within a single session. The parallels of the ETT® samadhi process and meditation are carefully explored.

The ETT® samadhi process is next compared to prayer. It most closely resembles the category of meditational prayer. Christian centering prayer is explored to be a process that also may yield states of samadhi. Then the outcomes of samadhi are compared to one scale of characteristics of NDEs. This comparison shows a very close parallel.

An in-depth examination of the specific characteristics of samadhi is described. The production of synesthesia is described. The production of synesthesia by the ETT® samadhi process also parallels that of long-term meditators. An examination of levels of states of consciousness is carefully explored and a new hypothesis for the continuum of these states is presented.

Next, the chapter compares the state of consciousness produced by certain drugs with the euphoric states of consciousness produced by the ETT® samadhi process. It is notable that these positive states can be reached through the ETT® samadhi process without the risk of breaking the law, side effects, or addiction. The case example described a woman who had a positive "hallucinatory" experience by means of the ETT® samadhi process without the risky use of hallucinogenic drugs.

Chapter Six

Hearing Voices

Spiritual or Psychotic?

Throughout history people have reported hearing voices when no one else is speaking, and the debate regarding the positive or negative value of hearing voices is a longstanding one. As far back as 1050 BC these voices were viewed as medical conditions or caused by negative supernatural forces (Scurlock & Anderson, 2005). However, as early as 399 BC Socrates heard positive voices according to his pupil Plato (Long, 2009). The Christian Bible is filled with numerous accounts of people hearing voices. The prophet Ezekiel heard voices a total of ninety-three times, Moses heard God's voice (Exodus 23), and Jesus heard God's voice. In fact, the founders of most major religions reported hearing divine voices. The position of cessationists is that while events that took place during Biblical times were true, spiritual events of that type have since ceased to exist in modern times. Today, if a person reports hearing voices, these voices are usually understood to be symptoms of a psychological thought disorder. However, with the increased interest of people who are "spiritual but not religious" and especially with the increased use of meditation, more and more direct spiritual experiences such as voice hearing are being reported. Both spiritual experiences and psychotic experiences have in common that they are both non-logical, which opens the possibility for one being mistaken for the other. Hearing positive or spiritual messages in the form of an audible voice has occurred during or after Emotional Transformation Therapy® (ETT®) sessions.

Let me clarify what is meant by hearing voices. It means the perception of an auditory verbal experience without the physical or electronic presence of another person who was the source of the verbalization. It does not mean remembering how a voice sounds, nor does it mean a message in the form of a thought. Many people have self-critical thoughts or intuition in the form of thoughts. While people often refer to these messages as hearing voices, they are not literal auditory perceptions. In psychiatry, these perceived voices are often referred to as auditory verbal hallucinations (AVH). However, the term "hallucination" can often be misconstrued as fabricated. These inner voices are clearly heard voices.

When ETT® is being used, especially the ETT® samadhi process, people often report perceived verbal hallucinations as part of their spiritual awakening. I shall use the phrase "auditory verbal hallucinations" to indicate this phenomenon. This awareness of voices can be frightening when one lives in a society in which AVHs are viewed as symptoms of psychosis. Sometimes these experiences are attributed to inner guides, angels, God, or deceased people. Since ETT® possesses the capacity to unearth psychological activity at such an in-depth level, experiences can arise that are far beyond events in conventional face-to-face talk therapy. When negative or destructive voices emerge, it is important for therapists to be well-informed about the types of voices possible and how to differentiate between constructive versus destructive voices. An exploration of the history and the therapeutic meaning of these voices as well as a review of the latest brain research about inner voices follows.

RELIGIOUS HISTORY AND HEARING VOICES

For centuries the experiences of Christian saints and mystics who have heard voices has been well documented. Hildegard of Bingen (1098–1174) was a medieval German mystic who heard God's voice in which He commanded her to speak and write specific things. Her voices were authenticated by the church (King-Lenzmeier, 2001). The French mystic Joan of Arc (1412–1431) first heard God's voice at age thirteen. She was initially very afraid of it and seldom heard it without seeing a light. She heard it every day and led the French army to many victories due to being guided by God's voice (Obermeier & Kennison, 1997). The English Christian mystic Julian of Norwich (1342–1416) was the first woman to ever write about hearing voices in English. Saint Teresa of Avila (1515–1582) was a Spanish Christian mystic who heard voices after intense prayer over time. According to McCarthy-Jones (2012), Saint Teresa characterized divine voices by the following characteristics:

- voices bore a sense of power and authority
- a great tranquility bears upon the soul
- words do not vanish from memory for a long time
- the words possess a complete certainty (p. 46)

At one point, AVHs were viewed as spiritual, and then they were seen as either demonic or a function of medical pathology. Politics raged for and against AVHs. People were burned at the stake for them or heralded as saints for the voices they heard. In 1882, a survey of 17,000 normal participants was conducted in London and 2.9 percent of people reported hearing voices (Sidgwick et al., 1894). An Italian psychiatrist named Tamburini (1881–1990) was the first to suggest that hearing voices was a function of brain activity and correctly identified the brain mechanisms that we now know are involved in AVHs (Berrios, 1990). In the late 1800s, there was a popularity of viewing AVHs as symptoms of insanity, but the first president of the American Psychology Association, William James, disagreed. He said that the medical pathologizing of hearing voices

> finished up Saint Paul by calling his vision on the road to Damascus a discharging lesion of the occipital cortex, he being an epileptic, snuffs out Saint Teresa as a hysteric, and Saint Frances of Assisi as an hereditary degenerate. (James, 1902 in McCarthy-Jones, p. 71)

PSYCHIATRY AND VOICE HEARING

Modern psychiatry ushered in AVHs as symptoms of mental disorders. Kraepelin (1919) originally named hearing voices as a symptom of what he called Dementia Praecox and Paraphrenia in the early 1900s. Bleuler replaced the term Dementia Praecox with the term schizophrenia (1950). Even Freud described hearing voices (1901/1958, p. 261). Freud thought the AVHs were fantasies or wish fulfillments recreating experiences that were lost earlier (Eigen, 2005). Carl Jung (1963) thought AVHs were caused by repressed complexes and were related to dreams.

In the 1940s, Kurt Schneider identified symptoms of voice hearing that he believed were special diagnostic symptoms of schizophrenia. "These were voices conversing with one another, and voices that kept up a running commentary" (McCarthy-Jones, 2012, p. 85). These symptoms came to be known as Schneiderian first rank symptoms and were part of the *Diagnostic and Statistical Manual* (DSM) I, II and III manuals as symptoms of schizophrenia.

In the DSM V, under "schizophrenia spectrums and other psychotic disorders," AVH is described under "Hallucinations" as the following:

> Hallucinations are perception-like experiences that occur without an external stimulus. They are vivid and clear, with the full force and impact of normal perceptions, and not under voluntary control. They may occur in any sensory

> modality, but auditory hallucinations are the most common in schizophrenia and related disorders. Auditory hallucinations are usually experienced as voices, whether familiar or unfamiliar, that are perceived as distinct from the individual's own thoughts. The hallucinations must occur in the context of a clear sensorium; those that occur while falling asleep (hypnogogic) or waking up (hypnopompic) are considered to be within the range of normal experience. Hallucinations may be a normal part of religious experience in certain cultural contexts. (American Psychiatric Association, 2013, pp. 87–88)

In the DSM V, there are four diagnoses that list hallucinations as primary symptom options:

- Brief Psychotic Disorder
- Schizophrenia
- Schizoaffective Disorder
- Substance/Medication-Induced Psychotic Disorder

While these are criteria for diagnoses today, these diagnostic criteria are not really complete information about hearing voices according to the scientific research.

HEARING VOICES AS PSYCHIATRIC SYMPTOMS

In one study, fifty percent of posttraumatic stress disorder (PTSD) patients reported hearing voices (Anketell et al., 2010). In another study, sixty-seven percent of PTSD patients reported hearing voices (Brewin & Patel, 2010). Yet these symptoms are not even significantly noted for this population in the DSM V. Combat veterans often have voices with themes of guilt and tend to hear voices of dead comrades that are not simply flashbacks of events. However, the most disturbing message these voices of veterans often communicate is "kill yourself" (Mueser & Butler, 1987).

People who have experienced childhood sexual abuse have shown a higher propensity to exhibit hearing voices than others. Among people diagnosed with bipolar disorder, those who had childhood sexual abuse had three times more AVHs (seventy-three percent) than those without childhood sexual abuse (twenty-three percent) (Hammersley, Dias, Todd, Bowen-Jones, Reilly, & Bentall, 2003). In another study with psychiatric patients, auditory hallucinations were three times more common with those who had histories of childhood sexual abuse. Furthermore, these patients had commenting voices six times more often and commanding voices seven times more often than those without childhood sexual abuse (Read et al., 2003). These findings and others make it abundantly clear that at least one contributing factor toward the production of some forms of AVH's is early life trauma.

Significant scientific research also identifies the proportion of AVHs in several different psychiatric populations:

- In schizophrenia, the prevalence of AVHs is approximately seventy percent (Baethge et al., 2005; Thomas et al., 2007).
- Seven percent to twenty percent of patients with bipolar disorder heard voices (Hammersley, Taylor, Mc Govern, & Kinderman, 2010; Baethge et al., 2005).
- Studies indicate that about thirty-two percent of people diagnosed with borderline personality disorder heard voices (Yee et al., 2005; Kingdon et al., 2010).
- Alcoholic AVHs occur in about seventy-six percent of people with delirium tremens (Platz, Oberlander, & Seidl, 1995).

It is interesting that research findings of psychiatric disordered populations do not necessarily match with the DSM V diagnostic criteria.

In addition to these populations, in one study, about twenty eight percent of people with Alzheimer's heard voices (Craig et al., 2005). As many as fifty percent of people with moderate to severe head injuries report AVHs (Fujii & Ahmed, 2002). People with Parkinson's disease hear voices on the average of eight percent of the time (Holroyd, Currie, & Wooten, 2001; Matsui et al., 2006). A small percentage (2.5%) of elderly deaf people reported hearing voices (Cole et al., 2002). Interestingly, those were normal adults who literally could not hear another person speaking in their physical presence.

VOICE HEARING IN CURRENT RELIGIONS

Research suggests that hearing voices occurs in every country on earth (Murphy et al., 1963). However, these voices are not always viewed as psychopathology in many cultures. Even when hearing voices has been seen as a symptom of schizophrenia, the resolution of these conditions was actually more successful in third world countries than in "advanced societies" that used psychiatric medications (WHO, 1973, 1979). Dialogue with deceased ancestors accounts for much of the AVHs in third world societies but not in the United States and highly industrial societies. It should be noted that in the DSM V allowance was made for hearing voices as normal in religious experiences within certain cultural contexts. This recognition is an official departure from viewing AVHs as simply a symptom of psychological disorders. Also in non-Western cultures hearing voices is more likely to evolve into visual hallucinations (Al-Issa, 1978).

AVHs are formally recognized in many established religions in the United States and around the world according to religious doctrine:

- Both the contemporary Catholic church and the Anglican church recognize voice hearing.
- Islam recognizes voice hearing and attributes the voices to an entity they call the "Jinn" (Blom, 2010).
- Fifty-nine percent of members of the Evangelical Christian church compared to a control population reported hearing voices (Davis, 1976).
- The majority of an English Pentecostal church reported hearing God's voice in response to prayer (Dein & Littlewood, 2007).

Hearing voices has long been a part of most religions, but there is great controversy concerning whether the voices heard were from a source that was divine or evil. The Catholic church still follows the categories for differentiating different types of divine voices developed by Saint John of the Cross (1542–1591) that were called locutions (McCarthy-Jones, 2012). However, Quakers seek the still, quiet voice from within that is believed to be found in a quiet mental state (Fox, 1808).

HEARING VOICES IN HEALTHY POPULATIONS

So far in this discussion, sources for AVH have been largely viewed as a symptom of psychiatric disorders, medical conditions, and religious sources. However, substantial research validates AVH in healthy subjects without any psychiatric disorders, religious, or medical sources to which they might be attributed. In a large study of healthy voice hearers who have no psychiatric disorders, seventy-one percent had never heard negative voices and twenty-five percent heard both positive and negative voices (Sommer et al., 2010). The category of healthy voice hearers completely changes common stereotypes of AVH.

Even the DSM V identifies one category of voice hearing that is not considered a symptom of a psychological disorder. This category concerns AVHs when they occur during hypnopompic or hypnogogic states. Hypnopompic states occur when a person is in the process of waking up in the morning but is neither fully asleep nor fully awake. Hypnogogic states occur when one is in the process of falling asleep but is neither awake nor asleep. There is substantial scientific evidence that hearing voices takes place within normal populations. From 2.4 to 49 percent of normal populations hear voices during these states according to a range of studies (Ohayon, 2000; Jones & Ferryhough, 2006). The most common occurrence in these states is hearing a person calling their name.

On a personal note, I do most of my writing in the early hours of the morning. As I was writing I heard my wife call out, "What? What do you want?" I replied, "I didn't say anything." She replied, "I thought I heard you calling my name." My wife does not have any type of psychological disorder, nor does she hear God or evil voices speak to hear. This occurrence drove home to me the commonality of hearing voices during hypnopompic states. Since voice hearing is not a complaint-based issue in normal populations, it does not receive as much attention as a research topic and as a result skews the usual perception about voice hearing in the general population.

BRAIN RESEARCH ON AVH

Substantial scientific research on the nature of brain activity during AVH now exists. The research generally finds distinctly different brain mechanisms involved immediately preceding AVH as opposed to during AVH activity. Most of these studies involve the use of neuroimaging of the brain, and there are numerous studies on this topic. Most of these studies were done on schizophrenic patients. The following are the findings:

Preceding AVH

- The parahyppocampal gyrus is activated. This brain mechanism normally functions to identify the social context of linguistic elements of verbal communication.
- The insula is activated. Its usual function is to facilitate perceived embodiment of emotion.
- The inferior frontal gyrus including the left side referred to as Boca's area is activated. This mechanism is involved in language production and verbal comprehension as well as "go/not go" decisions (Diederen et al., 2010; Sommer et al., 2008).

From this it can be seen that the brain is developing a social context for the voice, preparing a physiological experience and providing permission to move forward in the activity of language reception. Apparently, it is necessary for the brain to activate in this way before actual AVHs can occur.

During AVH

- The inferior frontal gyrus activates language production and verbal comprehension.

- The superior temporal gyrus activates the capacity for the sensation of sound and processing of speech so it can be understood as language. It is also involved in perception of emotion in faces.
- The insula activates the bodily experience of emotions.
- The cerebellum activates motor activity.
- The supramarginal gyrus in the parietal lobe activates language processing (Diederen et al., 2010; Sommer et al., 2008).

It appears that the brain is basically utilizing similar mechanisms that would be involved during normal hearing of other speaker's voices that were physically present. However, there are some differences. For example, when dysfunctional negative voices are being heard during AVH, there is a lack of congruity between the right and left brain hemispheres (Diederen et al., 2010). Nonetheless, the fact that these brain mechanisms are activated during AVH verifies that a unique occurrence is taking place and that AVHs are not fabricated falsely.

THE NATURE OF AVHs

Research on the nature of voices heard by people diagnosed with some form of psychosis reveals information that may or may not conform to common beliefs about hearing voices. There have long been diagnostic issues pertaining to whether voices are heard inside the person's head or outside. In a study of voice hearers who consisted of eight-one percent schizophrenics, it was found that twenty-eight percent heard voices outside their heads, while thirty-five percent heard them in inside their heads, but thirty-eight percent heard both inside and outside voices. Inside voices were perceived to be equally as real to the hearer. Whether voices are perceived to be inside or outside does not seem to be of diagnostic significance. However, ninety-one percent were more likely to resist commands perceived as coming from outside their heads compared to seventy-six percent who heard voices inside their heads. A total of fifty-three percent of schizophrenics had "command" AVHs and of those who cooperated with the commands, thirty-three percent committed a violent act in which eighteen percent were self-injurious and fifteen percent were violent acts toward others. However, of the people who were able to ignore these commands, the strategy used most frequently was prayer (Lee et al., 2004). This finding is important because it shows that the person hearing negative voices can change them.

Regardless of the philosophical approach to treatment, it is always imperative to take appropriate measures for the safety of the client and those people around them. These measures may at times include medications. However, strange, peculiar, or odd thoughts do not necessarily equate to dangerous risks. Many more clients commit suicide and/or homicide that do not hear voices than people who do hear voices.

One thing that has been overlooked most often is the fact that people with psychotic diagnoses also experience positive voices. Various studies have found that the number of positive voices is as high as eighty-three percent of the psychotic population (Honig et al., 1998). The fact that positive voices bring forth healthy functioning contradicts the concept that hearing voices within psychotic patients is dysfunctional.

Do psychiatric medications stop AVHs? Psychiatric medications do not usually eliminate AVHs. However, there is a tendency for these medications to help people feel less bothered by these voices. Psychiatric medications that target reduction of voices tend to produce an experience of detachment from client AVHs (McCarthy-Jones, 2012, pp. 375–383). A conventional psychiatric approach to these voices is to ignore them so that the existence of the voices will not be reinforced.

There has been substantial research on the conventional process of labeling clients with a psychiatric diagnosis, medicating them, and hospitalizing them. Research findings include the following:

- After a diagnosis of some form of psychosis there tends to be a significant loss of hope (Pitt et al., 2009).
- Side effects of antipsychotic medications often include disruption of eating and sleeping patterns as well as physical pain (Rofail, Heelis, & Gournay, 2009).
- Loss of a sense of safety and security emerges from hearing voices at times but is amplified by being hospitalized (Gee, Pierce, & Jackson, 2003).
- The consequence of loss of social and romantic relationships has a severe negative impact (Redmond, Larkin, & Harrop, 2010).
- Being stigmatized as a lesser person that other people should stay away from tends to make negative voices worse and makes people avoid mental health services (Judge et al., 2008).

Theorists have attempted to classify different types of AVHs because both the possible sources of stimulation and the nature of voices can be so completely different. The following list offers distinctions of AVHs:

- Hypervigilant voices are heard during exposure to unpatterned sound and perceived to be from outside the head (Dodgson & Gordon, 2009). These types of voices occur in two ways:
  A. Voices with repetitive content
  B. Voices with extended novel content; complex in form; ongoing inner dialogue

- Memory-based voices tend to occur in two ways:
  A. Reenacted memories—verbatim memories or parts of memories of actual events
  B. Reactivated memories of novel complex content that are thematically related to trauma
- Transcendent sources of complex dialogue unrelated to outside noise, but highly relevant and meaningful in one's life events

While this is not a complete list of options for categorizing AVHs, it acknowledges different types so as not to assume that all inner voices are the same, nor is it simply a choice of good or evil. This is an attempt to simplify complex findings and rigid philosophical positions that may not be able to be explained by simple assumptions. Some people may have only one type of AVH, but most of my clients have had several of these types of AVHs.

Psychiatrist Clancy McKenzie suggests that the massive scientific research on schizophrenia characterizing schizophrenia as (1) a brain disease that can be verified by brain scans, (2) a genetic condition, and (3) a chemical imbalance, have confused cause and effect. In other words, these conclusions are drawn based on evidence of the effects of a casual event. Dr. McKenzie has identified the casual events as specific early childhood trauma that disrupted brain development and then became latent until a stressor triggered reactivation in later life. McKenzie is not blaming poor parenting, because traumatic events can occur in the best of families. Therefore AVH's in schizophrenia may simply be a part of an array of coping mechanisms in response to certain traumas in early life. Dr. McKenzie's treatment for schizophrenia involves little or no medications and has been successful with schizophrenics (McKenzie, 2004, personal communication; McKenzie, 2009).

The facts that some psychotics can change the voices and those positive voices tend to exist in most of them leads to the idea that these positive resources can be therapeutically valuable. The cross-cultural evidence shows that when people experiencing AVHs are supported by their culture, the nature and function of these "negative" voices can be changed. In the early 1980s, I had a case in which a woman was prone to having psychotic episodes.

BARBARA'S CASE

Barbara was an attractive, married, forty-year-old woman who sought counseling due to psychotic breaks from reality, but she did not want to take medication. These psychotic states involved manic states in which she talked incessantly. Much of the content of her psychotic dialogue was "word salad" that made no logical sense. The expression during psychosis often included Christian religious content. While I had not actually seen her in these states, she brought writings that occurred during these states. As I listened and supported her struggle, she had fewer of those types of states.

One day she told me that she and her husband were going on a cruise to Europe. A few days later, Barbara called me from New York harbor where she was about to board the ship. Barbara was beginning to enter a psychotic state and felt undecided about boarding the ship. Barbara decided to board.

Weeks later I heard from Barbara. She told me that she was largely confined to her cabin on the ship where her husband listened as she talked rapidly for hours each day during her psychotic episodes. However, by the time she arrived in Europe the psychotic episodes had subsided. Barbara reported that by going through this state with support, she was able to complete it. Years later Barbara reported that her psychotic states never emerged again.

As a young therapist, this event took place contrary to all I had learned about schizophrenia and psychotic conditions. How could a genetically based brain disease be healed through supportive expression? Due to this experience, I viewed psychosis differently, but my understanding was not validated until many years later when I came across the work of John Wier Perry.

SUPPORTING VOICE HEARING

Jungian psychiatrist John Wier Perry viewed psychotic states as part of a spiritual renewal process. A cultural perspective similar to that view is held in several third world countries. From this vantage point AVHs have value as a part of the breakdown of identity that possesses a spiritual movement toward the goal of a new identity. If these people undergoing "renewal" are supported and understood through empathetic responses, it is believed that the psychotic states progress and function as transitional states. Dr. Perry developed a government-funded "sanctuary" in which people in these psychotic states lived and were supported instead of medicated. Research on the outcomes of this approach showed the following results:

> The three year follow-up on eighty-one cases in the Agnew Project showed 73% recurrence of the psychosis in patients treated with medication both in and out of the hospital, but only 8% recurrence for those treated without medication both in and out. The personality profiles were even more striking: those on medication showed arrest in emotional development over the three years of the follow-up, while those off medications showed no such plateauing of the growth curve, but a continuous upward rise. (Perry, 1999, p. 27)

Although these research findings are stunning, the field of psychiatry is largely unaware of them, and the information can hardly be found in any textbooks. While people in psychotic states are often seen as shamans or people undergoing a spiritual upheaval in many third world cultures, they are usually labeled, shunned, and seen as outcasts here. Therefore, it's not surprising that these people struggle in the United States, even with medications. When research validated the non-medicated approach, it was largely discarded in the United States because that approach was viewed unfavorably in this culture. In fact, research has shown that third world countries that do not use medication for psychosis have better outcomes than first world nations (WHO, 1973, 1979).

Dutch psychiatrist Marius Romme went on a Dutch television program to appeal to voice hearers to contact him, and four hundred and fifty voice hearers replied. From this initial contact, meetings took place, and the first conference for voice hearers occurred in 1987. Subsequent to this conference, the International Community for Hearing Voices was launched, and voice hearing communities were established around the world. These groups are now internet based and advocate the liberation of voice hearers (Romme et al., 2009). While it is recognized that some voice hearers possess unresolved issues, the voices themselves may largely become problems due to the person's reaction to them and to society's reaction to them (McCarthy-Jones, 2012, pp. 90–95).

WORKING WITH INNER VOICES

Strategies exist for working with people who hear voices—strategies that achieve results without the use of medications. Initially, people in the United States are often frightened by hearing voices because they tend to judge them as an abnormality. Therefore, a normalization of the experience by an accepting therapist tends to be stabilizing, as demonstrated in two large studies (Mosher, Vallone, & Menn, 1995; Perry, 1999, p. 27). In an office setting, I have witnessed psychotic states stabilize temporarily as quickly as within a single session by simply empathizing and normalizing the client's psychotic dialogue. This tendency can be further established by the use of ETT® tools.

A second therapeutic challenge is to understand the meaning of AVHs. John Wier Perry suggests that most psychotic dialogue is meaningful, but it represents meaning through symbolic language characteristic of classic myth and allegory. However, a different meaning appears for some people to be a more literal reenactment of traumatic interpersonal events. If a person possesses a religious orientation in which voices are accepted, inner voices may be attributed to learned beliefs. When AVHs emerge as a consequence of ETT®, especially the samadhi process, AVHs may emerge as spiritual voices whether a religious background exists or not. Regardless of the source attributed to these voices, an exploration of their meaning to each person is valuable.

Once these first two principles of either symbolic or memory re-enactment are established, a therapist can encourage engagement with these inner voices with the goal of transforming negative or destructive voices. The first engagement strategy is to help a client engage with his or her own voices constructively. The second strategy involves the therapist engaging with a client's voices. This usually involves empathizing with destructive voices. Although these destructive voices can be very hostile, narrow-minded and rude, it is important to note that they are essentially psychological defenses. This suggests that their origin may have been perceived to have been functional at some time in the client's life or in the client's imprint of a parent's life. If they currently exist as a hostile defense, there is likely to be a vulnerable emotional part that these voices are defending. Therefore, after rapport is established, and trust between the client and destructive voices, and/or the therapist is developed, then the vulnerable emotional aspect underlying the psychological defense can emerge. When this opportunity occurs, emotional transformation can be facilitated by ETT®. When this takes place, negative voices can become constructive voices.

HEARING VOICES AS POSSESSION

In the vast majority of countries around the world, the phenomenon of demonic or spirit possession is an accepted condition. Often the experience of hearing voices is attributed to possession. People who have spiritual orientations that include possession may often label dissociative identity disorder and symptoms of hearing voices as possession. Within these religious traditions, the remedy for symptoms of possession is deliverance. I have observed that people who report or exhibit features of possession often have a history of poor interpersonal boundaries derived from intrusive childhood experiences. Therefore, their experiences of perceived intrusions in their lives extend into their spiritual lives. However, I have witnessed that far too many people have a limited belief system and tend to attribute almost any negative symptom to evil intrusions of a spiritual type. The following strategy is an alternative to deliverance as a strategy. When an opportunity to engage and transform destructive voices occurs, the possibility of transformation of these voices into constructive voices can occur. A transformation of destructive voices to positive voices often leads to a healing integration of a formerly fragmented person—an integration that tends to have long-term benefits. By engaging and transforming negative voices as well as strengthening interpersonal boundaries through concluding intrusive traumas, the possibility of making the person immune to potential future intrusions is insured. The major key is to transform the client's fear.

JANE'S CASE

Jane was a forty-five-year-old married woman diagnosed with dissociative identity disorder. At the time I was working with Jane, I was supervising an Episcopal priest who was pursuing his license as a Licensed Professional Counselor. At one point during treatment, Jane reported the presence of demons in her psychiatric hospital room. The priest confirmed that demons were indeed present in her room. This frightened Jane even more. When the priest reported this experience to me, I decided not to debate his spiritual orientation or the existence of demons. However, I knew that if the fear of these demons was reduced, the client's ability to cope would improve. Therefore, I recommended that the priest use his religious authority to reframe these demons into lesser threats. I had the priest tell this client that demons were present but they were like gnats. When he did this, her fears diminished and symptoms immediately receded. Then it was easy to cast them out later.

In this case whether the priest's religious orientation and detection of demons was accurate or not, we concurred with the goal of reducing the client's fear. A therapist, using the following active steps, can resolve conditions identified as possession:

- respect and operate within the client's religious orientation
- process fear to conclusion
- if there are inner voices, engage them and shift them from destructive to constructive voices
- access the client's own inner resources for use in the therapeutic process
- collaborate with a priest or religious authority if appropriate
- correct poor interpersonal boundaries and related core issues
- strengthen the client's sense of self

SPIRITUAL VOICES

Subsequent to ETT® sessions, many clients have experienced hearing the voice of what they perceived to be God. These clients could not be categorized into one of the four diagnoses for which the DSM V lists AVHs as a symptom. In none of these cases did the idea of seeking to hear God's voice occur in a discussion preceding the hearing of it. People who heard God's voice talk to them had a diverse array of religious/spiritual orientations from complete atheists/agnostics to Christian, Jewish, "spiritual but not religious," Buddhist, and others. In many cases the initial hearing of God's voice was quite shocking. AVHs occurred after a series of ETT® sessions for some people, but sometimes it happened during or after the ETT® samadhi process took place. In almost all cases, the message of the voice was therapeutically beneficial to the client. The voice was typically masculine, but in a few cases it was feminine or undetermined. Some of the qualities that God's voice produced for clients included

- comfort
- reassurance
- new perspectives
- answers to questions perplexing to clients
- love or affection
- recommendations of things to be done

Some people saw a visual appearance of the God whose voice they heard. The hearing of God's voice occurred only once in some cases, a few times with others, and for some it became a continuous occurrence. So far the message of God's voice has never been punishing, critical, or demanding. Most people accepted the message of God's voice after an initial inability to accept it as valid. However, some people argued with it, rebelled against it, or mistrusted it when it occurred repeatedly, but in all cases, so far, they eventually accepted God's voice as speaking from a vantage point of truth. Doubt about the validity of God's voice occurred when the events in a person's life were tragic or negative. From a psychological perspective people projected their own attachment deficits onto this voice of God, but God's message functioned as a secure attachment relationship when clients were not projecting onto this relationship.

In many cases, clients heard voices of angels, spirit guides, deceased loved ones, and spiritual leaders such as Jesus, various gurus, or ascended masters. In some cases, clients were unable to identify the source of a spiritual voice, or when told about its identity by the voice, the client was unfamiliar with this entity. These spiritual guides were almost always helpful to the therapeutic process by concurring with the therapeutic direction or adding valuable support and understanding. However, these voices did not always tell clients what they wanted to hear. These voices often brought messages about resolution to a client's issues that did not provide relief as quickly as the client sought. Nonetheless, answers eventually occurred, and they were valid for a resolution over time. Essentially, ego needs were not always secured when and how the client wanted them to take place.

No one can definitively confirm that these perceived spiritual voices are valid, based on logic alone, because their basis is a matter of faith. However, the fact that spirit guides or God's voice has been functionally beneficial is a measure upon which they score extremely high. The "downside" is that these voices may create chaos in a person's belief system that is disturbing for some people and becomes a therapeutic issue in and of itself. However, the nature of growth is that disruption tends to occur before new psychospiritual growth can take place.

On rare occasions the perceived voice of God has changed to a more critical, negative voice. However, it was typically discovered that a client's negative projections had contaminated the voice, and this situation was subsequently corrected.

CAN GOD'S VOICE BE FACILITATED?

Cross-cultural and religious church evidence clearly shows that the development of hearing spiritual voices is a possibility. As described earlier in Chapter 4, ETT® has facilitated the perception of hearing God's voice, and in Chapter 9 it will be described for the use of facilitating hearing voices of deceased entities. However, there are some variations, risks, and inauthentic possibilities regarding this issue. First of all, many people will never hear an audible voice from within because spiritual messages may occur only in the form of thoughts. Secondly, destructive voices can masquerade as God's voice due to influences from traumatic events in a person's past or other factors. Third, the perception of hearing God's voice is well known in certain churches, in part, because these churches provide a supportive community for hearing voices. In a community in which psychiatric pathologizing of hearing voices prevails, even if one did hear God's voice, its development and manifestation could become problematic due to a negative social reaction. Fourth, other spiritual voices such as that of perceived angels, spirit guides, deceased people, or religious leaders may occur instead of God's voice for certain people. Among these other options dialogue with deceased people, especially ancestors, is the most universal, cross-cultural phenomenon.

Depending on these aforementioned factors, one should weigh the risks of encouraging the development of hearing God's voice. In most cases, the ETT® facilitation of hearing God's voice occurred spontaneously, usually when the ETT® samadhi process was used. The initial reaction to this occurrence is frequently, "Am I going crazy?" Once support is provided and a way to fit this experience into one's life has occurred, it tends to become an incredibly valuable part of one's positive resources.

Historically, the method used by Saint Teresa of Avila during the 1500s comes closest to how spiritual methods parallel ETT® for the development of hearing voices. Saint Teresa describes the four stages of prayer—a form of Christian centering prayer—that by most definitions parallels the process of meditation that we know today. Over years of consistent daily prayer, Saint Teresa experienced the evolution from prayer as initially laborious to the point where the process became more natural, followed by the arrival of spiritual gifts, and finally the presence of God occurring powerfully and clearly, often in the form of God's voice (du Boulay, 2004, pp. 46–55). The ETT® samadhi process amplifies the typically long meditation process into a swift procedure.

The basic concern for most people is how to distinguish psychopathology from authentic spiritual voices. As one can see from the previous research cited, it is over simplistic to assume that all voices of a spiritual source are legitimate. To add to the complexity of this issue some people who possess clear psychological disorders simultaneously may also possess authentic spiritual voices. On one level it is easy to distinguish psychopathology from authentic spiritual voices in that authentic spiritual voices are not critical, caustic, hopeless, fearful, nor generally do they tell people to kill themselves or others (except for Joan of Arc) or to conduct deeds that oppose consensus acceptability. However, they may tell people to do and say things that may not match with everyone else's religious ideas. In some cases, the person hearing negative voices may conceive of them as coming from God, but to outsiders these messages are easy to assess as pathological or destructive. Therefore, there is value in sharing the messages from these voices with someone who is unbiased but ethical. However, the fact that a message comes from an inner voice is not enough evidence to conclude that it must be problematic. Sometimes, in fact, simply empathetically listening to the voices by clients can change a negative voice to a positive one.

The vast majority of people in inpatient psychiatric facilities include religious dialogue in the expression of their symptoms, but the vast majority of schools of psychiatric training do not provide teaching about religious issues except for religion as a defense. This means that religious issues are filtered through psychiatric conceptions, which usually leaves all hearing voices in the category of pathology. This results in direct conflict between practice and what most scientific research has found. The fact that there are positive and negative voices, spiritual and destructive voices, voices that are a result of trauma, and voices that are a result of medical conditions leaves our understanding fragmented. Furthermore, those people who experience some psychopathology—psychosis, bipolar disorder, and other disorders—often experience positive ecstasy at points.

Isabel Clarke has offered a model that could integrate these disparities. However, in her "discontinuity model" she had to develop a conceptualization and language to make sense of it. The following provides the general idea. One can classify modes of thinking into two general categories:

- The logical mind of ordinary consciousness, which is Teasdale's propositional cognitive subsystem (Teasdale & Barnard, 1993).
- Perceptual/relational mind that views things as wholes with emotional meaning and involves sensory modalities and the person's inner world, which is Teasdale's implicational cognitive subsystem (Teasdale & Barnard, 1993).

Then if this perceptual mind can be seen as a category that incorporates both psychotic states and spiritual states, a term that comes close to describing this category is Thalbourne's "transliminality" (Thalbourne et al., 1997). Since people who hear voices can enter psychotic states and also enter spiritual states, and people who hear spiritual voices often enter into what Western medicine would label as pathological states, to categorize them as totally separate does not often match the reality. However, states exist in which a continuum from the psychotic to the spiritual and back and forth could occur, it appears that these voices are linked. This matches the reality of what is seen in these clients. In addition to the previously cited research that supports this perspective, viewing "psychotic" and spiritual voices within this context provides a basis for the therapeutic benefits. While it might be in the client's best interest to diagnose them as schizophrenic, for example, in order to access insurance reimbursement, research has shown that a diagnosis of some form of psychopathology is detrimental to the therapeutic process. This is especially true since many believe transitional psychotic states represent a shift in the formation of the inner self. If the transliminal states are understood to be an internal quest for growth that simply includes excursions into turbulence on the way to ultimate states, the presence of the turbulence can be expected and understood instead of its presence creating yet another trauma. This process can be likened to the biological birth of a baby. In the case of biological birth, it is not viewed as a medical illness per se, yet having discomfort is expected and accepted as part of a transitional process. Normalizing the process eases tension rapidly.

The transliminal domain concerns hypersensitivity to one's own psychological issues and susceptibility to both psychotic states and mystical states. This sensitivity makes these clients susceptible to a fluctuation to and from these qualitatively different states. However, these states are not random and potentially possess an impetus in a direction of growth, although the journey could be long and circuitous. Clients can be directed to use their own inner positive resources to encounter negative states of mind.

Turbulent voices can be encountered with empathy and validation. Once a bond is formed between problematic voices and the therapist, a previously frightening voice can become vulnerable and available for transformation via the same ETT® process used to transform other emotional distress. Some voices are more rigid than others. Joining into the client's transliminal states and operating within the context of their perspective can yield functional outcomes. Most clients in the United States have incorporated the current view of hearing voices that our society has adopted, which leaves them judging their own voices by the standards of psychiatry. This situation creates inner conflict. Therefore, an acceptance of these voices can often lead to the client accepting his or her own voices through the therapist's example. I have recently discovered a psychotherapy process using ETT® that can rapidly integrate the perceptual/irrational mind with the logical mind of ordinary consciousness that results in the elimination of negative psychotic states in just a few sessions. The process uses a form of memory reconsolidation only after a rapport with the inner negative voices has been built. Memory reconsolidation facilitates permanent changes, but I will continue to observe these clients to see if longevity of changes does, in fact, occur. Of course, scientific research needs to take place to verify the consistency of this technique.

Most psychological treatment approaches are designed to reduce or stop psychological symptoms, which ignores the possibility that unpleasant symptoms may simply represent turbulence in the wake of a positive growth experience. If distressing symptoms are embraced instead of resisted, voluntary neural circuits may engage involuntary distress neural circuits, resulting in cooperation with the growth impetus of the system. Paradoxically, this strategy often yields a conclusion of the distress but with the benefit of encouraging, and supporting the inner growth impetus. Most ETT® processes work by validating and amplifying a symptom in such a way that it speeds up the emotional transitional state into transformation.

Hearing voices appears to be an extended human capacity that can occur for a variety of purposes. Evil versus good are relative issues that vary from one culture to another. According to Perry, McKenzie and others, psychosis itself can be viewed as something other than true pathology. In third world cultures, where hearing voices serves as part of a special spiritual process, so-called malicious voices can signify an internal renewal process in which one's identity is breaking down for the purpose of deepening and growing into a new identity. Evidence suggests that if psychotherapy adopted support of this transformation, almost all inner voices could become allies for the client.

CHAPTER 6 SUMMARY

This chapter opened with a historical perspective of the centuries' long debate about spiritual vs. psychotic voice hearing. This controversy has occurred since 1050 BC and continues today. Then definitions of voice hearing and the phrase AVH were introduced. The high points of voice hearing in religious history were identified, and then an exploration of voice hearing in the history of psychiatry was the focus. Research on hearing voices in psychiatry was summarized. Then research on AVH's in current religions was examined.

The phenomenon of hearing inner voices in healthy populations was carefully explored. These voices may be from neither psychiatric conditions nor from religious sources. Scientific research on the nature of brain activity during voice hearing was explained. Then theories about the nature of voice hearing took place in some detail. A case study of healing from pathological voice hearing provided an example of how to therapeutically change negative voices. The approach of supporting various types of voice hearing was acknowledged. Then a therapeutic approach to working with inner voices was described.

Construing inner voices as possession was acknowledged since many cultures adopt this perspective. A case study illustrated one way to approach voices perceived as possession. Next, recognizing and working with spiritual voices was discussed. The facilitation of positive spiritual voices through ETT® was explored and the concept of transliminality was described as a context for conceptualizing the negative versus positive spiritual voices.

Chapter Seven

Cancer as a Rebirth Opportunity

Of all medical conditions, cancer is the one most often associated with death by the general public. The intimation of death often evokes questions of an existential nature: Why am I here? What is the meaning of life? What does death mean? What is the spiritual nature of life and death? Therefore, spiritual issues are thrust into people's awareness to a degree surpassing anything that might have occurred before a life-threatening illness. In response, many people hold dearly to their previously learned faith, testing its capacity as a resource, while those without religion are motivated to ask spiritual questions they have not faced before. Atheists and agnostics may not speak in spiritual terms when confronted with cancer, but questions regarding the meaning of existence and death certainly arise. These profound challenges to a person's understanding can bring about a fundamental shift in personality—a shift some would call a rebirth.

To what do cancer survivors attribute the cause of their cancer? Research with cancer survivors shows that they primarily identified biological and lifestyle issues as the cause of their cancer, and psychological factors were the least commonly identified factors (Ferrucci, et al., 2011, pp. 121–140). However, research has demonstrated that psychosocial factors are significant contributors. Another study showed that nonwhites were more likely to attribute the cause of cancer to supernatural forces (Landrine & Klonoff, 1994, pp. 181–193).

CAN THE MIND CAUSE CANCER?

Spiritual and religious issues arise in coping with cancer after it is diagnosed. Before that diagnosis, however, something else has transpired. Scientific evidence exists that psychological and social issues often play a role in the actual causation of cancer. Regrettably, this information is seldom provided to most cancer patients by conventional medical doctors. When this information is known, it is far too often misused as a means to self-blame, which may contribute to worsening the journey of life and possibly worsening medical conditions. The scientific evidence of psychosocial factors related to cancer shows that it contributes to cancer development, but this information should provide the knowledge for understanding and prevention. There are many scientific studies that focus on psychosocial factors as a contributing cause of cancer (termed prospective studies) and research that focuses on the development and/or progression of cancer (called retrospective, quasi-prospective, or case control studies). These studies all involve adult populations only. The following information regards psychosocial causative factors in cancer.

One study of 6,848 people found that people who were socially isolated were at a higher risk for cancer (Kaplan & Reynolds, 1988, pp. 1–13). Cancer research is considered more valid if there is a long-term follow-up. This study was followed up for seventeen years. Another study found that "rational-emotional behavior" was a causative factor in cancer in a study of 1,353 people (Grossarth-Maticek, 1982). This means that people who tend to avoid the acknowledgement and expression of unpleasant emotions by rationalizing or intellectualizing reactions are at risk for developing cancer. In psychological terms, these people exhibit not conscious denial but a form of repression of emotions. What is peculiar to psychotherapists is that there is often a tendency for cancer patients to appear less depressed than people in general, but this is often due to repression according to research (Dattore, Shontz, & Coyne, 1980). In another study of 1,300 people who were followed up at intervals for forty years, it was found that people who reported a lack of closeness to their parents during childhood were at a higher risk for cancer. It also found that loners were sixteen times more likely to develop cancer than those who were socially active and who expressed their emotions to others (Bleiker et al., 1996). A different study found that early life events such as the death of one's mother or depressive episodes occurring as long ago as twenty years earlier predicted the occurrence of cancer, but in those cases there was little evidence of recent or current depression in these patients. Another study found that possession of high negative emotion coupled with high social inhibition or nonexpression of emotions predicted a higher incidence of cancer (Denollet, 1998). These studies offer a compelling profile of psychological and social factors that may cause cancer.

In an era in which most people initially go to their primary care physicians for an array of mental health conditions in order to acquire psychiatric medications for their symptoms, the possibility of more frequent repression increases. Psychiatric medications may alleviate some symptoms but generally do not resolve psychological conditions. This often leaves core emotional memories unresolved and out of conscious awareness, leading the person to believe that no psychological problems exist. In this era, most people are using psychiatric medications alone and never even consider going to psychological counseling. This inadvertent collusion between doctors and patients to repress emotions has hypothetically placed more people at a higher risk for cancer development. Psychiatric medications tend to mask emotions, not uncover them. While there is a place for psychiatric medications, the reduction of distress symptoms keeps people from pursuing in-depth psychotherapy. This tends to place people, who may already be at risk for cancer, at an even higher risk by contributing to block conscious awareness of relevant core emotions.

THE ETIOLOGY OF CANCER

Based on substantial scientific research, de la Pena has produced a hypothesis about cancer causation. He suggested that when there is a mismatch between environmental incoming information and the information organizing capacity of the brain over time, it promotes disruption of the system. This mismatch can be either boredom (information underload) or over excitation (information overload) (de la Pena, 1983, p. 25). Information underload could be understood as the experience of a person going through the motions of living a life that is not congruent with his or her authentic self. Le Shan (1990) suggests that cancer is related to one not living according to one's true purpose, which can be exhibited as boredom. However, information overload could become problematic when stressors are too much and occur too often while simultaneously repressing the associated emotional turbulence to cope with it. Either mismatch is seen as potentially a cause for the development of cancer (Temoshok, 1985).

Just because it has been scientifically established that psychosocial factors contribute to cancer causation, it does not mean that other contributors do not exist. For example, chemical substances such as cigarette smoke and other environmental carcinogens are known contributors. Radiation agents such as x-rays and radioactive isotopes are known contributors. Viruses have been thought to be factors. Stomach cancer has been prevalent in Japan, colon cancer occurs more in English-speaking countries, and oral cancer is more prevalent in India. This is considered to be due largely to differing nutritional customs (de la Pena, 1983). Genetic predisposition has also been shown to be a contributing factor. However, recent research has shown that genetic expression is changeable through environmental factors such as the psychosocial environment.

SCIENTIFIC RESEARCH ON THE PSYCHOLOGY OF CANCER

It may sound like a stretch to conceive of cancer in psychological terms. While psychosocial factors related to cancer are scientifically validated, psychotherapy tailored to those factors known to be related to cancer is rarely addressed by most psychotherapists or doctors.

There are research findings about the mind's role in the progression and survival of cancer. These studies largely focus on people who have already been diagnosed with cancer and what factors either retarded the healing process or advanced it. One study found that people who exhibited more anger but without a loss of emotional control survived better than other cancer patients (Stavraky et al., 1968). Another study showed that people who had closer personal relationships survived longer (Weisman & Worden, 1977). Women who had breast cancer survived much longer when (1) they expressed their distress more often and (2) they required more adaptation to having cancer (Derogatis, Abeloff, & Melisaratos, 1979). Another study found similar results with melanoma patients (Rogentine et al., 1979). People who were nonexpressive of emotions were found to have a worse progression of cancer (Temoshok, 1985). In addition, less expressive patients had thicker tumors, tumors that progressed faster, and tumors that had fewer lymphocytes (protective immune cells) attacking the tumor (Temoshok, 1985). People having a passive response style to their diagnosis and appearing more well-adjusted had a worse cancer prognosis (Levy et al., 1991, 1987, 1985). This evidence strongly supports the importance of the expression of emotion in psychotherapy for cancer patients. It was also found that those people who survived cancer the longest expressed more joy (Levy et al., 1987). This evidence suggests that a procedure like the ETT® samadhi process, that facilitates extreme well-being, is valuable.

Other factors shown from scientific research include a patient's high need for sympathy while simultaneously having a reserved personality that made the person less likely to seek support. These people could be mistakenly seen as "strong" and "never complaining" about their condition, but the research has shown that they are in fact at a higher risk for not surviving (Stavraky et al., 1988). It would be in the cancer patient's best interest to redefine strength to mean a willingness to pursue, face, and express related unresolved emotions.

Another study found that people who had a variety of severe life-threatening events, previous to a cancer diagnosis, were five times greater to be at risk for death than other cancer patients (Ramirez et al., 1989). When life-threatening events are coupled with ineffective coping styles found in the Stavraky study, the evidence suggests that these people are at a higher risk for death by cancer.

One of the coping styles studied was coping by sharing with confidants. Specifically, the number of close confidants that a cancer patient had was evaluated. Among breast cancer patients the survival rate was fifty-six percent survival with no confidants, sixty-six percent with one confidant, and seventy-six percent with two confidants (Maunsell, Brisson, & Deschenes, 1995). This factor hypothetically validates that disclosing to a psychological counselor boosts survival rate by ten percent. If the counseling process enhances the client's ability to find and use other people as confidants, the survival rate is boosted ten percent for each new confidant the cancer patient has!

Whether the client was measured to be psychologically distressed or not was found to have no bearing on the length of disease-free survival or overall survival in one study (Tross et al., 1996). This finding indicates that repression of unresolved emotions may not be exhibited consciously, which provides the appearance of no distress because other studies that look for nonexpression of emotion find repression to be the reason for the patient to appear distress-free.

THE EXPERIENCE OF THE CANCER TREATMENT PROCESS

Many times the cancer treatment that people choose may have miserable, painful side-effects for which medicine has only minimal remedies. Most types of chemotherapy, radiation, and surgery have unpleasant side-effects. In these cases, ETT® can provide procedures to neutralize these symptoms if the client is physically able to make it to the office. Typically, the side-effects of a chemotherapy treatment can be neutralized in one or two ETT® sessions, making the healing journey far more comfortable. The intention of these types of sessions is simply to eliminate unpleasant symptoms, not to pursue any deep underlying factors. Essentially, as the client describes emotional distress, physical pain, or other symptoms, the therapist uses wavelengths of light and/or ETT® modalities to target and alleviate each symptom, one at a time. Even if ETT® is not used for anything else in the cancer patient's treatment, this offering can make the treatment bearable and maintain an improved emotional state.

As described in one of my previous books, ETT® possesses a unique capacity to eliminate physical pain (Vazquez, 2013, pp. 83–200). In one case, a cancer patient attending an ETT® session had forgotten to take his prescriptions for oxycodine and morphine. He was doubled over in severe pain during the session. I applied the use of the peripheral goggles. Within about ten minutes his severe pain had been reduced to zero. When I asked him if he had ever felt pain relief that quickly, he remarked that this method was faster and better than oxycodine or morphine! Of course, with this method there are no drug side-effects.

If the scientific research has so clearly identified psychosocial factors that contribute to cancer, why do most doctors seem unaware of these factors? Lawrence Le Shan may have conducted more exploration on the psychological attributes of cancer than anyone else. He looked back into the medical history of cancer diagnoses and was surprised to find that, in the 1800s in the United States, cancer was largely viewed as a psychologically generated condition. At that time family doctors often conducted home visits, and doctors got to know the patients personally and know the family as well, which made psychosocial factors known to the doctors. With the passage of time, x-rays, magnetic resonance imaging (MRI), positron emission tomography (PET) scan technology, and lab tests largely became the diagnostic tools for cancer. While these tools provide a greater understanding of the body, the interpersonal component between doctor and patient became largely systematically eliminated over time (Le Shan, 1990). Without this interpersonal contact and familiarity with the patient, a physician has little or no basis to identify the psychological factors in cancer. In some cases, psychological counseling has filled this interpersonal void. However, with the recent increase in the use of pharmaceuticals as the singular means to treat psychological issues, personal counseling has often been omitted. This leaves the medical team without any awareness of psychological factors in the diagnosis.

Many cancer patients report enormous stress build up when they are awaiting the results of a body scan or lab tests that may indicate if the cancer is progressing or declining. Patients describe a continuous worry for weeks on end until the next diagnostic meeting with the doctor. Many patients report not sleeping the night before a doctor's appointment. I suppose waiting periods cannot be helped; nonetheless, they create a torturous waiting with the client's life in the balance. These waiting periods can become traumatic experiences in and of themselves and produce stress hormones that contribute to the cancer. There are few greater ways to elevate fear, worry, and distress than to have a life-threating condition and then to have to wait to know if the news is good or bad. In one scientific study of patients undergoing allogeneic bone marrow transplant for acute leukemia, an attitude of "anxious preoccupation" was found to result in a shorter survival time and poorer quality of life after the procedure (Andrykowski, Brady, & Henslee-Downey, P. J., 1994). Therefore, it is of great therapeutic value to resolve worry, not just for comfort but for relieving the stress that might contribute to the cancer itself. In one instance—after a single Emotional Transformation Therapy® (ETT®) session—a woman's stress changed from anxiety and sleeplessness preceding the previous medical report to complete sleep and calmness as she anticipated the next scan report. Wavelengths of largely yellow light were used in conjunction with expressive catharsis to achieve this relief.

THE ROLE OF AUTHENTICITY IN HEALING

Does positive thinking affect the progression of cancer? One study found that pessimistic expectations of the future were a significant risk factor for mortality (Schulz et al., 1996). However, this finding, by itself, does not necessarily endorse positive thinking. A different study found that people with either low anxiety or high anxiety but with higher constraint of emotion predicted an earlier death (Weihs et al., 2000). In other words, if positive thinking was misused to suppress emotional expression, it placed cancer patients at a higher risk. This verifies that one cannot or should not fake being positive or force a hopeful attitude in order to improve survival chances. This scientific evidence suggests a case for authenticity, genuineness, knowing one's inner self, and then expressing emotions congruent with one's inner self. However, two studies found that cancer patients who minimized the impact of their cancer survived better (Butow, Coates, & Dunn, 1999; Butow et al., 2000). When these results are taken together, it would mean that while a patient must be authentic in emotional expression, a sense of authentic empowerment regarding the cancer demonstrates higher survival rates.

In many cases, cancer patients appear to be appropriately outgoing and expressive of emotions. In fact, these clients may appear to have a close network of family and friends. In these cases, the cancer patient may have withheld unpleasant emotions from family and friends and instead projected fears and anger onto society or institutions like politics, religion, or even medicine. While these institutions can possess some corruption, the generalization of total corruption is an assumption without factual support. When these clients are engaged about these topics, enormous fear and rage may surface. While these patients are not often aware that their withheld emotions regarding family and friends have been redirected to a more distant target, making them less likely to be resolved, they can view their emotions as justifiably intense. In many cases, the intensity of their reactions suggests that these institutions or public figures are triggering a primal concern that already exists, such as a lack of safety in the world and a consequential desire to escape living in such a threatening world. Of course, if this fear and anger can be accessed and resolved, growth from the experience can usher in a new life perspective.

Not only do people repress automatically, but they often build an entire philosophical position around avoidance of unpleasant emotions. They may use quasi logic to ask themselves why anyone would want to recall and feel the negative experiences of the past. The phrase, "I have put an unpleasant event behind me," often really means, "I have repressed it." Some people may say, "There is nothing I can do about it now, so I don't want to think about it." While past events are, in fact, over, the emotions from these events often continue to be present but repressed and may contribute to physical conditions such as cancer. The fortunate fact is that these emotional remnants are available for change through psychotherapy. One of my clients with stage IV cancer had Bible verses memorized that he used to immediately counter every "negative" emotion that arose. This is very different from using religious scriptures for inspiration and support. An assessment for possible repression of emotion through dissociation revealed that he was dissociating by means of using Bible verses. This means his thoughts and emotions were directed away from his emotional distress, leaving his unresolved distress intact and contributing to physical symptoms. He developed this response to a very high level until this form of suppression became automatic, a very skillful repression. Since repression contributes to cancer, this strategy could be seen as the misuse of religion.

If most of a person's relevant emotions are not conscious, neither is one's authentic self. It is the strength and purpose of the ETT® samadhi process to penetrate psychological defenses and to reveal the authentic self, as described in previous chapters. ETT® is used to access unresolved emotions and bring them into conscious awareness and then resolve them. Therefore, ETT® possesses the exact process necessary for facilitating the types of psychological change that can have the best impact on cancer.

The cancer patient's network of relationships can aid the healing process, or interfere with it, or both. As cited earlier, dysfunctional interpersonal patterns in relationships may be a contributing cause of the cancer or a factor that exacerbates the condition (Quinn & Herndon, 1986, pp. 45–48). During the treatment process the journey toward healing may entail financial strain, logistical support strain, and emotional strain. Consequently, other people attempt to be supportive of the cancer patient. However, many cancer patients either do not know what type of interpersonal support they want, or they are ill at ease communicating what type of support they do not want. People who have been very private most of their lives may not be prepared to handle a barrage of well-wishers, especially when the patient is fatigued from either the cancer or the treatment. People related to the cancer patient usually have positive intentions, but they often have no idea what type of support the cancer patient actually wants. Therefore, it is important to help the client identify what would be helpful from other people, from the client's perspective, and encourage the client to communicate these needs to others to insure proper interpersonal support.

One particular way that cancer patients repress emotions is through a role reversal attachment pattern in which excessive empathy and focus on other people sacrifices self-awareness and self-care. This is particularly documented in the profiles of breast cancer and melanoma patients. While people who focus on pleasing others are often well-liked and continually get reinforced for their selfless behavior, this omission of self-awareness can be a means for repression and ignorance of one's own emotions. One breast cancer patient put it this way: "Basically, I am everybody else's tit." These people tend to be drawn to the helping professions like nursing, psychology, special education, and others. Almost all cancer patients I have seen are primarily worried about the loved ones that would be left behind if the cancer patient died, not themselves. This characteristic misplacement of focus must shift to one of self-healing in psychotherapy so that the psychological factors then enhance survival. This change is often seen by the client as selfish, but it is intended to be self-awareness and self-love instead. The issue can be viewed as an interpersonal boundary issue. When clients take other people's emotions into their own personal space, they crowd out their own emotions and self-perception. For example, many cancer patients describe a scenario in which relatives come into town and stay at the cancer patient's house to "be supportive." However, when extra people are in the house, it may often make the cancer patient more stressed, especially if the cancer patient is too polite to speak out against this perceived intrusion because he or she would feel guilty. This sacrifice often leaves the cancer worse. This psychological issue provides an interesting parallel to what is taking place on the biological cellular level during cancer growth.

Normal cells are able to recognize one another when, in formation of tissue, they come together, transmit information, and cease to divide. One cell recognizes its neighbor's "personal space." The cancer cell, in contrast, is anarchistic. It divides regardless of neighboring cells and penetrates other tissue to establish colonies.

A crucial feature of a tumor is that it grows progressively in size (Berenblum, 1974). It never reaches growth equilibrium.... Even more striking is the erratic spatial relationship of the cells to one another (Berenblum, 1974). The more malignant a tumor, the greater the degree of tissue disorganization (de la Pena, 1983, p. 7).

This description of cancer cells bears too strong a resemblance to the interpersonal dynamics of cancer patients in which perceived intrusion into one's personal space presents a parallel too striking to be accidental. People in different fields of study rarely risk crossing over to another field in the understanding of a phenomenon. However, the integration of information between biology and psychology is necessary due to the research that links psychosocial factors with cancer. Based on this linkage it may be possible to facilitate change in the interpersonal dynamics of cancer patients that might become reflected in the parallel activity of the cancer cells' interaction with other normal cells. Repression could be responsible for psychological inner chaos that manifests physically as chaotic expression of cell growth because distress was not allowed an outward emotional expression. Then this psychological chaos is reflected in the cellular activity at the site in the body that symbolically represents a relevant issue for which appropriate psychological growth has been inhibited.

POTENTIAL FOR PSYCHOSPIRITUAL GROWTH FROM CANCER

The disruption of cancer in one's life is a substantial change which can result in a new reaction. The new reaction can form strength to overcome the disruption, which parallels some concepts from chaos theory (Prigogene & Strengers, 1984). Illya Prigogene, Nobel Prize winner for chaos theory, has shown "how living organisms utilize energy available in their environments to reorganize themselves to increasingly higher orders of complexity" (Combs, 2002). The principle of disrupting a system of any type—geological, cellular, or psychological—and then reorganizing it into a higher order system is known to be a universal phenomenon. In religious or spiritual terms, it could be seen as a death-rebirth cycle. Frederich Flach has made explicit a process similar to chaos theory that he calls "The Law of Disruption and Reintegration."

Flach's theory provides an avenue for improvement. When disruptive events occur, a person must accommodate the events—emotional upheaval, interrupted work, and home disorganization—and descend into chaos. However, through expression and working through the distress, a reorganization of the psyche can potentially construct a more resilient being. Biological evidence for the idea of rebirth lies in the presence of a hormone that only emerges with pregnant women and cancer patients. It is the human chorionic gonadotropin hormone. If this death-rebirth cycle occurs well, a person becomes more able to process future disruptions. However, Flach also describes what he calls "Illness Option A: The Failure to Disrupt" (Flach, 1988, p. 39).

When stress impacts a person—instead of enduring the emotional turbulence leading to change—the person fails to adapt, which leads to disordered behavior, or stagnation, and the increased vulnerability to stress. For example, in the event a loved one dies and people near to the beloved do not grieve or adjust their life to this change, attempting to assert control, they risk psychosocial and spiritual disorders and vulnerability to physical illness.

In the case of a cancer patient, an attempt to stay in control during times of distress may block potential transitional periods of distress. This blocking may occur by means of intellectualization, denial, rationalization, or other means of repressing emotions. When this means of coping occurs often enough and/or long enough, unresolved emotional neural circuits in the brain may re-route into somatic neural circuits until the patient's physiology bears the symptom.

A second illness option concerns "The Failure to Reintegrate Successfully" (Flach, 1988, p. 40). According to Flach, this occurs when a person descends into chaos but becomes fixated at the point of the worst chaos, which results in chronic destabilization and a dysfunctional system. People who fit this category would be those who have chronic illnesses, not necessarily cancer, unless they get cancer over and over.

At the center of this cancer profile is the repression of emotion, meaning that emotions are buried and out of conscious awareness. The result is that people who enter my office with cancer often exhibit no significant emotional distress. Most cancer patients only come to me for therapy because an unusual doctor told them that the physical, psychological, and spiritual factors must be addressed. Since these clients tend to report few if any psychological or spiritual symptoms, outside of the disturbance of being diagnosed with cancer, these clients are usually unlike all of my other clients. Therefore, these clients require education about psychosocial factors related to cancer as well as therapeutic strategies that can penetrate psychological defenses like repression. Since most of the cancer patients I receive are already at the last stage of cancer progression, these people also require a form of psychotherapy that can work rapidly. These factors make ETT® the ideal form of psychotherapy for cancer patients. An objective is to uncover and process repressed material quickly enough to impact psychological changes that will facilitate changes of the physical attributes of cancer.

INITIAL SESSION WITH A CANCER PATIENT

Several important objectives must be accomplished during the initial session with cancer patients. Standard intake information—personal history of family, relationships, medical history, drug or alcohol use, religious orientation, and so on—should be acquired as it is with any new client. Of course, empathy and understanding should occur as part of the interpersonal bonding. Then questions specific to cancer are asked. For example, an exploration of limiting beliefs about the cancer should be asked, such as the following:

- Does the client believe cancer is genetically based and assumed to be unchangeable?
- Does the client view cancer as strictly a medical condition that has no connection to psychological factors?

- Is the diagnosis of cancer viewed as a death sentence?
- Is the cancer thought to be a consequence of the client's bad deeds or mistakes or bad luck?
- Does the client possess a belief about the reason for the cause of this cancer?
- Does the client believe that his or her current treatment will heal the cancer?
- Does the client view the cancer cells as negative intrusions that must be fought?
- Is the client aware of the research regarding the link between nutrition and cancer?

These questions will provide information about a person's overall perspective concerning cancer. Some people will have definite beliefs about cancer while others may say, "I don't know," in response to all of these questions. Answers to these questions will help to isolate any limiting beliefs about healing cancer as well as highlight areas where the person needs appropriate education about the known facts about cancer. The answers to these questions provide a context for understanding the beliefs that may have contributed to emotions or nonemotional reactions to cancer. Of course, if the client has limiting beliefs, the ideas are explored toward the goal of reducing limiting beliefs. If there is a lack of knowledge about cancer and treatment, education is provided.

Another focus of the session should be concerned with the person's reaction to having cancer and going through treatment. Some patients may be in shock and may feel few emotions, a situation requiring ETT® procedures such as the spectral resonance technique to activate awareness and alleviate emotions. Others may feel overwhelmed, afraid, and verbally expressive, which would require a different approach such as peripheral goggles. Still others may possess some form of repression but have little awareness of emotion at all, which might require a different ETT® retrieval strategy. The patient's reaction to his or her current condition would dictate which therapeutic approach to pursue first.

It is very important to find out the stage of cancer development. There are usually four stages, one through four, with four being the last stage before death. However, there are different rates of progression of cancer, often referred to as grades. This information dictates the immediacy of a need for treatment. For example, stage IV with an aggressive rate requires immediate sessions multiple times per week, whereas stage I or II with a less aggressive cancer may require only weekly sessions. This frequency of sessions helps to provide a therapeutic impact before the body is overcome by the cancer progression. Since I receive most cancer patients after they have attempted conventional medical approaches and are attempting alternative approaches, they are usually already at stage IV when they enter therapy. Then the challenge is to get these patients psychologically better fast enough to overcome and contribute to reversing the rate of cancer progression. This requires immediate frequent sessions of ETT®.

PSYCHOTHERAPEUTIC TREATMENT FOR CANCER PATIENTS

If the diagnosis of cancer was a surprise to the patient, it could be that the shock and subsequent trauma are likely to produce continuous stress hormones. If this is the case, these stress hormones tend to contribute to the progression of cancer. Therefore, it is important to relieve the shock defense so that emotions will not be blocked from awareness. However, many cancer patients view the upheaval of emotions, subsequent to the removal of shock, as getting worse psychologically. Therefore, educating the client is important. Removing the shock symptoms of numbness may lead to more emotional expression which can be seen as psychological progress. These emotions must be processed quickly and effectively in order to benefit from the upheaval. Wavelengths of far red visual light stimulation are particularly valuable for helping to remove the symptoms of shock. Then a variety of other wavelengths of light are used to process other emotions that emerge.

Cancer patients are often surprised by their initial diagnosis. In many cases, there is an entire medical history of surprise diagnoses. This strongly suggests a deficiency of mind–body awareness as well as evidence for the tendency to repress emotions. In one case, a man believed all of conventional medicine was corrupt, so he avoided doctors as much as possible and was convinced that he knew his body well even after several medical "surprises." His fear led to a stereotype of all conventional medicine, which in reality supported his avoidance defense. By the time the cancer was diagnosed, it had progressed so far that there was not enough time to treat it effectively. Therefore, it is important to pursue overcoming avoidance tendencies and heighten the client's awareness of the mind–body relationship throughout treatment.

This lack of mind–body awareness is often complicated by having been diagnosed with cancer. Since cancer patients may have missed the bodily signals that something was wrong, many patients begin to associate any physical symptoms with the fear that these symptoms may indicate worsening of their cancer. This results in frequent fearful thoughts each time a body symptom arises, which is not the type of mind–body awareness needed to improve recovery. Therefore, it is important to focus treatment on alleviating the trauma of the diagnosis and the hypervigilant response to bodily symptoms.

Since it is not uncommon for clients to see cellular structures in the light during these sessions, one way to facilitate improved mind–body awareness is to encourage dialogue to and from the cancer during visual brain stimulation. The objective is to enhance awareness of the relationship between the mind and body and ultimately to develop the skill of altering bodily symptoms through mental processes. The ability to do this opens up the possibility of actually changing cancer activity.

While this process of talking to the cancer may initially be viewed as strange, ridiculous, or even absurd to many clients, once they are encouraged to try it, significant impact can occur. One technique involves writing a letter both to and from the cancer. In one instance, I gave this homework to a cancer patient who responded in protest that she was not creative, did not know what to say, and believed that she could not do it. I explained that this process appears to link neural networks in the brain that connect mental process to bodily ones. I told her to try it and just see what happens because it could work. The following are her two letters:

Dear Disease,

I've chosen to address you as "disease" rather than cancer because I think you are much more than tumors growing inside my liver, and more than a crazy cell lurking somewhere in my body waiting to catch me by surprise. I think you are something that has been growing inside me for years.

For now you may truly be the life-threatening tumors in my liver, but you represent so much more. You're the force that is taking away all the magic inside of me that I never used.

You're eating up that part of me that wanted to dance like all the other girls, but wouldn't because someone might laugh. You've just about destroyed the part of me that wants to throw my popcorn box on the floor at the movies but wouldn't because someone else might fall. And I can't even remember the last time I felt passionately enough about anything to argue about it, except maybe my son. Maybe I should have fought more for him than with him.

I've let you take away almost all my rainbows, and the unicorns have been gone a long time.

If I don't find some magic somewhere, you're going to win this horrible game. I never liked games. I never learned to have fun and now there may not be time to learn how.

I hate what I've let you do to me.

Your host

Dear Host,

It's a shame that it took you this long to realize that you had value. It was easy to take away your magic. After all believing in magic means taking some risks, and you've never really been very good at that.

You're right. I didn't just happen. I've given you warnings over the years, but you always had to finish just one more little task.

Your epitaph should read, "She always met her deadlines." I'm not sure it's not too late for you to change but I'd like to see you try.

Dominantly yours,
Reality

These letters to and from her cancer revealed this patient's inner struggle and many of the characteristics seen so often in cancer patients. It reveals the interplay between psychological features and physical activity. People often feel a change in their physiology during or after the letter writing. This letter writing or verbal dialogue may need to be executed several times for some people to enhance mind–body awareness.

WHY DOES CANCER OCCUR AT SPECIFIC BODY LOCATIONS?

It has been my experience that the specific body site where the cancer initially manifests is not a random location. Therefore, it is valuable to explore the meaning of that body site to each client. Humans are inherently symbolically oriented beings. The body site of the cancer is likely to possess a particular meaning for each person. While Louise Hay and others have lists of body sites and their associated psychological meaning, I prefer to help each client identify these meanings individually, instead of assuming these body sites mean the same for everyone. Through the use of visual brain stimulation via the spectral chart or the light device, a search for meaning is conducted. This involves asking the client questions such as the following:

- What does (body part) mean to you?
- Why do you think your cancer occurred at (body part)?
- What do you think the (body part) represents?
- If we can assume your cancer is sending a message, why do you think it selected (body part)?

When a client answers these questions, I recommend trusting whatever responses emerge and validating the client's ideas. Pursue these responses to elicit further detail. Then this leads to issues that can be pursued to resolution.

LORI'S CASE

Lori was a sixty-year-old married woman who presented with stage IV uterine cancer and was undergoing ITP chemotherapy as well at ETT®. After working on the distress that cancer had caused in her life, she sought further change. While Lori was viewing wavelengths of indigo, I asked what her uterus represented to her. Lori said motherhood. Then I asked how her motherhood was going. Lori suddenly burst into tears. She explained that she was a devout Catholic and all three of her adult children had left the Catholic Church and now believed in past lives. Then Lori said that she felt like a complete failure as a mother and just wanted to die. We proceeded to process this distress until it was alleviated within two sessions. Eventually, her cancer receded until it was gone.

The Christian church originally included reincarnation as part of its theology, but in the third century AD leaders of the Catholic Church decided to eliminate reincarnation from the doctrine. In addition, any member of the Catholic Church who believed in reincarnation was henceforth to be excommunicated from the church. This rule continues to be a part of Catholic doctrine today.

This case represents how the disruption of a core issue by means of other people's experiences affected Lori to the extent that a death wish emerged. She went into internal psychological chaos, and she repressed emotions. Theoretically, this resulted in the development of cancer cells possessing chaotic growth at the bodily site that represented motherhood to Lori. When Lori grew psychologically from the disturbance, her body gradually responded by developing normal cells. Her cancer activity diminished.

Some of the most common and potentially destructive emotional experiences of cancer patients are the emotions of helplessness, hopelessness, or powerlessness. These emotions produce stress hormones that contribute to the progression of cancer. Therefore, these emotions should be engaged and brought to transformation. However, people who repress emotions may believe they are already hopeful, but this hope may often be a superficial veneer. The real helplessness may be totally outside of conscious awareness. Helplessness may be projected onto the medical community, political figures, religion, or corporations, or whoever may serve as a scapegoat. Transformation of these emotions involves primarily the use of wavelengths of yellow light.

SELECTING A FORM OF CANCER TREATMENT

Typically, most cancer patients lack an awareness of the psychosocial and spiritual factors related to cancer. This occurs because very few physicians either are aware of the research or do not inform the cancer patient about areas outside of their specialty, other than to make some kind of vague reference to the idea that illness is "stress-related." However, the specific type of stress or emotion related to cancer is usually unknown, so this does not inform cancer patients enough to allow them to target and resolve the psychological, social, and spiritual aspects of cancer. One type of education that I provide is the Type C Questionnaire, which pinpoints psychological characteristics known to be related to cancer by scientific research (Temoshok & Dreher, 1993). As soon as client characteristics known to be associated with cancer are identified, treatment targeted to those features directs the treatment plan unless current distress warrants immediate pursuit. If there is significant repression and/or lack of emotional awareness, treatment begins with the spectral resonance technique.

The cancer industry is an enormous financial endeavor. Whenever there is a desperate need for resolution and people are willing to pay large amounts of money for treatment, there will be all types of treatments available. Cancer treatment can be a controversial issue to the point that people have been legally prosecuted for methods that are not accepted by conventional medicine. One major study reviewed all of the research studies on alternative spiritual interventions and their outcomes with cancer patients. While nondrug spiritual and religious interventions all produced small to moderate effects compared to the control group, only the therapeutic use of psychedelic drugs produced large effect sizes (Kaplar, Wachholtz, & O'Brien, 2004). Since the ETT® samadhi process has been shown to produce this same effect, it might offer a natural alternative for spiritual enhancement for cancer patients. The peculiar thing about cancer is that I have personally known people who have acquired long-term relief of cancer through a wide variety of methods. These range from surgery, chemotherapy and radiation, to absolutely no treatment, nutritional treatment, prayer, and raw food diets. These results would cause one to wonder how could so many different types of treatment work for the same condition. First of all, while the term cancer is used, in fact, there are many different kinds of cancer, and they vary in ways that might make one form of treatment work for one person and another one for the next person. Given the array of treatments available, how does a patient select the optimal treatment?

Frequently, I encounter cancer patients whose doctors have recommended one form of treatment, but then a spouse was sure another method was necessary, but a friend urgently recommended a different treatment and warned against the doctor's recommendation. Some cancer patients report that their oncologists reprimanded them for trying a form of treatment outside of their recommendations and told clients that they would die quickly if they did not do what the doctor said. Many of the cancer patients I see have already tried conventional medical approaches that have failed and are looking for another option. Sometimes their type of cancer is inoperable or not appropriate for chemotherapy or radiation, and they are forced to look outside of conventional medical options. Often the cancer patient is shocked and confused about the cancer in the first place and is only more confused when several different people advocate the pursuit of different forms of treatment. In the context of this pressure and confusion, I recommend that counselors do not further the confusion by expressing a preferred treatment. Instead, it is the counselor's job to help these clients listen to their own inner inclinations and find the treatment they believe in. Often cancer patients are so unaware of their own inner selves that they cannot base a preference on that information. This requires processes like the ETT® samadhi process to access an authentic sense of self below the patient's psychological defenses. Once this inner self is accessed, decisions can be made that allow a person's belief in a choice of treatment to become congruent and powerful.

The placebo effect regards a person's expectation and belief about the effect of a strategy that will heal physical pain and illness. It is very powerful and has been scientifically documented to heal a vast array of illnesses. It verifies that the human body possesses the inherent capacity to heal itself. However, these beliefs must be authentic. In fact, the placebo effect is so strong that every drug must surpass the placebo effect in two scientific studies in order to be approved by the FDA. However, most pharmaceuticals do not actually show superiority over the placebo effect until many trials have occurred. The conclusion to be drawn in this case and in many others is that the placebo effect is a more potent healing agent than many pharmaceuticals. Given the strength of the placebo effect, I recommend therapeutically attempting to activate it by using strategies to (1) access the patient's inner self, (2) identify the patient's most compelling beliefs about healing, and (3) strengthen those beliefs. Therefore, after educating a patient regarding the options, whatever a person chooses to use as a treatment approach should be supported. It is often the placebo effect that can account for the success of a wide variety of methods being used to treat cancer.

DEATH ISSUES AND CANCER PATIENTS

When people have cancer, it often occurs that while the possibility of death is on people's minds, few people talk about it with the cancer patient. In an effort to be positive, the issue of death and dying is often avoided. In this situation, the cancer patient, family, and friends all engage in a superficial dialogue to avoid talking about what is actually on their minds. This façade is damaging to cancer patients who are already too willing to avoid unpleasant emotions. I recommend that therapists ask cancer patients about their understanding of death and their fears regarding death and dying. For some people, discussions about what happens after death are important. These "discussions" provide an opportunity for the clients to express themselves while the therapist provides empathy, validation, and understanding. If emotions emerge, ETT® modalities can assist processing these emotions. Fears related to death tend to provoke both the fight-or-flight response and stress hormones, which tend to make cancer worse, especially if the fear is continuously present but unexpressed. The fear of death is inherent in the human experience because it is a survival mechanism. Paradoxically, facing the fear of death increases a person's chance of survival. For example, when death fears are processed to resolution, the reduction of stress hormones usually aids the healing process. Those who have experienced this resolution report feeling as if an enormous weight has been lifted off their shoulders.

After psychotherapy has occurred for a few sessions, underlying issues can emerge that were totally unknown to the client initially. Often, clients become aware of a death wish. This can occur as a result of some intolerable event from which a person wishes to escape so badly that death appears to be a way out. For example, faced with the death of a loved one, some people lose their will to live and cannot work through their grief. In other cases, a feeling of intense shame for past mistakes produces a belief that they do not deserve to live. In one case, a simple incident of jealousy preceded a diagnosis of cancer. Even though these types of intense emotion and consequential beliefs appear fixed by clients, a process like ETT® can usually facilitate change of these emotions within a brief series of sessions. Eliminating this death motive is vital. Even if medical interventions succeed, the possibility of either relapse or an unpleasant life might continue to be intact. When psychotherapy sessions involve these issues, it is not only valuable to eliminate death wishes but also to seek clarity about reasons for continuing to live. When these therapeutic endeavors are successful, the individual often exhibits a substantial transformation.

APPROACHES TO CANCER TREATMENT

If the client views cancer as an enemy to fight against, the fight-or-flight response is likely to produce stress hormones that can worsen the cancer. Cancer is not, in fact, an evil source entering the body from the outside in the way that bacteria might infect the body. Instead, cancer is the result of the patient's own cells growing chaotically. Therefore, to view cancer as an evil source is to operate against oneself and produce further internal division. An alternative way to view cancer is to see it as a messenger. Then the task is to understand the messenger and ultimately heed its message. For example, breast cancer patients may have lost themselves in a quest to please others. Prostate cancer patients may have lost their sense of power or possess unresolved guilt about sexual issues. The basic message might be to recognize, face, and work through these issues to grow into a higher level of integrity and self-worth. The life-threatening nature of cancer can force people to attend to themselves in new ways.

Scientific research has shown that expressive group therapy and self-hypnosis for pain doubled the survival rate of breast cancer patients! This was not just a support group but a leader-led group in which emotional expression was the weekly focus for one year. The study was particularly valid because it involved a large number of participants as well as a control group and was followed up for ten years (Spiegel et al., 1989). This study represents strong evidence that interpersonal psychological interventions alone can improve the survival rate of cancer patients.

Meditation and prayer have been widely believed to account for the alleviation of an array of medical conditions. However, there are mixed scientific findings about the effectiveness of intercessory prayer, so most scientists would not completely affirm its success (Hodge, 2007, pp. 174–187). One scientific study with 3,851 participants examined the use of private religious activity such as prayer and its effect on prolonging survival. While a small positive effect was found, a greater change was evident for those people who had been previously using prayer than for those who began to use it when their health began to decline (Helm et al., 2000). However, the widespread popular belief that prayer heals physical bodies is in itself an important factor because it may, in part, be the result of the placebo effect. Even if prayer can change medical conditions, if it does not address the known causative factors, recovery by this means alone risks relapse. The following is a case I know about personally.

MARK'S CASE

A Protestant minister had an adolescent son, Mark, who was diagnosed with cancer. This minister believed in the healing power of prayer and acquired the help of his entire congregation to pray for his son. Mark's cancer remitted within a relatively short period of time, and the recovery lasted for a few months. Then the cancer returned again. The congregation again prayed for his healing and the lab tests and scans again showed a complete recovery from cancer. Then a few months later the cancer returned, and the congregation prayed again. This time the young man did not recover.

In this case, prayer was apparently a factor that had impact. However, hypothetically, since the minister did not know about contributing psychosocial factors, the young man was at risk for a relapse. Based on the cancer research, if the core emotional memory was repressed and not addressed, the boy was at risk. Intercessory prayer has merit as a healing tool, but it might not be enough to complete the job in some cases. This type of occurrence could cause the general public to view prayer as a healing agent while simultaneously allowing scientists to point out the mixed reviews of prayer as a marginal means to heal.

I have had the good fortune to develop psychospiritual nontouch healing skills (further description of this ability occurs in Chapter 9). In a couple of cases, I had the opportunity to use this skill on people who had cancerous tumors that they could feel with their hands because they were near the surface of the skin. Within twenty minutes this psychospiritual healing approach was able to eliminate the cancer tumors to the extent that they could no longer be seen or felt. While this was a remarkable occurrence, unfortunately these tumors later returned. This bears a similarity to the prayer experience aforementioned. In my view, these kinds of physiological changes risk not being sustained because the underlying contributing factors have not been completely resolved.

Meditation practices are well documented to have a wide range of benefits for physical health. Hypothetically, meditation should be very helpful for cancer patients because of its propensity to penetrate psychological defenses such as repression and to provide access to one's inner self. However, most forms of meditation only yield this benefit after many weeks, months, or years of consistent daily use. Therefore, a procedure like the ETT® samadhi process that yields the same benefits as meditation—but accomplishes them in a very short time—has provided an optimal intervention for patients experiencing advanced stage cancer.

It is considered unethical to make claims of cancer cures without scientific research to support these claims. However, anecdotal reports of cancer cures are valuable because they provide leads for new scientific studies—studies which could either rule out the effectiveness of a method or validate it. It is postulated that many people who overcome cancer never go back to their doctors, which leaves the successful cases undocumented. However, Paul C. Roud investigated eleven cases of people with severe medical conditions, all of which were expected to rapidly progress to a certain death, but did not. He documented the medical reports, the personal stories, and the fact that all of these people totally recovered and did not relapse (Roud, 1990). Most of these people had some form of cancer. An examination of these stories reveals that in most cases these exceptional changes cannot be attributed to medical interventions alone. In each case, some type of significant inner psychological shift occurred that appeared to make these cases end differently.

In most cases, when ETT® was applied to cancer patients, those patients were undergoing some other form of medical or alternative intervention. It would be unethical to ask these patients not to participate in whatever other medical treatment had been chosen. Therefore, while I have observed many people undergo dramatic healing, it cannot be attributed to only one factor, although these patients often believe ETT® was the key factor. As a result, I have had only two opportunities to work with cancer patients in which ETT® was the only intervention that was used. In both cases, their cancer went into complete remission and has not returned after six years in one case and ten years in another case.

JACK'S CASE

In one ETT® case, a sixty-five-year-old male physician sought help for his advanced prostate cancer and chose to use no other treatment modality. He was aware of the effectiveness of ETT® and had known me personally years before. Since this case was over ten years ago, I do not recall every detail. However, I recall his issues partly involved a sexual affair that took place outside of his marriage. This affair had remained a secret from his wife for several years, but his guilt from it continued to be prominent. He processed this issue to completion within four sessions. Subsequently, his prostate cancer gradually ended, and it has not returned in over ten years now.

PAULA'S CASE

Paula, a bright fifty-five-year-old woman, was diagnosed with rectal cancer. She had tried a number of cancer treatments. She even had rectal cancer surgery, but the doctors were unable to eliminate all of the cancer. Her cancer grew back after this. We had spent several sessions helping her to make treatment selections because she was confused about all the options and lacked self-confidence. She had also worked on certain traumas that preoccupied her. Identifying and expressing her emotions was difficult. After much progress had been made on these issues, the physical experience of her cancer was pursued.

Multidimensional eye movement was the modality used. Paula described the kinesthetic awareness of pressure at the site of her cancer. After about fifteen minutes of using far red at a four o'clock angle, Paula described a lessening of the pressure. In a subsequent session, the same procedure was replicated. This time the physical sensation at the site of the cancer was completely eliminated. Since Paula could not feel her cancer for the first time, she wondered if it was actually gone.

Paula made an appointment with a new colorectal doctor whom she saw within a few weeks of that session. Paula had not used any other interventions but ETT® during that time. He reported that if he had not seen her medical records, he would have had no idea that she ever had rectal cancer before because there were no signs of it. This healing has lasted six years as of this writing.

These two cases represent a new possibility for the healing of cancer. Although the psychosocial issues targeted by their treatment are based on substantial scientific research and are not new, the strategy used in treatment offers an exciting new possibility (Dreher, 2003; Vazquez, 2013). Of course, at the time of this writing there is not yet scientific research to substantiate the use of ETT® as the sole means to treat cancer. It is not yet known if these anecdotal findings could be replicated in a large sample of cancer patients. However, it is time to conduct such research in search of a better way to heal cancer.

One of the therapists who attended my training in 2014 about the psychosocial and spiritual aspects of cancer patients reported a dream related to the information received in that session. What follows is first a record of her dream and then a day later her reflections on the dream and on cancer.

REBIRTH DREAM

> I had a dream that I walked into a hospital and was going to see my daughter. I wasn't aware of why she was at the hospital. It was like a delivery room. I wasn't worried or aware of sickness. I got to her room and she wasn't in her bed, it was made, and she was gone. My first thought was "someone took her" and I was terrified, and then I thought "she ran away," and I was sad and afraid I'd never see her again. I kept searching the hospital, desperately searching (but full of doubt about finding her). I turned the corner and I found her sitting on the floor playing alone and content. I was relieved.

It was at that time, I was awakened (actually awake, not dreaming about being awake) by my daughter who snuck into my bed to snuggle between her Daddy and me, which she does frequently in the early morning hours.

I was lying there feeling the warmth of her little body and listening to her breathing, feeling her little toes against the back of my leg. She rubs them together exactly like her daddy does to soothe herself back to sleep. I was remembering the conversation that we had when I tucked her in last night about how much I loved her. We argued about who loved who the most. I told her that I loved her more because she lived inside my body. She asked me about what I ate when I was pregnant with her. She said, "I was hungry, and saying Mommy hurry up and feed me and I was kicking you in the ribs to get your attention." She had been told these stories, but this time when she was telling me about it, it was really like she remembered. She asked me about what I liked to drink and I confessed that I really loved the taste of Coke and Dr. Pepper and that I would have it sometimes even though I wasn't supposed to. She said that she loved it and that's why she gets crazy when she drinks Dr. Pepper today.

I fell back asleep thinking about this special moment with her, and when I woke up I had this new awareness that was so clear and strange. I was aware that the dream was about being pregnant with my own soul, that my soul requires the same love and care as the child growing in my stomach. That everything we put into our bodies and our minds profoundly affects our soul in the same way the pregnant mother feeds her baby through the umbilical cord and everything she feels, hears, tastes, and touches is communicated to the baby directly. I realized that in the dream my daughter leaving the bed and finding a place to play alone to take care of herself represents what I did as a little girl to survive my family environment. And then it all came to me that our parents are responsible for teaching us about caring for our souls when we are infants. They either pour engaged affection into us, nourishing us and "seeing" us, reflecting back love and affection in their eyes, or they do something else that ranges from inconsistent love and affection to neglect and rejection. We adapt to cope with whatever circumstance we are born into, but our soul has an innate desire to thrive. These "defense/coping mechanisms" or attachment styles might be our soul's way to attempt to thrive in an environment not conducive to life. So the little girl in my dream went away to play alone, to find peace. I was terrified that I wasn't going to find her, but I did, on so many levels that make sense. When we don't feed our soul, pay attention to it, "see it," it's like we are starving the growing child inside us, only this child finds creative ways to get our attention and to take care of itself. Sometimes it will kick us in the ribs, and sometimes it gives us cancer, but it will keep trying to get our attention.

THE NEXT DAY SHE CONTINUED

I am back to explain the rest of the awareness about the dream. I was also aware that since we are pregnant with our soul, that when we die, we are giving birth to our soul. I have never thought about it that way or heard it explained in those terms. I've heard that "it's a new beginning," but when I woke up from this dream it was like I was given this vision and it was like everything made sense. It was crystal clear. If the soul has this drive to live and thrive and be known and seen, if we don't feed it, nurture it, and "disclose" it by actively expressing our authentic self, it will first attempt to get our attention. Pain and sickness are effective, given that we are so good at ignoring gentler forms of communication from our soul, like the voice that whispers in your ear telling you, "No, don't do that, it's not good for you!" or "Go for it, make that change" or "Tell that person what you really think!" And finally, if that doesn't work, if you don't cooperate and allow the soul to be expressed and to live here on earth within you, it will find a way to be born "prematurely." Unfortunately, that means that we die (or at least the host body for the soul dies), but the soul gets to finally live.

CHAPTER 7 SUMMARY

This chapter identified how the life-threating nature of cancer tends to provoke spiritual, religious, and existential issues. Then the question of whether the mind can cause cancer was addressed through a substantial number of scientific research findings. These findings confirmed psychosocial factors as major contributors to cancer. Next, summaries of research about the mind's role in the progression of cancer as well as psychological factors in survival rates of cancer were described. Among the most frequent factors involved were various forms of coping that involved repression and suppression of unwanted emotions.

The psychological and social issues related to the experience of the conventional cancer treatment process were identified. Issues of physical pain and its psychological component were explained. The psychological trauma of waiting to find out medical test results and the treatment for this resulting stress were explored. The psychological issues involved in healing from cancer were closely examined, including the following: discovering one's authentic self, learning to identify and express one's emotions constructively, and learning how to participate in constructive relationships.

The potential for participating in the challenge of healing from cancer in such a way that recovery can lead to a transformation or rebirth was described. Recommendations for how to optimally conduct an initial session with a cancer patient were covered in some detail. Treatment planning issues, questions to ask, and issues typical of cancer patients were reviewed. Helping cancer patients to develop better mind–body awareness is an important objective described through theory and case studies.

The question of why cancer occurs in specific body locations was explored and illustrated in a case study. Then the issues related to selecting a form of cancer treatment were carefully reviewed. The issue of facing the possibility of death is a very important challenge to undergo for most cancer patients. Therapeutic approaches for dealing with potential death were covered. The role of spiritual approaches to healing cancer was explained through theoretical concepts and case studies.

Two case studies that used no other form of treatment but ETT® were provided. While it is acknowledged that scientific research supporting this approach does not exist yet, nor is ETT® purported to be a cure, these case studies, however, yielded resolution of the cancer. They provide a basis for the possibility that cancer can be brought to remission by resolving psychospiritual factors alone through the use of ETT®.

Chapter Eight

Resolving Spiritual Differences in Couple Relationships

Profound, spiritually transformative experiences can now be facilitated and old issues resolved; unfortunately, new issues tend to emerge. One area of great concern is the impact of spiritual transformation upon couple relationships and the family. No matter how blissful a spiritual experience may be, some people wonder if it is worth it when its impact results in a divorce or an adverse consequence for a relationship. A strong devotion to one's religious or spiritual orientation can impact a couple's relationship in a number of different ways. The children of these couples are also subject to a range of adverse effects. This chapter is devoted to the issues that religion or spirituality may provoke in couple relationships. Under consideration will be the variety of ways one partner can respond to another partner's spiritual orientation.

The United States is experiencing a rising trend in religious intermarriage. The Pew Research Center (2015) has found that nearly four in ten people are in mixed religious marriages compared to half that number in 1960, and more couples are mixed with a Christian spouse and a nonreligious spouse than ever before. This increasing tendency may be the basis for producing more religious conflicts in couples.

UNDERSTANDING SPIRITUAL/RELIGIOUS DIFFERENCES

It is important to assess how partner A is responding to partner B's spiritual/religious orientation. The most extreme response to partner B is one in which partner A actively opposes partner B's spiritual perspective. In these cases, responses are not subtle. To have a primary relationship in which partner B knows that partner A vehemently opposes this position tends to activate an almost continuous discomfort in the relationship. If it is unresolved, it might be the focus of couple counseling.

Another level of difference exists if partner A completely disagrees with partner B's spiritual view but respects it. However, the ability to respect differences must be authentic or passive-aggressive remarks may contaminate the relationship. There is a difference between disagreement and complete opposition. This distinction should be clarified if it is a relevant issue. Most couples are going to disagree on at least a few issues, so the better the couple learns to tolerate and respect these differences, the more likely the relationship will endure at a quality level. Spiritual or religious orientation may simply be one of several areas where tolerance and respect occurs in a couple's relationship.

There are a few people who have partners who are actually neutral to the other's spiritual viewpoint. In these cases, the partner neither disagrees or agrees and is generally not very philosophically oriented. As long as a person's spiritual orientation does not significantly alter what the other partner needs in the relationship, this neutral partner tends to be satisfied. This response by a partner can make religion a nonissue.

There is another degree of response to partner A's spiritual viewpoint in which partner B may strongly support partner A's spiritual orientation, although partner B may not share partner A's view. This response is like that of an interested spectator who likes what he sees but would not do it himself. Of course, this partner response is usually constructive.

Finally, there are those partners who agree with each other's perspective and actually support each partner's religious/spiritual perspective. Of course, we seldom see these couples in counseling. Unfortunately, many people who long for this type of response from their partners discover that they are simply not congruent in this way. Problems occur when one of the partners changes his or her stance and disrupts this unified position due to either a loss of faith or a spiritual awakening.

Depending on which of these aforementioned responses a partner may have, psychotherapy can be adapted to resolve it. Assessing each partner's response to the other partner's spiritual orientation with unbiased empathy is important in order for people to be understood and for an appropriate treatment plan to be custom-tailored. The importance of these five degrees of partner responses cannot be overstated. For some people hundred percent agreement is important, for others a general agreement is okay, others are okay with only fifty percent agreement and still others do not need much agreement from their partners at all. After identifying the differing needs for agreement, couples can explore the motives for these needs in their attempt to fully pursue conflict resolution.

While some people link agreement with perceived love by the other partner, others do not. If this is the issue, it can be pursued in therapy. If a person conceives of his or her spiritual orientation as an essential aspect of identify, then rejection of this orientation can be received as a personal rejection. This point may not be understood by the other partner. Therefore, couple counseling focused on this understanding can help. When the emotions related to these issues are accessed and resolved, the issues tend to diminish or disappear altogether.

The level of commitment a person needs from a partner is a crucial factor in pursing any conflict occurring as a consequence of that person's commitment to religion/spirituality. For example, if a person is a minister or priest in a faith, the level of importance for spousal support may be at a high level. However, partners can hold their faith activities to be central in their lives even if they are not professional religious leaders. When this is the case, their needs become a significant aspect of the couple relationship. Even coworkers can become involved when a couple's relationship interferes with a role deemed to be a shared commitment.

HARRY'S CASE

Harry was a Protestant associate minister. Harry's wife preferred to attend a nondenominational church. The senior minister at Harry's church told Harry that he had never heard of a minister's wife not attending that minister's church and that the congregation expected the minister's wife to be active in the church. Harry did not want to force his wife to attend the Protestant church, but it put him in a bad position having to explain his wife's whereabouts. Therefore, in therapy we worked on resolving Harry's distress about the matter through Emotional Transformation Therapy® (ETT®). When it surfaced that Harry's wife liked the stable income that they received from his job, it was brought to her attention. At that point his wife conceded and agreed to participate at Harry's church for most important events, but also acknowledged that she might attend the other church when it did not interfere with Harry's main church activities.

In this case, we found an important common interest—income —that helped the couple to place their differences secondary to this common interest. Fortunately, this could be done without complete sacrifice by Harry's wife. The fact is that Harry was already a minister when Harry and his wife married, and she knew the expectations and had initially accepted them. Some people have trouble with the perceived confines of a new marital relationship. It was also true that Harry's wife wanted to be in contact with her previous husband

and with her single girlfriends, a fact that was upsetting to Harry. Therefore, there were boundary issues for her in general. The church attendance issue was simply a symptom of a greater boundary issue. Success in this matter was essential, and it made the resolution of other issues more likely.

In an attempt to accommodate their partner's needs, some people decide to change religions by joining their partner's religion. In many cases, this unified religious participation is believed to be a way to strengthen the bond, and it works. However, for some people this sacrifice may be too great for the partner who is changing faiths. When the new faith is not congruent with a person's authentic religious/spiritual experience, it can forge an internal psychological split between pleasing the partner and being true to oneself. When this occurs, the discrepancy within can be pursued. Sometimes simply talking it through with a third party relieves the incongruence. In some cases, both the internal conflict and the consequential conflict with the partner escalate to a higher level. In these cases, both individual and couple counseling may be useful. In any case facilitating resolution of the emotions involved via ETT® often results in a cognitive resolution.

In couple's counseling, if significant spiritual differences are identified by one or both partners as an issue during the first session, therapy can be focused on this matter. At the end of the first session, it is valuable to give both partners the homework task of writing a description of their individual spiritual viewpoints, to be brought to the second session. This task serves several purposes. First of all, it may help clarify a person's perspective to write it out. Second, this task indirectly communicates that someone (the therapist) is interested in their viewpoint and wants to understand it. When each viewpoint is read in the second session, if empathy and understanding is provided by the therapist, clients often experience the empathy they have not received from their partners, thus enhancing the therapeutic bond. Third, it is possible that the partners may understand each other's viewpoint more clearly. This exercise places all the parties into the same position of understanding the viewpoints, which provides a foundation for further interventions. The therapist can challenge each partner to describe the other person's viewpoint to the satisfaction of the partner who wrote the viewpoint. This may yield a fulfilling sense of being heard by the other partner.

Appendix A of this book contains a questionnaire for identifying "Partner Spiritual Differences." This questionnaire can be used to quickly identify precise issues concerning partner spiritual issues.

ETT® AND CONFLICT RESOLUTION

One of my licenses is that of a licensed marriage and family therapist. In this specialty, a system's perspective is prevalent, meaning that couples and families are treated with a view of how relationships in the couple system impact the individuals. When a change in one individual occurs, even if it is a good change, it may impact the couple system in a variety of ways, perhaps giving rise to negative consequences. Spiritual and religious issues are one of many topics that can alter the couple system. For further information about the ETT® couple counseling approach, see my second book, *Accelerated Ecological Psychotherapy* (Vazquez, 2013).

The use of ETT® for couples counseling has its own place in the field. Couple conflict is one of the best applications for ETT®. In most forms of couple counseling, a long, drawn-out interactive process may or may not alleviate the emotional distress, although understanding is often achieved. When a couple in conflict reaches an impasse, it is usually because the intense emotions of at least one partner are fixated. ETT® techniques can typically eliminate this emotional intensity within minutes. Often when this takes place, the conflict impasse is easily facilitated to conclusion. ETT® elevates the art form of couple therapy to new levels, especially conflicts.

HIGH-RISK RELIGIOUS CONFLICT

Assessing the degree of hostile behavior that results from religious disputes is extremely important. For example, some people may have participated in verbal abuse or physical confrontations. In fact, some people have committed suicide or homicide due to these disputes. Therefore, it is important to rule out dangerous risks with these couples during the early phase of therapy. If dangerous risks are evident, this will change the course of treatment to include more frequent sessions as quickly as possible. In these cases, individual sessions designed to reduce the intensity of affect and tendencies to act out can be treated with ETT® modalities. Typically, psychological triggers exist due to unresolved previous experiences. These experiences can be resolved via ETT® processes. Pargament (2011) cites a case in which a man murdered his wife, three children, and his mother for what he believed to be religious reasons:

> With (my daughter) being so determined to get into acting I was also fearful about what that might do to her continuing to be a Christian....
>
> Also, with (my wife) not going to church I knew that this would harm the children eventually.... At least I'm certain that all have gone to heaven now. If things had gone on, who knows if this would be the case.
>
> It may seem cowardly to have always shot them from behind, but I didn't want any of them to know even at the last second that I had to do this....
>
> I am only concerned with making my peace with God and of this I am assured because of Christ dying even for me. (p. 151)

In this case and many others, it appears that the real issue for therapeutic purposes is exercising tolerance when loved ones behave in ways outside of one's control. Many family members behave in ways that differ from one's religious viewpoint, but very few people commit murder to control these behaviors. People often project their dysfunctional thinking onto religious ideas. The cognitive distortion in this man's thinking is apparent to most people but seemed reasonable to him. If there had been an opportunity to work with this man before this tragedy, the emotional intensity of his religious conviction might have been diminished, potentially softening this thinking, without changing his basic spiritual orientation. Although some people fear that their loved ones may not go to heaven, few people murder them to prevent this from happening. However, this anecdote illustrates how the need to control family member's behaviors, when coupled with inflexible religious moral beliefs, could become dangerous.

EXTERNAL INFLUENCES ON COUPLE CONFLICT

The spiritual perspective of someone close to one member of a couple might have a negative impact on the couple's relationship. The parents of either or both spouses may object to the couple's spiritual perspective. The parental objection may place partner A in the awkward position of being placed in the middle between partner B and his or her parents. This conflict may escalate to the point that partner A, who is caught in the middle, may demand that partner B make a choice: Give allegiance to me or your parent. This conflict may often continue to exist without resolution, or if a choice is made, the party who is not aligned may feel alienated and respond with hostility. ETT® work targets the dissolution of intensity of emotions involved, which typically alters rigid stances as a result.

Sometimes siblings have an impact upon a couple. People who have had particular roles of influence in a partner's family of origin may affect the partner. For example, a sibling or siblings who have dominated the particular sibling that is in a couple relationship may criticize or use guilt manipulation to assert opposition to a certain spiritual viewpoint. This can result in distress for the couple. An evaluation of the couple's boundaries may yield a means to change that can help this predicament.

Sometimes close friends can impact one partner to such an extent that it may provoke a disturbance in the couple's relationship. For example, well-meaning friends may encourage one partner into a religious or spiritual orientation that results in opposition by the other partner. In other cases, concerned friends may oppose the couple's spiritual perspective, which could disturb the couple's relationship. In some cases, deep friendships may have existed long before the couple bonded. These friendships may have involved confiding to a level beyond that of the couple relationship and thus its influence may be greater than that of the partners in the couple. In this case, it is imperative that the couple relationship grow as a separate entity and establish its own strength and interpersonal boundaries, which may develop new limitations for the older friendship. The ETT® process can assist resolving distressing emotions regarding these issues and typically leads to clarity concerning how to adapt to these changes in relationships.

One of the other issues that can strain the couple's spiritual/religious views pertains to the couple's children. If there is a difference in viewpoint, many couples are forced to decide which viewpoint they wish to teach the children or whether to share with the children that they have different religious perspectives? If the latter is chosen, it is important that it does not become a competition between the parents for the children's perspective. As children grow older they may tend to question the parent's religious perspective. If the couple had previously been avoiding their spiritual differences, this questioning can expose the couple's issues. In this case, couple counseling can often help couples work through their differences. When couples have adult children who may have chosen a different religion, it may become a significant problem for the couple as illustrated in the following case.

ROBERT'S CASE

Robert was a fifty-year-old, successful Jewish businessman who was divorced. Robert's family of origin was Jewish, and his mother died when Robert was ten years old. This contributed to Robert becoming more dependent on his father, yet hypersensitive to abandonment. Since Robert's family was not very active in the Judaic tradition, Robert sought a faith that provided more involvement. Therefore, Robert became a messianic Jew who involved Jesus in his faith. Robert's choice was unacceptable to his father, to the extent that he rejected any further contact with Robert. When I met Robert, he had had no contact with his father for ten years and did not expect any contact for the rest of his life. Psychologically, this left Robert feeling abandoned by both his mother and father, which contributed to his becoming very "clingy" in relationships. This tendency, over time, ultimately led to several women breaking up with him. I observed that this case fits the syndrome Mellody (2003) calls "love addiction," but the long-term key was to resolve Robert's unresolved emotions about his mother's death. Otherwise, trauma re-enactment would likely continue. In this case, Robert's lost relationship with his father, due to a change in Robert's religious orientation, was a key factor in furthering Robert's alienation, resulting in obsessive-compulsive and depression tendencies.

In Robert's case, religious differences between him and his father exacerbated his abandonment pattern in his relationship with women. Instead of continued hostility, Robert's father chose to simply eliminate Robert from his life in an effort to cope with Robert's religious change. While the father's coping mechanism was not murder, suicide, or continuing harassment, nor illegal, the psychological consequences were devastating in different ways.

The aforementioned issues pertain to the effect that people external to the couple can have on a couple's relationship. They generally pertain to ineffective interpersonal boundaries, miscommunication, and poor adjustment skills by either the couple or the influential people outside the couple. ETT® couple counseling or individual ETT® counseling can help. Religious/spiritual intolerance is frequently a factor. These issues are well-known couple issues, whether the theme is religion or not, but when religion is involved, passion may escalate more than in other issues.

The majority of all couples who get a divorce cite finances as one of the primary issues. When religious or spiritual activities involve significant expenditure, finances can become an issue even when the couple shares a similar religious orientation. When religious viewpoints involve expenditures and the couple does not share the same viewpoints, money can become a greater issue. Most Christian faiths recommend donating one tenth of one's income to the church. This can be significant when the other partner does not share that view, and particularly if that partner has had experiences that contribute to making him or her hypersensitive to financial issues anyway. Negotiating skills can become important in these matters, but when ETT® processes ease the emotional intensity, the magnitude of the issues often dwindles. Finances often concern one's sense of security. When the sense of insecurity is corrected, the problem with religious differences and finances often becomes tolerable. This focus during ETT® processes can reduce distress.

One of the most significant consequences of spiritual/religious differences upon the couple occurs when this issue impacts affection between partners. Some people cope with stressors by withholding affection. Loss of affection between partners is a major factor in the dissolution of a relationship. Even though a couple may appear to be going through the motions of a constructive relationship, without appropriate affection, depression, anger, or anxiety may occur. However, in many cases religious difference only serves as an excuse to increase the distance from the other partner when the authentic motive is fear of affectionate closeness. In these cases, couple therapy focused on affectionate intimacy may help. Individual sessions can target core emotional memory that blocks the expression and/or reception of affectionate intimacy. When hostility about a partner's religious orientation diminishes affection, this conflict often reaches a dangerous level. The emotions of the avoidant or upset person can be flushed to the surface, expressed, and reduced through basic ETT® processes. Then they have a chance to be resolved.

Another variation on this theme occurs when spiritual/religious issues interfere with a couple's sexual relationship. For example, one partner can avoid sex or reject the other partner as a means to enact retribution on that partner due to the other partner's religious position. When a male partner views the female's religious enthusiasm as opposition that he cannot compete with, erectile dysfunction may occur. Many religions focus on the evil of sexuality to the extent that one partner may lose comfort with being sexual, even with his or her partner. This position may increase the resistance of the partner with a greater sexual desire to oppose a partner's religious position. These issues are often about boundaries between religion and the couple's sexual fulfillment. The use of sex as the battleground for religion can unnecessarily heighten conflict. ETT® processes can be used to reduce emotional intensity.

TRIANGULATION WITH RELIGION

Many issues of couple conflict concern triangulation. This term is normally used in conjunction with a third person bonding with one partner in such a way that the two-person bond is reduced or disrupted. However, a church or a spiritual focus can parallel triangulation as if it were a third person. Triangulation can leave one partner jealous, envious, or hostile to the partner's spirituality or church as if it were an affair. This type of reaction may have its roots in earlier life triangulation in the family of origin in which dad bonded with the child against mom or mom bonded with the child against dad. Then triangulation with a religion can serve as a trigger to unresolved family dysfunction from early life. When this has been the case, the intensity of emotion regarding triangulation can be great. As in many previously mentioned issues of religion or spirituality, the core issue is often really not about religion or spirituality, but about other issues projected onto religion or spirituality.

HUNTER AND ALEXIS

Hunter and Alexis were a forty-year-old married couple who came to marriage counseling due to a religious conflict. Both Hunter and Alexis identified themselves as Christians, although their versions of Christianity were different. Alexis felt passionate about her Bible church. Hunter thought her church was too focused on getting money from the church's participants and viewed it as phony. This seriously disturbed Alexis because she believed his criticism was not justified. The passion Alexis felt for this church was obvious when she spoke about it. However, Hunter saw it as taking up too much of her time, energy, and money and he felt angry toward it. ETT® process reduced the emotional intensity.

Through processes of shared expression both partners were guided to empathize with each other's perspective. During individual sessions it was discovered that each of them had previous experiences of triangulation in their family of origin that left them with unresolved emotions. Once these emotional memories were resolved, tolerance for each other's perspective became less emotionally intense, leading to more flexibility about each other's different religious perspectives. Alexis continued to go to her church but reduced her level of involvement. Hunter even agreed to attend church with her on occasion and cease criticism of it.

THE SHAMAN COUPLE CASE

I saw one couple, Ben and Jane, who were about fifty years old. Both Ben and Jane had been following a shamanic spiritual leader for about ten years, and both of them held this man in high esteem. Their twenty-year marriage had been very passionate. However, it appeared that Jane's bond with the shaman was one of total devotion, and Ben became uncomfortable with that relationship. As a result, he developed close friendships with certain women in the group to cope with his perceived abandonment. Jane viewed Ben's relationships as inappropriate, while Ben felt rejected by Jane and uncomfortable with her relationship with the shaman.

When the couple came to see me as a marriage therapist, I knew I could become the next source of triangulation. Therefore, I made strong efforts to deal with them evenhandedly while providing empathy for each of them. At first I mediated several truces while they temporarily followed through on homework. Ultimately, however, Ben rejected me, possibly because of Jane's bond with me, and he was unwilling to continue couple therapy. In Ben's mind, our relationship probably replicated a projection of a similar triangulated relationship that occurred with the Shaman.

This example illustrates how therapists risk becoming an object of couple triangulation. In this case, their spiritual orientation was contaminated by couple triangulation, and it was projected as a trauma re-enactment. If I had it to do over, I would have reframed their perspective of the issues and searched for previous triangulation issues in the form of core emotional memories related to it. With these core memories resolved, the intensity of triangulation could have been eased.

While it is important for couples to resolve their differences for the sake of their relationship, it is also important because of its potential impact on the couple's children. Research findings make it clear that children can be profoundly affected by parental discord. Additionally, new research in epigenetics suggests that altered levels of circulating stress hormones can affect genetic expression. Research provides evidence that these changes in genetic expressions can be found in the offspring of the couple's children and in the grandchildren, who may or may not even know the grandparents. This cross generational link can place generations of people at risk. Therefore, resolution of conflict can make a difference for many people connected to the original couple (Di Christina, 2015, p. 10).

THE IMPACT OF SPIRITUAL AWAKENING ON THE COUPLE

One of the consequences of spiritual awakenings can be a perception of "oneness" with everything. This perception can manifest as a loss of interpersonal boundaries. When appropriate boundaries are lost, the other partner may experience a violation of personal space and discomfort about the manner in which the awakened partner interacts with others.

Spiritual or religious issues pertaining to the use of ETT® typically involve ETT® facilitating a profound spiritual change. In many cases, ETT® strengthens spiritual or religious perspectives by facilitating a direct experience with perceived spiritual realities. However, there have been several cases of couples who were atheists when an ETT® experience facilitated a profound spiritual event in one partner. This type of event can challenge a couple's stability. In those cases, there often was not an overt attempt to create spiritual experiences. Instead, the depth level of ETT® processes risks these spontaneous occurrences. In almost all of these cases, the person who had the spiritual awakening was pleased with it. However, this profound change had effects on that person's relationships. Until a person adjusts to the effects of these changes, a spiritual transformation cannot be successfully integrated into his or her life.

HILLARY'S CASE

Hillary, a married adult woman, was a parent of three children. Her husband Mark grew up with a schizophrenic mother who often talked about unusual religious ideas. When Hillary had her spiritual awakening, she gradually demonstrated an array of spiritual gifts, including precognition, several unusual physical symptoms accompanying her Kundalini arising, and a variety of nonordinary states. While these events were generally positive, a variety of unresolved emotions from her past surfaced during this purification process. These unusual spiritual phenomena and Hillary's emotional unrest repeatedly triggered in Mark the same responses he had had to his mother earlier in his life. This meant that at times Mark felt angry, anxious, and helpless. Fortunately, Mark possessed good wisdom and common sense and went through a few sessions to help him cope with this challenging predicament. His distress, however, complicated Hillary's spiritual process. Nonetheless, several ETT® sessions alleviated much of this distress.

This case demonstrates how a profound spiritual awakening can spur very challenging adjustments to a couple's relationship. The effects of a spiritual awakening ripple outward to all relationships of the awakened person. Anytime a person undergoes a profound change of any type, it impacts that person's sense of identity and risks the dissolution of relationships. Some people who are in relationships with the awakened one simply cannot or will not accept this change. Historically, people have been burned at the stake, crucified, or murdered when a spiritual awakening took place within an intolerant community. However, spiritual awakenings have impacted humanity as strongly as any other events in human history.

The spiritual awakening of one partner in a couple presents a challenge. Answering that challenge hinges upon the nature of the couple's spiritual issues before the awakening and the readiness of the partners to cope with such change. In many instances, couples may not have given religion and spirituality much importance, and they may not even have discussed it over the years of their marriage. Then when a spiritual awakening suddenly ushers this new topic into the couple's dialogue, it can be greeted as an intrusion by the other partner. In some cases, it can be seen as just another odd, temporary trend by the other partner who has become calloused to the partner's instability. A third reaction may be curiosity, fascination, and intrigue. A fourth and pragmatic reaction is concerned with how this change might impact the other partner, and once that is clarified, then a response may occur. Some partners fear that the awakened one might become famous, and fear the threat of abandonment. A fifth response might involve a complete discrediting of the partner's awakening as if the partner is delusional and a victim of manipulation. Finally, a partner could view the awakened partner with awe, wonder, and a high level of respect. The point is that rarely is an awakening seen as a neutral event from the view of the other partner.

Therapists involved in facilitating an awakening need to assess its impact on the other partner and encourage collateral sessions with the couple when needed. If the couple was not stable before the awakening, its continuity may be at greater risk. However, even a very stable couple relationship may lose its balance when a change like this occurs. As one partner stated, "This is not the person I married, and it feels like we need to begin our relationship again." Much of the success of these adjustments depends on previous coping skills. If a partner has had an unpleasant experience with major change in his/her past, such as a divorce of parents during one partner's childhood, this change could reactivate coping experiences from that time. If this does occur, one's reaction to significant change in a partner may become disproportionately intense to the current change. While spiritual awakenings can involve the most potent positive experiences known to humankind, change itself can be a blessing, a problem, or anything between these two extremes. However, change in general is inevitable, and good skills in adjustment can allow the most important growth in life.

It would be shortsighted not to mention those rare cases in which a spiritual awakening is simply too great of a change to maintain the relationship bond between the partners. This is illustrated in the Buddha leaving his wife and children to follow his quest for enlightment. For this decision millions of people are forever grateful. When a spiritual awakening occurs, one might recognize that the marriage was built on false premises in which one partner joined the relationship for inauthentic reasons or that one partner refused to grow and change. While divorce is not advocated, there are rare times when it might be seen to be in everyone's best interest. Most often working through issues with the opposite sex is simply part of the spiritual path. In the type of awakening called Kundalini, one experiences the unity of masculine and feminine transcendent inner aspects. Therefore, it requires authentic resolution of the masculine and feminine issues on all levels in order to achieve ultimate spiritual levels.

Many Christian churches have taken on the role of marriage counseling with the clear agenda of placing Christ at the center of the marital relationship in order to unify the couple relationship. This movement has been activated to reduce the divorce rate by facilitating reconciliation between partners. This approach succeeds more often when both partners already agree on religious philosophy but are stagnated on the relationship conflict. For some people this approach can work well, while others may be too uncomfortable discussing issues like sexuality with people in a church. For example, there appears to be a disproportionate number of sexual addicts involved in fundamental Christian churches who participate in secular sexual addiction treatment facilities. Nonetheless, dispute resolution, meditation procedures, and marital therapy for conflict are important needs. It is hoped that this methodology is helpful to both couple relationships and spiritual growth.

Ideally, a couple could be encouraged to share with each other by making spiritual and religious issues a focus for growth, exploration, and adventure. Once both partners recognize how their tendencies to trigger early life issues can occur, they can more easily separate religion from those issues. If an openness and curiosity about spiritual growth could not only be tolerated but encouraged, the spiritual journey could become a source of fun and inspiration instead of control and conflict. When spiritual awakenings are supported by the people closest to the awakened one, growing pains are less and both partners win.

This approach is not only about how to alleviate couple conflicts, but also about the possibility of transforming conflicts into an actively charged couple spirituality. What if a couple's relationship actually enhances each partner's spirituality? A spiritual awakening by one partner could potentially awaken the other partner, or the couple could become awakened by the relationship itself. In many cases, people who have experienced a spiritual awakening through ETT® have contributed to awakening their partner and in some cases other family members as well. Through enhanced couple communication and mutual spiritual practices, couples can reach new levels of spirituality. Even couples who continue to differ in their spiritual viewpoints can enhance each other.

CHAPTER 8 SUMMARY

Research has shown a dramatic increase in the number of couples who have differing religious/spiritual perspectives with each other. Therefore, when a method can strongly impact a partner in a positive way, it risks the possibility of more conflict within the relationship. This chapter first examined specific ways in which couple conflict about religion/spirituality can manifest. This examination was followed by a case study about how religious difference can occur in a couple when one partner has a major contrast in religious views with the other partner. In order to custom-tailor treatment, assessing the nature of each couple's religious/spiritual orientation is explored.

Following assessment, the use of ETT® in conflict resolution is explored. Then the chapter explores those religious conflicts that are at a very high risk for violence, suicide, or divorce. Sometimes the risk of elevating a couple's conflict can be due to people outside the relationship who exact a strong influence on one partner of the couple. A case study in which a parent disowned his adult child because he left the parent's religion is explored. Then a brief survey of different types of couple conflict took place.

Many couple conflicts over religion/spirituality can be conceptually understood through the construct of triangulation. This construct was illustrated in two case studies. Ideas about how to manage and therapeutically resolve triangulation were described.

The impact of spiritually awakening one partner in a couple relationship is carefully explained. A case study illustrated one way in which this type of profound awakening can affect the marital relationship. This type of adjustment is a primary concern because ETT® tends to facilitate spiritual awakenings. Then the chapter considers not only how to resolve religious conflicts but also how to foster a more spiritually charged couple unity.

Chapter Nine

Extended Human Abilities

A growing amount of experientially based, psychospiritual activity has been shown to yield certain functional benefits. These activities include, but are not limited to, various forms of meditation such as mindfulness meditation, transcendental meditation, and Christian centering prayer. Additionally, using various forms of yoga and a variety of psychedelic drugs has become more frequent. While people anticipate the familiar benefits of relaxation, insight, or temporary joy derived from these activities, they are often not prepared when spiritual awakenings are accompanied by an array of spiritual "gifts" or extended human abilities. These types of awakenings and gifts also occur with the use of Emotional Transformation Therapy® (ETT®). While most of these gifts are seen as good, these abilities are typically quite surprising and disorienting due to their sheer peculiar nature. Since most people who have not had these experiences do not believe them, the person thus gifted often feels alone, alienated, and suspected of being a liar or psychotic. This outcome often leaves the gifted person in a more problematic condition than before the awakening. Most psychospiritual practices do not provide adequate preparation for the intensity, peculiarity, or range of possible capacities that can develop from these experiences. This chapter is about the nature and scope of these awakened spiritual gifts.

Before further exploration of the spiritual gifts resulting from psychospiritual activity, it is important to address the issue of the scientific reality of these abilities. There was a time when only anecdotal evidence about these spiritual abilities existed. Within the last three decades scientific research concerning some of these abilities has been compiled in significant quantities and at a high level of qualitative rigor. It is now a fact that a wide variety of extraordinary human abilities exists and has been scientifically validated (Benor, 2001; Murphy, 1992; Schwartz, 2007). Without personal experience of these abilities, many people assume that they are not real. However, arguing against the existence of these capacities on the basis of a lack of scientific evidence has become, at the least, questionable, because scientific evidence for some of these gifts clearly exists.

Historically, most major religions have experienced controversy regarding the exact significance of psychospiritual gifts. In the Christian tradition, "miracles" reported to have been performed by Jesus are generally accorded validation as a sign of his connection to God. However, these same activities performed by someone who is not Christian may be considered as evil by some Christians.

PEGGY'S CASE

Peggy came to me for psychological counseling. In our initial interview of her personal history, she reported having had a life-threatening medical condition that was unresponsive to conventional medicine. Out of desperation, Peggy decided to see a Filipino psychic surgeon. She reported to me that the psychic surgeon completely cured her condition, and it had not reoccurred in ten years. However, Peggy now attended a Christian church where the minister told her that the psychic surgery was not conducted within the Christian perspective and must be considered evil. Peggy accepted that view in spite of the fact that she was alive and symptom-free due to the Filipino healer. In this case, Peggy's Christian minister failed to see in the Filipino healer's gift a connection to God.

Spiritual gifts such a psychic abilities, precognition, psychokinesis, healing abilities, and others are viewed in various ways by different faiths. Within the various forms of Buddhism, there are different perspectives on these matters. For example, Theravada Buddhism minimizes metaphysical gifts, whereas Mahayana Buddhism maximizes the importance of metaphysical gifts (Smith, 1991, p. 126).

In Hinduism, "siddhis" are supernatural abilities that appear as by-products of spiritual development. Although certain tantric and yoga practices are designed to develop these abilities, almost all of the great Hindu teachers have cautioned against seeking siddhis for their own sake.

Ramana Maharshi, for example, warned people repeatedly against attachment to "siddhis" and makes no use of them himself, while other great masters, such as Sai Baba of Shirdi, employed siddhis for the welfare of his followers and their spiritual instruction. However, for those who have not reached a similar level of spiritual development there is a clear danger of misuse of power in the employment of siddhis, which would negate all previous spiritual efforts (Schuhmacher & Woerner, eds., 1994, pp. 333–334). These precautions about the use of supernatural abilities in conjunction with spiritual awakenings are addressed in one passage of the Bible:

> If I speak in the tongues of men and angels, but have not love, I am a noisy gong or a clanging cymbal. And if I have prophetic powers, and understand all mysteries and all knowledge, and if I have all faith, so as to move mountains, but have not love, I am nothing. If I give away all I have, and if I deliver by my body to be burned, but have not love, I gain nothing. (1 Cor. 13:1-3 English Standard Version)

While extraordinary abilities are known in most forms of Hinduism and Buddhism, the Vajrayana or "Diamond Vehicle" school of Buddhism, which developed out of Mahayana Buddhism, identifies eight specific siddhis, or supernatural powers, which are the following:

1. the sword that renders itself unconquerable
2. the elixir of the eyes that makes gods visible
3. fleetness in running
4. invisibility
5. the life essence that preserves youth
6. the ability to fly
7. the ability to make certain pills
8. power over the world of spirits and demons (Schuhmacher & Woerner, eds., 1994, p. 334)

It is possible for people to possess any of these spiritual gifts and still be immoral, addicted, or malevolent in any number of ways. The possession of extraordinary skills does not automatically mean a person is closer to God than anyone else. However, people of some faiths would disagree with this view. A friend of mine grew up in the mountains of West Virginia where churches conducted snake handling as a religious ritual. Congregants believed that people who could handle poisonous snakes and not get bitten possessed greater faith than those people who either did not participate in the ritual or those who were bitten. However, there are many well-known cases in which people with spiritual gifts have broken laws or moral codes, or used their skills to profit from others.

However, there are also people who possess spiritual gifts who are highly enlightened, deeply spiritual, and authentic. Some people develop spiritual gifts as a by-product of activities along their spiritual path and then lose their way spiritually. The acquisition of spiritual gifts requires a highly challenging adjustment. In fact, it can and often is traumatic.

EXTENDED HUMAN CAPACITIES

A case has clearly been made for the idea that all humans possess capacities that are largely untapped and exist as natural potentials for use. Utilizing this great potential of our minds may simply be a way to enhance the evolution of our species, a perspective suggesting that these genetic endowments exist for the purpose of our advancement. While precautions about the potential misuse of these powers are certainly warranted, if our affectionate and moral development occurred alongside the development of extended capacities, the risk of harm would be diminished markedly. Assuming that the moral and ethical use of these abilities is developed, let's look at some of the capacities developed through the use of ETT® that could be harnessed for the further advancement of humankind.

In 1992, Michael Murphy documented evidence for what he referred to as extraordinary human capacities in the following list:

1. Extraordinary perceptions of things outside the organism including apprehensions of a numinous beauty in familiar objects, voluntary clairvoyance, and contact with entities or events that are inaccessible to the ordinary senses.
2. Extraordinary somatic awareness and self-regulation.
3. Extraordinary communication abilities, including the transmission of thoughts, volitions, and ecstatic states through extra-somatic modalities.
4. Superabundant vitality that is difficult to account for in terms of ordinary bodily processes.
5. Extraordinary movement abilities.
6. Extraordinary capacities to alter the environment including exceptional hand-eye skills and abilities to influence things at a distance without reliance upon direct physical actions, as for example in spiritual healing.
7. Self-existent delight, which does not depend upon the satisfaction of needs and desires in the manner of ordinary pleasure, and which persists through sickness and other adversity.
8. Supreme intellectual capacities evident in some works of genius, by which great artistic or other productions are apprehended *tout ensemble*, all at once; and the unitive knowledge inherent in mystical experience, which differs radically from ordinary thinking.
9. Volition exceeding ordinary will, which unifies separate impulses to produce extraordinary actions.
10. Personhood that simultaneously transcends and fulfills one's ordinary sense of self while revealing one's fundamental unity with others.

11. Love that transcends ordinary needs and reveals a fundamental unity with others.
12. Alterations in bodily structures, states, and processes that support the experiences and capacities just noted. (pp. 27–28)

While these extraordinary capacities have been demonstrated, very few people possess all of these qualities. However, as mind-altering techniques such as meditation and ETT® become more popular, the number of people possessing these skills should increase. As this occurs, it becomes important for psychotherapists to recognize and understand these phenomena.

People who have had near-death experiences often report profound transcendent experiences which bear a similarity to other mystical states derived from contemplative techniques. Research on the after effects of near-death experiences has shown the production of spiritual gifts as a consequence (Atwater, 2003, p. 36). It has been estimated that about 15 million people have had near-death experiences in the United States and a significant portion report these experiences.

When an awakening on the spiritual path occurs, unusual events may begin to take place as a consequence. Some of these events transpire in a way that Carl Jung would identify as synchronicity or meaningful coincidences. This might take place when events occur in a nonlinear or nonlogical juxtaposition, such that a person feels like the events happen at the right place at the right time. For example, two old friends who have lost contact for many years run into each other in a dog park in another state at the exact same time. The odds against that happening are extreme. Calling someone on the telephone at the exact second the other is calling you is another example. After a spiritual awakening, synchronicity tends to occur at a much more frequent rate. In some cases, this type of event may happen daily.

One particular variety of unusual occurrences pertains to a person's relationship with nature. Although this type of spiritual experience may seem very peculiar to many people, it is, in fact, very common and accepted in most Native American cultures as well as earth-based cultures around the world. While many people love their dogs and cats, spontaneous awareness and kinship with wild animals and plants is less common. In one case, after the experience of a spiritual awakening, almost every time this person went outside, a hawk appeared. I have had sessions in which profound spiritual events were taking place and a large number of birds flocked at my window. With respect to plant life, one former client had contact with a tree's sentient nature, an event that caused a profound feeling of change.

Many of these events occur after an experience of oneness with the whole universe because it tends to foster a perceived connection with everything around a person. While there is an impressive amount of scientific research documenting how eco systems move out of or into balance, Deep Ecology, developed by Norwegian philosopher Arne Naess, goes much further in its perspective of the natural environment. Deep Ecology conceives of an intimate subjective connection as if elements of nature were like relationships between people. Native cultures use phrases like "brother son," "sister moon," and "mother earth" to depict the intimate relationship quality of these elements of nature. While most people can feel an inspiration of some type looking at the grandeur of mountains or the beauty of an ocean beach, people who awaken spirituality often perceive extraordinary experiences in ordinary things. One client was potting a plant when it seemed like time spontaneously stood still and everything became interconnected, or one, in a way that left her speechless and awestruck.

While many people can appreciate something special in other people, plants, and animals, fewer people would expect a personal kinship with inanimate objects. As a child I developed a hobby of collecting rocks and minerals that were appealing to me. While I was initially drawn to their appearance, I also felt an unusual fascination and affinity with each distinct type of stone in a different way. I often felt euphoria while holding certain stones. I never told anyone about this experience at that time and had no way to conceive of it as "spiritual." Years later as an adult I am aware of many other people who describe various kinds of spiritual experiences via contact with stones. Many earth-based cultures name mountains, lakes, rivers, or even certain types of stones with human names. Spiritual awakenings can foster a unique contact and relationship with a variety of inanimate objects.

Although such experiences appear illogical to first world societies, they are commonly accepted in the belief systems of numerous third world societies. For example, Natalie Tolbert's anthropological description of the perspective of the Tukano people of the northwest Amazon basin in South America is striking:

> The Tukano believe in two interlocking worlds whereby the physical world of material things and the spirit world are discrete but coexist. Human beings interact with nature and with spirits: they are considered incapable of existing independently. Not only do Tukano people experience a kind of unity—interconnectedness between humans and nature—they also experience interconnectedness between nature and the spirit world. This concept of interlocking dimensions is common to many societies throughout the world and is found time and again. (2001, p. 30)

Tolbert believes "that spiritual or religious experience and certain symptoms of psychosis exist within a continuum. They are polarities of consciousness" (2001, p. 30).

Oneness by definition would need to include everything, even mechanical objects and people we have not liked. After one session when a woman was helped to remove spiritual blockages through ETT®, the next day she had a spiritual experience while driving on one of the busiest and most congested freeways in Dallas. She spontaneously felt as if everyone was flowing in unity, during traffic gridlock that would normally frustrate people, because she felt an experience of profound peace.

SPEAKING IN TONGUES

Glossolalia is referred to as "speaking in tongues" and involves vocalizing speech-like syllables that usually lack understandable meaning. Some people consider it part of a sacred practice (Cartledge, 2006). Sometimes glossolalia refers to xenoglossy, which is the speaking of a natural language unknown to the speaker. "Speaking in tongues" is considered a miraculous spiritual gift by some Christian groups. Glossolalists often think these verbalizations can be real, unlearned languages as well as the language of spirit, heavenly language, or the language of angels (Grudem, 1994, p. 1070). There are five passages in the New Testament of the Christian Bible which explicitly refer to "speaking in tongues."

Some Christians make distinctions in spiritual gifts related to glossolalia. The "gift of tongues" pertains to verbal utterances, whereas the "gift of the interpretation of tongues" is considered a separate gift. Another variation is "singing in tongues." The 12th century saint Hildegard of Bingen was reported to have spoken and sung in tongues. Some people would categorize automatic writing as a variation of glossolalia. Automatic writing involves spontaneous writing, usually in one's own language, that communicates information unknown to the writer. All of these gifts have been observed in some clients during or after their experience of ETT®.

Extensive evidence exists that glossolalia occurs in many different cultures around the world and in many different religions. Glossolalia occurs in Paganism, Shamanism, and mediumistic religious practices. In the God Light Association in Japan, glossolalia is used to recall past lives. Glossolalia has been observed in the Voodoo religion of Haiti and in Hindu gurus of India. It is best known in Pentecostal and Charismatic Christian churches in the United States (Goodman, 1972, pp. 3–23).

A linguist from the University of Toronto, Samarin (1972), conducted a five-year study of glossolalia in several different cultures. His extensive research revealed the following about glossolalia:

- It "consists of using a certain number of consonants and vowels … in a limited number of syllables that in turn are organized into larger units that are taken apart and rearranged pseudogrammatically with variations in pitch, volume, speed, and intensity" (p. 120).

- It "consists of strings of syllables, made up of sounds taken from all those that the speaker knows, put together more or less haphazardly but emerging nevertheless as word-like and sentence-like units because of realistic, language-like rhythm and melody" (p. 227).
- "The syllable form does not form words, the stream of words is not internally consistent and there is no systematic relationship between speech and concepts" (p. 2).

Therefore, Samarin described glossolalia as "only a façade of a language" (p. 128). These findings suggest that glossolalia is not an actual known human language but may indeed be a spiritually induced utterance.

It has been suggested that glossolalia occurs due to psychopathology. However, a scientific study in 2002 included 991 male evangelical clergy and found that glossolalia was not related to psychopathology (Francis & Robbins, 2003, pp. 391–396).

More recently neuroscientists have conducted brain scans on people while they were speaking in tongues. They found no significant brain activity in the areas of the brain associated with language function. However, regions of the brain related to emotion were activated (Newberg et al., 2006, pp. 67–71). Therefore, it is clear that the brain changed distinctly during glossolalia, suggesting that it is a distinct phenomenon.

There are certain Christian religions in which "speaking in tongues" or glossolalia is expected, commonplace, or required in order to become a part of that congregation. One client reported to me that he/she pretended to be speaking in tongues because of the social expectation in that church. However, in three other cases clients who were not involved in any church reported glossolalia. The first reported having no religion, another was Jewish and had been meditating for a long time, and a third described being spiritual but not religious. Since there was no social pressure to exhibit glossolalia, and these people did not even know what it was when it began, these cases seemed less questionable than those described by people whose church advocated speaking in tongues.

In the three cases of glossolalia mentioned, each occurred within different psychological dynamics. The first case mentioned happened to a client who was diagnosed with dissociative identity disorder and was an incest survivor. The "voice" emerged during ETT® as one of her dissociated parts. Other parts could interpret the voice's meaning. This voice had a very strong emotional tone. This inner part appeared to have developed as a consequence of having been thwarted in her verbal expression by her father in childhood. This inner part seemed to function as an attempt to get important information to me during sessions. It was apparent that her verbage was not an actual language.

In the second case, while the woman was Jewish, her spiritual orientation was strongly influenced by Eastern practices and her form of Judaism was not very orthodox. Her voices spontaneously occurred subsequent to ETT® sessions. When she was referred to me, it was clear that she possessed symptoms of a Kundalini rising. In the midst of this spiritual awakening, a voice emerged. This client was a "pleaser" and lost her capacity to voice her own authentic opinions in childhood. Her newly emerged voice possessed a strong emotional tone as if she were compelled to share an opinion but did not have permission to voice it in a normal way. She could often interpret the meaning of these utterances to me.

In the third case, a fifty-year-old woman client had been experiencing xenoglossy. When she spoke in tongues, linguists were able to identify her language as mostly Persian. Of course, this woman had never been to Persia nor had she ever taken a course in Persian. However, she came to therapy because she had lost her direct contact with the divine and wanted it back. This mystical woman was experiencing the "dark night of the soul." It emerged that several psychological wounds from her past had surfaced which we were able to process in psychotherapy. In her case, xenoglossy had already been present upon entry into therapy, and ETT® was used to restore her connection to the divine from which her gift was perceived to have emerged. A spiritual gift without a continuing relationship with the divine is often considered to be of less use.

PROPHECY

The current terms for prophecy are premonition or precognition, also referred to as future sight or second sight. It is a type of extrasensory perception that involves acquiring information about the future that cannot be known from normally acquired sense-based information. If one assumes that the future has not occurred, it would, therefore, be impossible to know about future events. This skill would appear to be impossible and irrational. However, a vast array of cross-cultural claims of precognition exists, and there are over 150 biblical references to prophecy (Nave, 1962, pp. 1009–1010).

With substantial evidence on both sides of the issue, controversy exists regarding the existence and accuracy of precognition. Mainstream psychiatry generally considers precognition to be hallucination (Blom, 2010, p. 421). In one study of 1777 dream-based and 1513 wakeful reports of the U.S. public, in seventy-five percent of dreaming and sixty percent of wakeful experiences people reported precognitive experiences (Stokes, 1997, pp. 6–87). A similar study in Germany found that the majority of participants reported precognitive experiences (Sannwald, 1959, p. 71). Nonetheless, most scientists generally do not accept the reality of precognition. Paradoxically, although much historical, cross-cultural, and case report evidence validates the existence of precognition, it is still not accepted scientifically. The problem may be narrowed to the idea that if people have not had a direct experience of precognition, it is extremely difficult to accept it, because precognition operates outside of our generally accepted concept of linear time. However, in most of the world's major religious traditions prophecy is a well-known phenomenon.

Certain types of spiritual awakening experiences serve as "gateway" experiences that open a person to a wide variety of spiritual gifts. Subsequent to these gateway awakenings, precognition skills can emerge and occur on a consistent basis. A few of my clients have experienced precognition that was eventually verified by the occurrences that followed. It is difficult to dispute precognition when the predicted events actually occur. ETT® clients who experienced awakenings have exhibited precognition.

In many cases, clients who later experienced precognition had a tendency toward anticipatory anxiety before their awakening. There was a preoccupation with a fear of negative events taking place in their future. If this habit was not resolved before a gateway experience people may inadvertently take their negative habits into a transpersonal level. People often fail to anticipate that there could be future events they do not really want to know about. When unpleasant precognition occurs, intense distress is often the result. This is an example of how extraordinary abilities may not be beneficial if one is not spiritually developed enough to accommodate the consequences.

Differentiating a fearful imagination from authentic precognition is important. The client may need help in this respect because both may seem equally real. Even if the client has developed true gifts of prophecy, no one is one hundred percent accurate. Discerning false prophecy is a key issue for people possessing this gift.

Precognition and other spiritual gifts have a tendency to attract inordinate attention from other people. If this tendency occurs when the gifted person has ego deficits, there is a strong risk that the person thus gifted will be drawn toward ego inflation and away from an authentic spiritual path. However, if it is ethically applied as just a different expression of one's potential, it can be beneficial. Therefore, it is important that therapists respond to this gift in an appropriate manner.

AFTER-DEATH COMMUNICATION

The Christian Bible contains numerous references to dialogue with deceased people, and after-death communication occurs in other religions as well, such as many Native American faiths and Shintoism. Studies have shown that sixty-six percent of widows have reported direct contact with their deceased spouses. As many as seventy-five percent of parents who have lost a child report seeing some kind of apparition of that child within a year (Moody, 1993, p. viii).

In some ETT® sessions, contact with deceased people occurs spontaneously without any attempt to elicit it. During or after the use of the ETT® samadhi process spontaneous contact with deceased loved ones can occur. However, a specific process of ETT® is designed to produce consistent after-death communication. This type of experience has been documented in other therapeutic procedures (Botkin, 2000).

In one study of the use of induced after-death communication as a psychotherapy process, seventy-one participants took part. This scientific research found that seventy-nine percent of the participants reported an experience of direct contact with a deceased loved one. Before and after the two-session protocol and six months later assessments revealed statistically significant improvements, including increase in positive coping, decreased anger and depression, and an increase in belief about the afterlife (Botkin, 2013, p. 1011). Although this study used EMDR to assist in the process, it bears a striking similarity to case study outcomes that used ETT®.

Moody (1975) coined the term "near-death experience" after having interviewed hundreds of people who returned to life after temporarily experiencing physical death. From these interviews several consistent experiences were found to have been described repeatedly. Among these experiences was direct contact with relatives and close friends known by the person during the near-death experience. Dr. Moody's work was acclaimed by many people, and numerous scientific studies by others followed his initial findings. Later, Dr. Moody wrote the book *Reunions*, in which he described how to facilitate dialogue between living people and deceased people (1993). This work was not generally greeted with universal acceptance, and his peers often thought this concept was too peculiar (Moody, 1995). In a lecture on the subject, Dr. Moody described how to facilitate this process, and I made the decision to build a "psychomanteum" according to his design (Moody, 1993). I wanted to use this process with clients who had substantial, unresolved issues with people who were deceased. To my delight it has worked almost every time!

Induced communication with people who have died is usually so compelling that clients are stunned by the perceived reality of the experience. This process is markedly different from most gravesite visitations during which a person expresses thoughts to the deceased person and no one is perceived to be responding. Gravesite expressions can be valuable because they allow people to express unresolved emotions. The use of an accomplished medium who serves as a channel for communication between the living and the dead is one means to accomplish communication. However, this method relies on a third party who may or may not be accurate. Whereas induced communication with deceased people provides direct communication between the living client and the deceased person that is consistently achievable and more difficult for the client to discredit. The therapist plays the role of organizing the event and supporting the communication between both parties, not the role of the medium.

Inducing after-death communication is fraught with political and religious challenges and is not for everyone. A therapist must know the client's religious/spiritual orientation as well as the client's openness to this approach. Presenting this approach may offend a client, and the therapist risks the loss of credibility and/or trust. Once the therapist determines that inducing after-death communication is appropriate, the procedure can be attempted. About half the world's population believes in dialogue with deceased people, but it is generally not acceptable in the U.S. population. Regardless of diverse reactions to this procedure, my only concern is whether it will provide a beneficial therapeutic outcome for clients. When used appropriately, the response to this approach has been a resounding "yes" to this question.

Dr. Moody used a psychomanteum based on Plato's "oracle of the dead" to conduct dialogue with deceased people (Moody, 1993, pp. 65–82). In 1997, I found that a modification of the psychomentuim that includes the ETT® light device was far more effective than other means of facilitation due to the ETT® method's capacity to process emotions during the experience. Through the ETT® method, specific variations of subjective experience were observed in clients during the after-death communication that include the following:

- receiving the thoughts of the deceased person's communication
- clients audibly hearing the deceased person's voice and unique intonations
- visibly seeing the deceased person's messages in the light from the ETT® device
- visibly seeing the deceased person's messages through spontaneous and changing internal visual imagery
- somatically feeling the presence of the deceased person's body within the client's own body that communicates messages to the client
- any combination of the aforementioned means for after-death persons communicating with the client

While the purpose of these communications is to achieve various therapeutic goals as a result of these exchanges, these dialogues themselves are likely to affect some aspect of the client's religious or spiritual perspective. For some people the communication validates viewpoints already held by the client. Other people experience surprise due to the realness of the communication, and it may initiate a spiritual quest for understanding. Some people develop a comfort about death after this communication. In almost every case in which induced after-death communication through ETT® was used, significant therapeutic gains were achieved.

SARA'S CASE

Sara recalled that she was repeatedly anally raped by her grandfather when she was four and five years old. This trauma was verified by medical examination years later. Throughout Sara's life this trauma produced complicated psychological dysfunction for which she had sought relief through years of psychotherapy and spiritual quests. However, the relationship and sexual abuse remained unresolved. Sara was open to an induced death communication session to pursue resolution. During the induced after-death session Sara found her grandfather to be receptive and willing to answer all her questions. Of course, it was an emotional session for her. However, the communication resulted in a level of resolution that all the years of psychotherapy and religious quests had not achieved.

DON'S CASE

Don originally had a six-figure income, a wife, and two children, all of whom were doing fine. Then Don received two driving while intoxicated charges and ended up in prison for two years. His wife divorced him, and he lost custody of his children. I discovered that Don never went to bars or did much of the activity associated with alcoholics. It turned out that Don felt intense anxiety so often that he drank alcohol to calm himself, especially when driving. When we pursued the source of his anxiety, the following trauma emerged:

> I always looked up to my older brother and wanted to be like him. One day, when I was eighteen years old, my older brother was driving when he had a terrible wreck. My brother died, and I was trapped under his dead body for an hour before the police and paramedics got us out! I have had panic attacks every since that wreck. So I drank alcohol to calm myself, especially when driving was about to take place.

We induced after-death communication between Don and his deceased brother. This communication appeared to be a profound interaction that was very emotional and finally began to resolve his traumatic grief. Don reported that he had seen his brother again after this session and completed his dialogue with him.

There are far more details involved in facilitating these induced after-death communications sessions. Dr. Moody described how to prepare a person for this communication. I conduct the session as a facilitator who structures and guides the dialogue between the person and the deceased person while providing support. Follow-up is also important. More detail about the facilitation process would be better taught in person.

Direct contact with deceased entities is not automatically a constructive experience. These events can be very distressing and are still a part of a therapy session and must be facilitated toward a beneficial end. When they are facilitated well, benefits can be very powerful.

SPIRITUAL WISDOM

Once rapport is built and clients have processed their psychological defenses, a spiritual wisdom often emerges during ETT® processes. The information that emerges often comes with a certainty and clarity that is not characteristic of the client's usual verbalization. The information is relevant and almost always congruent with what the therapist would view as constructive cognition. It is as if all the client's psychological defenses have been penetrated and his/her deepest inner self is verbalizing, based on listening to a higher wisdom. The client's voice tone is confident, and the words uttered are spontaneous, such that is seems obvious that the client is speaking absolute truth. The information is, of course, the answer to whatever the therapeutic issue is at the time. These messages are almost all unsolicited initially.

This spiritual wisdom may be understood by the client to come through a variety of spiritual vehicles, perhaps depending on a personal belief system or in some cases beyond a current belief system. The following are some of the spiritual vehicles to which clients have attributed their source of spiritual wisdom:

- the inner self
- angels
- spiritual guides
- deceased loved ones
- God
- inner child
- Jesus
- the light
- a spiritual leader of some type

A question one must ask is how do we know this "spiritual wisdom" is not a hallucination or a psychotic state? The main criteria used to determine this is whether the wisdom acquired is therapeutically relevant, valuable, and useful. Leaders within the field of psychology, such as Sigmund Freud and Albert Ellis, have long expressed the opinion that religion is a hallucination or irrational thinking. However, it is possible that when authentic spiritual wisdom does emerge from clients, we need to be open enough to recognize it, support it, and allow the client's spiritual potential to flourish, particularly when it aids the client's therapeutic goals. However, some clients might tend to allow their egos to attach to this higher wisdom in such a way that they see themselves as special or superior to others due to their connection to this spiritual vehicle. If that occurs, the client must be encouraged to place the spiritual wisdom into a more beneficial perspective.

Sometimes the spiritual vehicle for this wisdom appears in a visual form. One woman, who was spiritual, but not religious, spontaneously reported the following during viewing the ETT® light stimulation: "I think I see something moving in the light.... It looks like wings? I think it looks like an angel!" Then I told her to ask the angel if it had a message for her. It did, and the ensuing dialogue produced a rich wisdom that led her to the resolution of her issue.

Spiritual wisdom arrives in various forms. Many people receive messages in the form of thoughts that are perceived as thoughts that are not their own. In other cases, clients literally hear messages in the form of voices that are not pathological voices (described in detail in Chapter 6).

Sometimes a person simply penetrates psychological defenses to discover his/her authentic inner self. This discovery may appear so different from a previously learned way of thinking that it may seem ego alien at first. However, more often it occurs as a recognition of oneself, and previous perspectives may be identified as inauthentic.

SPIRITUAL "FLYING"

One of the eight siddhis is the capacity to fly. I have never seen or heard of an ETT® client physically flying. However, there is a long history of spiritual people levitating. The Christian saint Teresa of Avila was reported to have levitated many times in the presence of many observers (du Boulay, 1991, pp. 66–68). Hindu and Buddhist accounts are replete with reports of levitation. Participants in transcendental meditation have claimed to have achieved levitation. However, ETT® clients frequently report feeling lighter as well as feeling as if they were "floating." While these subjective self-perceptions are frequent and quite profound, so far I have not observed anyone physically leave the ground.

However, there is another phenomenon that could be construed as "flying." Many people describe having out-of-body experiences as a result of a shock (Alvardo, 1986; Noyes & Kletti, 1976, pp. 19–27). Out-of-body perceptions have also been consistently produced by researchers stimulating certain portions of the brain (Blanke, Ortigue, Landis & Seech, 2002). A voluntary form of out-of-body experience is referred to as astral travel. There has been other scientific research on astral travel (Smith & Messier, 2015; Braithwaite et al., 2013, pp. 793–805). This idea of flying is more related to "astral travel," which is a form of out-of-body experience that is purposely induced without the necessity of a shock. Robert Monroe's books about astral travel encouraged this form of spiritual activity (Monroe, 1977). The New Age religion Eckenkar is a religious orientation in which astral travel is a central point of their philosophy. Shamans are well-known to purportedly travel astrally for healing purposes. The concept of traveling the "astral plane" is not new and has been reported in many religions. ETT® clients have reported astral travel as a consequence of ETT®, although it is not a common phenomenon via ETT®.

The main reason astral travel is included as a spiritual gift is that it can occur as a result of ETT® processes in people who are educationally unprepared for it. In this case, astral travel can be quite frightening. People might think that they were near death during the experience or that they were having experiences of a psychotic episode, not to mention the havoc it might wreak on a person's religious or philosophical belief system. The fact is that astral travel is known cross-culturally and historically.

Even though this skill of astral travel may be fascinating to some people and quite compelling as a spiritual gift to others, one must question the nature of this gift. Why does one have this gift and what is it for? What is its purpose along one's spiritual path? Some people believe that astral travel can take one closer to God. Astral travel can be very attractive to the ego, and people have been known to see themselves as special or superior in spiritual evolution because of having developed this skill. This self-perception can contaminate further spiritual growth. If one's therapeutic goals are enhanced by astral travel, it can be helpful. More importantly the benefit of integrating this spiritual gift into functions of daily life can be rewarding.

In 1976, I had been meditating for years and had developed skills in altering states of consciousness. I had been in an atheist phase of my spiritual development for two years. Then I began reading Robert Monroe's book, *Journeys Out of the Body* (1971). On April 30, 1976, I had my first experience of voluntary astral travel. I did it again about a month later. These experiences ended my atheism and sent me on a spiritual quest for years to come. I knew the reality of a spiritual world through direct experiences but had not yet developed a specific spiritual philosophy. After this experience, I no longer focused on this skill, but the experience guided my spiritual direction.

Astral travel may be the mechanism for the skill of clairvoyance or remote viewing. This form of extrasensory perception involves the ability to acquire visual information about a person, object, or physical event at a different location outside of the range of human vision (Crookall, 1972). Scientific studies on remote viewing have found mixed results about its accuracy (Eliminate Kammann, 1978; Puthoff, 1996; Puthoff & Targ, 1976). In one study, the unique brain activity during remote viewing has been documented (Persinger et al., 2002).

TELEPATHY

One form of extrasensory perception is telepathy or radical empathy. This spiritual gift concerns the ability to detect accurately the thoughts and/or emotions of another person. Telepathy involves empathy but empathy is not often telepathic. Scientific research offers mixed findings on this subject.

A few ETT® clients have reported the development of telepathic skills, and in at least two cases clients exhibited this skill with me on repeated occasions. These clients had experienced a spiritual awakening during ETT® sessions. They had exhibited precognition as well. Even with highly skilled telepaths a person's own thoughts can contaminate the accuracy of the information received. Therefore, spiritual intention and potential contaminants must be evaluated from time to time.

It is important to understand the process of empathy to appreciate the nature of telepathy. Empathy can become dysfunctional in several ways. Some people lack development of empathy in autism, narcissism, anti-social personality disorder, and other conditions (Decety & Moriguchi, 2007, p. 22). However, role reversal attachment patterns involve excessive or inappropriate empathy. In this case, people tend to (1) take on the distress of worry, burden, sleeplessness, (2) experience the actual symptoms of the people with whom they are empathizing, and (3) inappropriately rescue others. These characteristics can become a person's identity as a caregiver, which can further provoke distress. In many cases, the caregiver loses awareness of his or her authentic identity.

Neuroimaging research on brain mechanisms involved in the experience of empathy reveal a very complex process. It is complicated because the person empathizing with another person undergoes brain changes that match the brain changes taking place in the other person. Therefore, knowing what the empathic person's brain is doing depends on knowing what the observed person's brain is doing. In one study, people empathizing with someone who had a physical pain that the empathizer had never experienced, elicited brain activity in the brain of the empathizer that matched the pain experience of the other person (Decety, Lamm, & Melzoff, 2009, pp. 362–376). Nonetheless, there are a few basic brain mechanisms that make various aspects of empathy possible.

One mechanism by which interpersonal influence is believed to occur is through mirror neurons. Research in animals has shown that mirror neurons fire both when an animal acts and when an animal observes the same action performed by another animal, or "mirrors" the behavior of another. Research with humans suggests that mirror neurons exist in the inferior frontal cortex and superior parietal lobe (Iacoboni et al., 1999, pp. 2526–2528). Eye-tracking measures in human infants suggest that the mirror neuron system develops before twelve months of age and helps infants understand other people's actions (Falck-Yetter & Hofsten, 2006, pp. 878–879). The mirror neuron system has been shown to play a role in the expression of empathy for other people's emotions (Carr, Iacoboni, & Dubeau, 2002, pp. 5497–5502). By watching another person, mirror neurons make it possible for the observer to actually experience and directly understand another person's experience in the observer's own body. The observer's understanding of another person is a direct experience involving the same neural processes as the observed person (Fadiga et al., 1996). It is actually an entire system of mirror neurons, not a single neuron that is responsible for this mechanism.

The experience of empathy in the brain consists of three phases: (1) affective arousal, (2) emotional understanding, and (3) emotional regulation:

- Affective arousal in empathy involves
  A. The amygdala, which alerts the brain and stimulates emotional reactions.
  B. The hypothalamus, which integrates information from different parts of the brain.
  C. The orbitofrontal cortex, which processes emotion and decision making.
- Emotional understanding in empathy relies on awareness about how one differentiates oneself from others and involves
  A. The medial prefrontal cortex, which interfaces between cognition and emotion.
  B. The ventro medial prefrontal cortex, which is the central emotional processing area.
  C. The temperoparietal junction, which identifies self versus other.
- Emotional regulation in empathy involves
  A. The orbitofrontal cortex, which is involved in decision making.

B. The medial prefrontal cortex, which is the interface between cognition and affect.
C. The dorsolateral prefrontal cortex, which executes executive control of affect.

The three brain mechanisms involved in emotional regulation connect to several subcortical limbic structures (Decety, 2011, pp. 92–108).

The first phase in the empathy sequence concerns emotional arousal. When this occurs in spontaneity that escalates to high intensity and is expressed dramatically, it may be dysfunctional in people. This heightened automatic response suggests that the person is taking in too much of the other person's experience, as if it is his or her own. It may indicate a loss of control of emotion by the listener, and while it is clear that the listener is attuning to the other person the emotional reaction may not be helpful. However, a neutral response with no affective arousal does not tend to be understood as empathy by the recipient.

The second phase of the empathic response concerns emotional understanding. This phase combines cognitive understanding with emotional sensitivity to the client. Telepathy is an extension of empathy.

The third phase is primarily focused upon the empathizer. Subsequent to phase one and two, what emotion is the empathizer left with? If one becomes too emotionally aroused by listening to another, there is a greater chance of possessing these emotions as one's own. If and when this occurs, how effectively will this listener regulate his/her own emotions? However, the third phase is largely dependent upon how effectively people handle phase one and two. Evidence of dysfunction in phase three may occur as (1) hyperarousal subsequent to an encounter, (2) night dreams about others, (3) worry or obsessive thinking about others, and (4) somatic symptoms subsequent to encounters. An ongoing experience of feeling burdened and/or experiencing a loss of energy suggests an inability to regulate emotions acquired from listening to other people.

A major problem that tends to emerge with the gift of telepathy is the characteristic difficulty most telepaths have with establishing boundaries between themselves and others. These highly sensitive people can become bombarded with other people's thoughts, feelings, and physical experiences, resulting in continual overwhelm for the telepath. These empaths are usually tormented with other's issues and may lose contact with their authentic selves in the process. I have worked with many empaths who had telepathic skills but were constantly overwhelmed with other people's distress.

For optimal functioning, a person needs the ability to turn on—and off—telepathic abilities when it is in his or her best interest. Unfortunately, I have found this skill to be the exception among empaths. Even if one understands the logic of appropriate boundaries, cognitive awareness often does little to change the experiential problem of allowing too much information into one's system. Telepathic skills are often rooted in empathy and one's care-taking attributes—attributes which people often treasure and for which they have been rewarded by other people's positive recognition.

While counseling clients with boundary issues, I discovered a range of very specific wavelengths of light within the red-orange frequency that can reverse this nondifferentiating function to create boundaries between the self and others. It is first necessary for the person to discharge accumulated stimulation. Then it is helpful to build personal boundaries. This process can restore and protect the telepath.

SPIRITUAL HEALING

Tom's case

Tom came into a session appearing visibly shaken. He reported that he had gone camping with a male friend. They enjoyed hiking and fishing together. Then one evening Tom's friend severely injured his arm and was in intense physical pain. Tom spontaneously placed his hands on the injury and healed the injury within a half an hour. While the friend was better, Tom was in shock about the experience. Tom possessed no experience in healing anyone at any time before. Tom entered my office a few days after the healing. All Tom knew about that type of healing was from biblical stories. This event caused Tom distress because he did not consider himself that religious, and he feared that he tapped into a real ability that he did not identify with.

He had no way of understanding or explaining the event and needed to talk about it. After listening to Tom, assuring him that it was okay, and providing him with scientific research about energetic healing, Tom appeared more relaxed and accepting of the event.

The ability to heal others by means of spiritual healing, energy healing, psychic healing, or various other terms refers to the use of an unseen force that passes from one person to another. This category of methods has a long history, even to pre-civilized society. It is known in virtually every major religion as well as Shamanistic approaches throughout the world. Instances of spiritual healing play a significant role in the recorded activities of Jesus. Currently, an impressive amount of scientific research both verifies its existence and has measured its effectiveness (Benor, 1992, 2001).

Linnie Thomas has documented sixty-six different types of energy medicine. She divides them into four categories (1) Eastern, (2) Western, (3) Spiritual, and (4) Shamanic (2010). The following is a list of some of the more popular and more documented methods:

Acupressure	Resonance Repatterning
Acupuncture	Shen Therapy
Emotional Freedom Technique	Therapeutic Touch
Qi gong	Spiritual Response Therapy
Reiki	Theta Healing
Thought Field Therapy	The Four Winds
Touch for Health	Reconnective Healing
Barbara Brennan School for Healing	Matrix Energetics
Body Talk System	Eden Energy Work
Core Energetics	Pranic Healing
Quantum Touch	Ernest Holmes Science of Mind

These types of healing have become popular within the last few decades and the number of methods has grown exponentially. There is substantial scientific research to validate some of these methods (Heidt, 1981; Keller, 1986; Quinn, 1988; Wirth, 1990). Most of these methods possess a theory about how energy is configured in and around a person, while some are dependent on the Chinese energy model, for example. Each system tends to claim the virtues of its own over others, but very few advocate the common ground among these models. In ETT® work, a gateway to a spontaneous spiritual awakening tends to occur and from that awakening extended human capacities or spiritual gifts may arise. If the healing ability emerges, it is often beyond a certain formula as epitomized by these methods. This is not advocating superiority over these formula methods, but simply that these ETT® gifts occur without a method. However, some people seek an accepted method such as Reiki to be the form through which to exercise their gifts. Nonetheless, this gift is not the goal of spiritual development, but instead a by-product that may enhance a person's spiritual journey. There is a strong tendency for people to become enamored with the power that the ability to heal gives them and to think of themselves as special due to this gift. In addition, the skill of healing can become a political problem when dealing with conventional medical personnel or people of certain religions.

MY HEALING JOURNEY

I have discovered that there is a distinct difference between energetic formula methods that anyone can learn and spiritual healing that emerges from a spiritual awakening. At one point I read a book on how to use Thought Field Therapy that involved physically tapping certain acupuncture meridians. After using this method for awhile, I accidentally tapped the wrong points on one occasion, and surprisingly it still worked. Clearly, I could heal certain emotions regardless of where, or if, I touched a person. I concluded that the power of healing was within my spiritual state of mind. Although I never attended another energy medicine training session, I actively pursued the development of my spirituality.

Some healers have a reputation that precedes them: the Christian healers, Father De Oreo, Frances McNutt, and the Brazilian healer John of God, and countless others. While no healer is one hundred percent successful, some are more successful than others. I have observed that people seem to have three types of responses to healers: (1) they are excited or amazed, (2) they are guardedly optimistic, or (3) they assume it is all fraudulent. I have conducted successful healings of many people directly in front of an audience, and it appears that the experience simply doesn't register as a fact to many people in spite of the evidence before their eyes. I recommend that direct factual experience be the consumer's guide to the skill of a healer. For example, I had two clients with completely positive expectations who went to Brazil to see John of God. One person had cancer and was told he was completely healed of it, but he came back to the United States where doctors told him that not only was the cancer still present but that it had metastasized. Another person allowed John of God to conduct surgery on her knee. When she returned to the United States it was worse, and the severe infection from the surgery took months to heal. Until I see direct successful evidence of the work of John of God, his work remains questionable for me. While belief in the healer is a factor, it has not been a prerequisite for me. The vast majority of people for whom I have facilitated healing did not have a belief in me, the process, or even in God on some occasions.

In the early 1980s, I took a course in Shen therapy that introduced me to the concept of energy medicine. Although I soon adapted this method with modifications of my own, I had not really experienced the spiritual gift of healing. Then in 1984, I met two of the well-known Russian healers, Victor Krivorotov in Tblisi and Djuna Davidashvilli in Moscow. During the flight back to the United States, I had a spontaneous experience of healing another person without even touching her. I had an authentic intention that dominated my being during the experience. I was as surprised as anyone! From that point on I was able to facilitate healing of a wide range of aches, pains, and emotional distress. I gradually integrated this skill into the professional counseling skills that predated this awakening.

JENNIFER'S CASE

In 1987, Jennifer was referred to me. She presented with seven to eight grand mal seizures per day, multiple sites of chronic physical pain, and complete blindness since her birth. During the first session, as a sequence of symptoms leading to a seizure emerged, I was able to stop the seizure by energetic means before it became full blown. This accomplishment never happened before or after that session because I never had another seizure client. Eventually, the number of seizures Jennifer was experiencing was reduced from eight per day to one per month. Next, we proceeded to eliminate her physical pain until it was permanently erased after a few weeks. Then, we finally had a session in which she asked if I could restore her vision.

It turned out that Jennifer was born prematurely as a result of a car accident that her mother was in. She appeared to regress to the event, and we processed this trauma to conclusion. Then as I worked on her eyes energetically, her vision gradually returned. There were witnesses, including her husband. I encouraged her to acquire an optometric evaluation, but she refused. Jennifer did not want to deal with the notoriety or skepticism involving the reversal of her blindness. She chose to continue to live the lifestyle of a blind person even though she could now see. However, the greatest impact seemed to be on me as the facilitator. This event dismantled my belief system and required an adjustment about possibilities.

Since that time my use of energy work has evolved. I have been the subject of scientific experiments where my brain was wired during an experience of healing others in an attempt to understand what was happening. In 2003, I was selected along with Barbara Brennan and John Pierokos to be in a scientific study about the internal nature of the healing experience. The author attempted to acquire the most advanced healers for this study. The results have since been published in the *International Journal of Healing and Caring, online* (Zeiders, 2003). At the time I called my method Confluent Somatic Therapy. However, I have focused more upon facilitating spiritual awakening since then.

LUCY'S CASE

Lucy was a fifty-eight year old married woman who was referred to me by a colleague in another state. At one point she was described as the most severely depressed patient in the history of a hospital that specialized in depression. At the time of the session described below, her husband had been diagnosed with a form of dementia. Lucy was experiencing physical pain at multiple sites in her body and was severely depressed. I had met with Lucy in person previously but after that our work was limited to energy medicine and contemplative approaches by telephone because we were two thousand miles apart. Lucy was an atheist prior to our work. In this case, I used energy emanation while in a unity state of mind. The following is Lucy's description of our session:

> The purist of white light bathed me with its brightness, intensity, and radiant warmth today during an incredible session with Dr. Vazquez. Standing with my eyes closed, my feeling of being weighted down eased as I began to feel weightless. My bodily pain dissipated out into the universe. It was as if I were floating on thin air. I felt light and airy. My eyes were closed, I experienced a horizontal line of the brightest light I had ever seen shoot across my visual field.... It was like a wide bolt of lightning, only horizontal from left to right ... a light of the purist pearl essence or opal white essence surrounded my whole body. This pure white light spun a cocoon around me. From my head down to my feet this gossamer blanket warmed my entire body. It made me feel protected and sage. Every fiber of my body heated to the point of releasing moisture, not perspiration but liquid healing energy. My tissues, muscles, bones, nerves, and soul, everything that makes us who we are, was caressed with pulsating warmth and healing today. I felt God's hands on me, his light, his compassion, his love. He actually touched me. I am overwhelmed by this experience today. I am deeply moved. This is the light I saw and felt when I had my near death experience at age 17. I experienced today that same feeling of being at peace and the embracing love of God and creation as I felt in a previous session. At this very moment I feel complete, at ease and in harmony. What a glorious feeling! My limited ability of expression to describe it is feeble at best. The emotional experience defies my description. Every fiber of my being remembers it, though. All I know is that I will do as my good and wise Dr. Vazquez has asked me to do and that is to meditate every day for 20 to 30 minutes (2 times a day if possible and preferably in the morning) on this experience and never forget it. God did touch me today. That's what I felt and that's what came from my lips. I heard my voice say it. That realization made me weak.... What an incredible release and powerful personal revelation. I need to focus on this experience and not on whether I am worthy of it. It happened today and it happened to me. It's not for me to question why, rather that I must accept it and build on it. I know not where this path is taking me. The light will shine on this path that I am on. I must try to continue to be willing to see it and trust in it. With Dr. Vazquez' wisdom, guidance, and compassion, I am more hopeful than ever that I will finally find my way in this life and all that lies ahead and beyond here and the blue horizon.

This session was one of many in which not only the psychological and physical distress was changed, but a spiritual state of extreme wellbeing was facilitated. These effects lasted for days, and its impact continues to exist for seven years now.

I have developed ethical concerns about these energy medicine techniques. This new field is not ethically regulated and virtually anyone can claim to be a healer. I submitted an article on ethical issues concerning energy medicine that was published by The International Society for Energy Medicine and Subtle Energies in 2001 (pp. 15–18). A few years later I received a phone call from a researcher asking me if I knew of any other published articles on the ethics of energy medicine. I said no. She informed me that my article was only one of two that she could find on ethics in energy medicine. Healers with no professional training can get in over their heads in either medicine or psychology. While it is wonderful to have these healing options, the field needs further development.

Nonetheless, energetic or spiritual healing can be a consequence of ETT® work. When viewed within the context of a spiritual path, it can serve to deepen and direct a person's spiritual inclination.

The role of spiritual gifts and/or extended human capacities has long been debated. Religions are divided among themselves about these matters, and scientists often scoff at the mention of such abilities while demanding scientific proof. Unfortunately, the newly gifted person arrives with these abilities and can rarely handle the adjustment appropriately. A plethora of issues greet the person often just after a spiritual awakening, sometimes leading the person to regret ever developing the abilities. However, the use of most of these abilities can help others in some way. Therefore, the spiritual psychotherapist is left with multiple challenges to help these gifted people. First, validation of legitimate spiritual gifts is important. Then teaching the client how to manage public relations issues is important because judgment by skeptics can be tormenting. For those who are gifted, a willingness to be a subject for scientific study might be helpful for others who may be in a similar situation; however, a person should be aware that no matter how good a scientific study may be it can always be discredited. Most importantly, it is important to help clients use their extended capacities to operate in conjunction with their authentic spiritual direction. For each person who misuses gifts for egoic gains there will be victims, and this could create more criticism for those with spiritual gifts who are already challenged by adjustment issues. Psychotherapists should at least help these clients to do no harm. If clients with gifts are led to use these gifts optimally, it may contribute to the spiritual evolution of the human species.

I expect skepticism and controversy when people read this chapter because many of the experiences of clients sound too unusual to be true. I am sure that therapists who have been working with clients for many years have never seen or heard of these experiences in their clientele, nor have many therapists experienced these things personally. However, in most cases these therapists have not experienced ETT®, so their assessment has been made without a comparable experience. It is our job to provide empathy and validation for people, unless we have confirmed evidence that the information is false. People who have unusual authentic experiences need to be believed and supported, whether therapists have had those experiences or not. In regard to extended human abilities, clients who nurture and develop these skills may produce ways to help and advance the human condition even more than those who lack those abilities. This author is not reporting these experiences of extended capacities to promote his own fantasy, but rather because these are exactly what these clients reported. To fail to report and explore them would be to deny the truth. However, reports in this sphere can be so different that it is important for therapists to have a map and guiding principles for this territory. It is hoped that this book will serve to humanely lead people through this territory.

CHAPTER 9 SUMMARY

This chapter begins by introducing the unfamiliar phenomena that occur when an authentic spiritual awakening produces extended human abilities or "spiritual-gifts." There is generally a lack of preparation for these abilities even in many spiritual practices. Within most major religions worldwide, the issue of extended human abilities is controversial, with certain faiths selecting a position against them and others viewing them as signs of higher spirituality. A case study illustrates this controversy. Then ethical positions concerning how to appropriately utilize these gifts are described. Specific documentation and description of the range of these types of gifts are listed.

Specific extended human capacities are described and include synchronicity and transcendent relationships with nature. Then a description of how the physical world of material things and the spirit world interact in many cultures is explained. Experiences specifically of perceived oneness or unity are noted.

The chapter explores the theoretical concepts of each spiritual gift as well as the scientific research about each gift. Next, therapeutic approaches to support, guide, and produce these abilities are surveyed. Glossolalia or "speaking in tongues" is a known phenomenon cross-culturally, and brain research on this phenomenon is described. Then three case studies in which glossolalia occurred were described.

The phenomenon of prophecy or precognition was described and scientific research findings were provided. Precautions and benefits were explained.

The purposeful facilitation of after-death communication was described. Scientific research on this was identified. A process by which ETT® can produce after-death communication was identified along with a description of the various ways in which it manifests. Then two case studies of after-death communication were described.

The capacity to access "spiritual" wisdom was explored. The ability to experience astral travel was recognized. The skill of telepathy was explored. The ability to conduct spiritual healing was thoroughly examined. Then a case study of this type of healing illustrated its outcome. All of these extended abilities were described with the inclusion of the related scientific research about them.

Appendix A

Partner Spiritual Differences Questionnaire

This questionnaire is designed to help you understand the differences that you have with your partner on matters of spirituality/religion. The term "spiritual viewpoint" is defined as the philosophy, values, and/or beliefs a person holds in matters concerning religion, spirituality, or issues regarding relationships to God. It is recommended that before responding to the questionnaire, one should describe in writing the major principles of one's religious/spiritual point of view in order to prepare to answer the questions. Please turn in a written summary of your spiritual viewpoint along with this questionnaire. If there are any questions that are not appropriate to your relationship situation, please write in "NA" (not applicable) instead of circling one of the letters. Otherwise, please circle the letter that best fits your answer.

Date_______________
Name____
DOB_________________________ Sex_______________________
Home Phone___________________ Business Phone_______________
Street Address____
City, State, Zip____

Please circle the letter that best corresponds to your experiences with each of the following questions:

1. What is your significant other's response to your spiritual position?
   A. Actively opposes your spiritual viewpoint
   B. Disagrees with it, but continues to respect your view

   C. Neutral
   D. Supports your spiritual viewpoint although he/she may not totally agree with your spiritual viewpoint
   E. Actively supports and agrees with your spiritual viewpoint
2. What role does your church/spiritual activity play in your daily/weekly priority of activities?
   A. Extremely important (commitment to the level of primary identity and/or vocation such as minister/priest)
   B. Very important (totally committed, with active religious participation that dominates your lifestyle)
   C. Important (deeply felt belief that does not dominate your lifestyle)
   D. Minimal (definite belief but does not include significant active participation in spiritual/religious ritual or activities)
   E. Not important
3. Ideally, to what degree do you prefer that your significant other is in agreement with you about your spiritual viewpoint?
   A. Total agreement—100%
   B. Largely in agreement of most beliefs—75%
   C. We should have some agreement, but it is okay to have some disagreements—50%
   D. It is okay if there is a lot of disagreement as long as we can respect each other—25%
   E. It does not matter if we are in total disagreement—0%
4. How important is it for you to have support for your spiritual viewpoint at this time?
   A. Very important
   B. Important
   C. Somewhat important
   D. Very little importance
   E. Not important
5. If your spiritual viewpoint is presently unclear and is in the process of developing, how important is it for your spiritual search/quest to be supported at this time?
   A. Very important
   B. Important
   C. Somewhat important
   D. Very little importance
   E. Not important

How important is your spiritual viewpoint to your relationship with the following people?

		SOMEWHAT	NOT	
	IMPORTANT	IMPORTANT	IMPORTANT	
6.	A	B	C	Spouse or Partner
7.	A	B	C	Parent/Parents
8.	A	B	C	Siblings
9.	A	B	C	Friends
10.	A	B	C	Coworkers
11.	A	B	C	Children

12. How does agreement in spiritual viewpoint affect issues of finances with your significant other?
    A. A great amount
    B. Significantly
    C. Very little
    D. Not at all
13. How does agreement in spiritual viewpoint with your significant other affect issues in the realm of affection?
    A. A great amount
    B. Significantly
    C. Very little
    D. Not at all
14. How does agreement in spiritual viewpoint with your significant other affect issues in the realm of sex and intimacy?
    A. A great amount
    B. Significantly
    C. Very little
    D. Not at all
15. How does agreement in spiritual viewpoint with your significant other affect issues in the realm of lifestyle (pace of life, nutrition, exercise, types of activities)?
    A. A great amount
    B. Significantly
    C. Very little
    D. Not at all

16. How does agreement in spiritual viewpoint with your significant other affect issues related to your children?
    A. A great amount
    B. Significantly
    C. Very little
    D. Not at all
17. How does agreement in spiritual viewpoint with your significant other affect issues related to his/her children?
    A. A great amount
    B. Significantly
    C. Very little
    D. Not at all
18. How does agreement in spiritual viewpoint with your significant other affect issues related your parents?
    A. A great amount
    B. Significantly
    C. Very little
    D. Not at all
19. How does agreement in spiritual viewpoint with your significant other affect issues related to your significant other's parent or parents?
    A. A great amount
    B. Significantly
    C. Very little
    D. Not at all
20. How does agreement in spiritual viewpoint with your significant other affect issues related to your work situation?
    A. A great amount
    B. Significantly
    C. Very little
    D. Not at all
21. Has disagreement about spiritual viewpoint contributed to violence or physical abuse with your partner?
    A. Often
    B. Occasionally
    C. Once
    D. Violence threatened but has not occurred
    E. Never occurs or threatened
22. Have emotional arguments or verbal abuse occurred between you and your partner about the issues of spiritual viewpoint?
    A. Often
    B. Occasionally
    C. Once

   D. Close to hostile emotions or verbal abuse but has not yet reached that level
   E. Never occurs
23. How does agreement in spiritual viewpoint with your significant other affect issues related to your partner's work situation?
   A. A great amount
   B. Significantly
   C. Very little
   D. Not at all
24. How much have you changed your spiritual viewpoint since the relationship with your significant other began?
   A. A great amount
   B. Significantly
   C. Very little
   D. Not at all
25. How much has your significant other changed his/her spiritual viewpoint since the relationship with you began?
   A. A great amount
   B. Significantly
   C. Very little
   D. Not at all
26. How unwilling is your partner to participate jointly in your religious or spiritual activities (worship, rituals) with you?
   A. Claims that he/she will never participate
   B. Has never yet participated
   C. Has seldom participated
   D. Often participates
   E. Always participates
27. How important is it that you feel free to express your spiritual viewpoints in your major relationships?
   A. Very important
   B. Important
   C. Somewhat important
   D. Very little importance
   E. Not important
28. How strongly do you perceive your need to be in control in your relationships?
   A. Extreme need to be in control
   B. Important need to be in control
   C. Normal/average need to be in control
   D. Minor/little need to be in control
   E. No need to be in control

29. How do you think your significant other would perceive your need to be in control in your relationships?
    A. Extreme need to be in control
    B. Important need to be in control
    C. Normal/average need to be in control
    D. Minor/little need to be in control
    E. No need to be in control
30. How strongly do you perceive your significant other's need to be in control in relationships?
    A. Extreme need to be in control
    B. Important need to be in control
    C. Normal/average need to be in control
    D. Minor/little need to be in control
    E. No need to be in control
31. How important is it to you that your partner participates jointly with you in your religious or spiritual activities (worship, rituals, practices)?
    A. Very important
    B. Important
    C. Somewhat important
    D. Very little importance
    E. Not important
32. Does the difference in spiritual viewpoint have the importance to break up your relationship with your significant other?
    A. Strongly likely
    B. Likely
    C. Unlikely
    D. Not at all

Given a discrepancy between your spiritual viewpoint and that of your significant other, to what degree do you feel the following emotions?

	STRONGLY	*SOMEWHAT*	*NONE*	
33.	A	B	C	Anger/Resentment
34.	A	B	C	Frustration
35.	A	B	C	Sadness
36.	A	B	C	Loneliness
37.	A	B	C	Rejection
38.	A	B	C	Guilt/Shame
39.	A	B	C	Powerless/Hopeless
40.	A	B	C	Futility
41.	A	B	C	Hope
42.	A	B	C	Joy
43.	A	B	C	Other (Please write in.)

Appendix B

Emotional Transformation Therapy™ International Association (ETTIA)

Emotional Transformation Therapy™ International Association's (ETTIA) mission is to promote global awareness of the rapid and permanent resolution of emotional distress that can be achieved through Emotional Transformation Therapy™ (ETT™) and to support its member practitioners with quality professional development, therapeutic tools, and access to ETT™ research.

ETT® is an attachment-based interpersonal method whose outcomes are radically amplified by using precise visual brain stimulation. The method was founded by Steven R. Vazquez, PhD, LPC-S, LMFT. There are hundreds of professional trained in ETT® in the U.S. and abroad.

ETTIA is a nonprofit organization eligible to receive tax free donations to help in the promotion and dissemination of the use of the ETT® method. If you would be interested in acquiring information about ETT® training, information can be found on the website at www.ettia.org. Your interest and questions are invited.

Lynda Williams, ETTIA Board President, 2016
www.ettia.org

Appendix C

Visual Ecology and Psychotherapy Research Foundation (VEP)

WHAT IS VISUAL ECOLOGY?

Visual Ecology is the individual's moment-to-moment interaction with light stimulation of the brain through the eyes.

What does Visual Ecology have to do with Psychotherapy?

Adjusting the precise light wavelengths and patterns of light entering an individual's eyes when an emotional state is active can alter emotions in such a way as to substantially enhance the experience of a psychotherapy session. The safe, systematic method of integrating such factors as brightness, wavelength, and position of the primary light source as part of the interpersonal process is known as Emotional Transformation Therapy® (ETT®).

The Visual Ecology and Psychotherapy Research Foundation (VEP) is a 501(c)(3) nonprofit organization established in 2013 to facilitate research on the scientific study of ETT® and its effects. Donations to the VEP Research Foundation are tax deductible.

The VEP Research Foundation is reaching out to identify research partners, including scientists, academic chairs, and research institutions to facilitate the study of ETT® with research designs robust enough to yield meaningful results.

Information about current and future research projects on ETT® can be found at www.vepfoundation.org and by emailing info@vepfoundation.org.

References

Ai, A. L., Ladd, K. L., Peterson, C. C., Cook, C. A., Shearer, M. M., and Koenig, H. A. (2010). Long-term adjustment after surviving open heart surgery: The effect of using prayer for coping replicated in a prospective design. *The Gerontologist*, 50, 798–809.

Al-Issa, I. (1978). Social and cultural aspects of hallucinations. *Psychological Bulletin*, 84, 578–587.

Almaas, A. H. (1984). *Essence: The Diamond Approach to Inner Realization*. York Beach, ME: Samuel Weiser.

Almaas, A. H. (1986). *Essence with the Elixir of Enlightenment.* York Beach, ME: Samuel Wiser.

Alvardo, C. (1986). Research on spontaneous out-of-body experiences: A review of modern developments, 1960-1984. In B. Shapin & L. Coly (eds). *Current Trends in Psi Research: Proceedings of an International Conference Held in New Orleans, Louisiana, August 13–14, 1984*, Parapsychology Foundation.

American Psychiatric Association (2013). Diagnostic and Statistical Manual of Mental Disorders, 5th ed. DSM-5. Arlington, VA: American Psychiatric Publishing, 87-89.

Andrykowski, M. A., Brady, M. J., Henslee-Downey, P. J., (1994). Psychological factors predictive of survival after allogeneic bone marrow transplant for leukemia. *Psychosomatic Medicine*, 56, 432–439.

Angel, C. M. (2003). Repairing the harm, victims and restorative justice. *Utah Law Review*, 1, 15–42.

Angel, C. M. (2005). Effects of fact-to-fact restorative justice on victims of crime in four randomized controlled trials. *Journal of Experimental Criminology*, 1, 367–393.

Anketell, C., Dorahy, M. J., Shannon, M., Elder, R., Hamilton, G., Corry, M., MacSherry A, Curran D., O'Rawe B. (2010). An exploratory analysis of voice hearing in chronic PTSD: Potential associated mechanisms. *Journal of Trauma and Dissociation*, 11, 93–107.

Association for Spiritual, Ethical, and Religious Values in Counseling (2009).*Competencies for addressing spiritual and religious issues in counseling.* Retrieved from http://www.aservic.org/recources/spiritual-competencies/

Astin, J. A., Harkness, E., & Earnst, E. (2000). The efficacy of "distant healing": A systematic review. *Annals of Internal Medicine*, 132, 903–910.

Atwater, P. M. H. (2003). *The New Children and Near-Death Experiences*. Rochester, VT: Bear and Company.

Baethge, C., Baldessarini, R. J., Freudentha, K., Steeruwitz, A., Bauer, M, & Bschor, T. (2005). Hallucinations in bipolar disorder; characteristics and comparison to unipolar depression and schizophrenia. *Bipolar Disorders*, 7, 135–145.

Barker, R. B. (1968). *Ecological Psychology.* Stanford, CA: Stanford University Press.

Baron-Cohen, S., Johnson, D., Asher, J., Wheelwright, S., Fisher, S. E., Gregersen, P. K., Allison, C. (2013). Is synesthesia more common in autism? *Molecular Autism*, 4, 40.

Barrick, C., Taylor, D., & Correa, E. I. (2002). Color sensitivity and mood disorders. *Journal of Affective Disorders*, 68, 67–71.

Baylen, C. A., Rosenberg, H. (2006). A review of the acute subjective effects of MDMA/ecstasy. *Addiction*, 101, 033–047.

Benor, D. (1992). Lessons from spiritual healing research and practice. *Subtle Energies*, 3, 1, 73–88.

Benor, D. J. (2001). *Spiritual Healing: Scientific Validation of a Healing Revolution.* Southfield, MI: Vision Publications.

Berenblum, I. (1974). *Carcinogenesis as a biological problem*. Oxford: North-Holland Publishing Co.

Berrios, G. E. (1990). A theory of hallucinations: Auguste Tamburini. *History of Psychiatry*, 1, 145–50.

Blake, R. R. (2001). A primer on binocular rivalry including current controversies. *Brain and Mind*, 2(1), 5–38.

Blanke, O., Ortigue, S., Landis, T. & Seech, M. (2002). Stimulating illusory own-body perceptions. *Nature*, 419(6904), 269-70.

Bleiker, E. M., van der Ploeg, H. M., Hendriks, J. H., Ader, H. J. (1996). Personality factors and breast cancer development: A prospective longitudinal study. *Journal of the National Cancer Institute*, 88, 1478–1482.

Bleuler, E. (1950). *Dementia praecox or the group of schizophrenias.* New York: International Universities Press.

Blom, J. D. (2010). *A dictionary of hallucinations.* New York: Springer-Verlag.

Boguslaweki, M. (1980). Therapeutic touch: A facilitator of pain relief. *Topics in Clinical Nursing*, 2, 27–37.

Bono, G., McCullough, M. E., Root, L. M. (2007). Forgiveness, feeling connected to others, and well-being: two longitudinal studies. *Society for Personality and Social Psychology,* 34(2), 182–195.

Botkin, A. (2000). The induction of after death communications utilizing Eye Movement Desensitization and Reprocessing: A new discovery. *Journal of Near-Death Studies*, 18(3), 181–209.

Botkin, A. (2005). *Induced after death communication: A new therapy for healing grief and trauma.* Charlottesville, VA: Hampton Roads.

Botkin, A. (2013). Grief report: Psychotherapeutic outcomes reported by therapists trained in induced after-death communication. *Journal of Near-Death Studies*, 31(4), 1–11.

Braithwaite, J. J., Broglia, E., Bagshaw, A. P., & Wilkins, A. J. (2013). Evidence for elevated cortical hyperexcitability and its association with out-of-body experiences the non-clinical population: New findings from a pattern-glare task. *Cortex*, 49, 793–805.

Breiling, B. (1996). *Light Years Ahead.* Berkeley, CA: Celestial Arts, xix.

Brewin, C. R. & Patel, T. (2010). Auditory pseudohallucinations in United Kingdom war veterans and civilians with posttraumatic stress disorder. *Journal of Clinical Psychiatry*, 71, 419–425.

Brisch, K. H. (2002). *Treating attachment disorders: From theory to therapy.* New York: The Guilford Press.

Butow, P. N., Coates, A. S., Dunn, S. M. (1999). Psychosocial predictors of survival in metastatic melanoma. *Journal Clinical Oncology*, 17, 2256–2263.

Butow, P. N., Hiller, J. E., Price, M. A., Thackway, S. V., Kricker, A., & Tennant, C. C. (2000). Epidemiological evidence for a relationship between life events, coping style, and personality factors in the development of breast cancer. *J Psychosomatic Research*, 49, 169–181.

Byrd, R. C. (1988). Positive therapeutic effects of intercessory prayer in a coronary care unit population. *Southern Medical Journal*, 81, 826–829.

Canter, P. & Ernst, E. (2003). The cumulative effects of transcendental meditation on cognitive function: A systematic review of randomized controlled trials. *Wiener klinische Wochenschrift*, 115, 758–766.

Carr, L. M., Iacoboni, M. C., Dubeau, Mazziotta J. C., Lenzi G. L. (2002). Neural mechanisms of empathy in humans: A relay from neural systems for imitation to limbic areas. *Proceedings of the National Academy of Science USA*, 100, 5497–5502.

Carson, J. W., Keefe, F. J., Lynch T. R., et al. (2005). Loving-Kindness Meditation for chronic low back pain: Results from a pilot trial. *Journal of Holistic Nursing*, 23, 287–304.

Carson, J. W., Keefe, F. J., Lynch, T. R., Carson, K. M., Goli, V., Fraz, A. M., & Thorp, S. R. (2005). Loving kindness meditation for chronic low back pain: Results from a pilot trial. *Journal of Clinical Psychology*, 62, 373–386.

Carson, J. W., Keefe , F. J., Lynch T. R., Carson, K. M., Goli, V., Fras, A. M. & Thorp, S. R. (2005). Loving-kindness meditation for chronic low back pain: Results from a pilot trial. *Journal of Holistic Nursing*, 23(3), 287–304.

Carson, J., Carson, K., Gil, K., & Baucom, D. Mindfulness-based relationship enhancement. *Behavior Therapy*. 35, 471–494.

Carson, J., Carson, K., Gil, K., & Baucom, D. (in press). Mindfulness-based relationship enhancement. *Behavior Therapy.*

Cartledge, M. J., ed. (2006). "*Speaking in Tongues" Multidisciplinary Perspectives.* Paternoster. Waynesboro, GA: Paternoster Press.

Cashwell, C. S., Glosoff, H. L., & Hammond, C. (2010). Spiritual Bypass: A Preliminary Investigation. *Counseling and Values*, 54(2), 162–174.

Cashwell, C. S. & Young, J. S. (2011). *Integrating spirituality and religion into counseling: A guide to competent practice.* 2nd ed. Alexandria, VA: American Counseling Association.

Casteneda, C. (1998). *The Active Side of Infinity.* Hammersmith, London: Thorsons, 103–104.

Cohen, A. B., Malka, A., Rozin, P., & Cherfas, L. (2006). Religion and unforgivable offenses. *Journal of Personality*, 74, 85–117.

Cohen, R. S. (1998). *The love drug; marching to the beat of ecstasy.* New York: Haworth Press.

Cole, M. G., Dowson, L., Dendukrui, N., & Belzile, E. (2002). The prevalence and phenomenology of auditory hallucinations among elderly subjects attending an audiology clinic. *International Journal of Geriatric Psychiatry*, 17, 444–452.

Combs, A. (2002). *The Radiance of Being.* St. Paul, MN: Paragon House.

Cooperrider, D. L., Whinney, D., & Stavos, J. M. (2003). *Appreciative Inquiry Handbook.* San Francisco, CA: Berrett-Koehler.

Craig, D., Mirakhur, A., Hart, D. J., McIlroy, S. P., & Passmore, A. P. (2005). Across-sectional study of neuropsychiatric symptoms in 435 patients with Alzheimer's disease. *American Journal of Geriatric Psychiatry*, 13, 460–468.

Cranson, R. W., Orme-Johnson, D. W., Gackenbach, J., Dillebeck, M. C., Jones, E. H., & Alexander, C. N. (1991). Transcendental meditation and improved performance on intelligence related measures: A longitudinal study. *Personality and Individual Differences*, 12, 1105–1116.

Crookall, R. (1972). *Casebook of Astral Projection.* Secaucus, NJ: University Books.

Curran, H. V., Rees, H., Hoare, T., Hoshi, R., Bond, A. (2004). Empathy and aggression; two faces of ecstasy? A study of interpretative cognitive bias and mood change in ecstasy users. *Psychopharmacology*, 173, 425–433.

Curtis, R., & Robertson, P. (2009). Prayer and meditation: A review of research. *Counseling and Spirituality*, 28(2), 11–12.

Cytowic, R. (1998). *The Man Who Tasted Shapes.* Cambridge, MA: MIT Press.

Cytowic, R. (2002). *Synesthesia: A Union of the Senses, 2nd ed.* Cambridge, MA: MIT Press

Cytowic, R. E., Engleman, D. M. (2011). *Wednesday is Indigo Blue: Discovering the Brain of Synesthesia.* Cambridge, MA: MIT Press.

Dann, K. T. (1998). *Bright Colors Falsely Seen: Synesthesia and the Search for Transcendental Knowledge.* New Haven, CT: Yale University Press.

Darling, C. A., Hill, E. W., & McWye, L. M. (2004). Understanding stress and quality of life for clergy and clergy spouses. *Stress and Health*, 20, 261–277.

Darvish, A. S., Gudelsky, G. A. (2005). Evidence for a role of energy dysregulation in the MDMA-induced depletion of brain 5-HT. *Brain Research*, 21, 168–175.

Dattore, P., Shontz, F., Coyne, L. (1980). Premorbid personality differentiation of cancer and non-cancer groups. *Journal of Consulting and Clinical Psychology*, 48, 388–394.

Davis, J. M. (1976). Recent developments in the drug treatment of schizophrenia, Germany: Springer. *American Journal of Psychiatry*, 133, 208–214.

de la Pena, A. M. (1983). *The Psychobiology of Cancer.* South Hadley, MA: J. F. Bergin Publishers.

Decety, J. & Moriguchi, Y. (2007). The empathic brain and its dysfunction in psychiatric populations: Implications for intervention across different clinical conditions. *Bio Psychosocial Medicine*, 1, 22.

Decety, J. (2011). Dissecting the Neural Mechanisms Mediating Empathy. *Emotion Review*, 3(1), 92–108.

Decety, J., Lamm, C., & Melzoff, A. N. (2009). How do we empathize with someone who is not like us? A functional magnetic resonance imaging study. *Journal of Cognitive Neuroscience*, 22(2), 362–376.

Dein, S. & Littlewood, R. (2007). The voice of God. *Anthropology and Medicine*, 14, 213–228.

Delaney, H. D., Miller, W. R., & Bisono, A. M. (2007). Religiosity and spirituality among psychologists: A survey of clinician members of the American Psychological Association. *Professional Psychology: Research and Practice*, 38, 538–546.

Denollet, J. (1998). Personality and risk of cancer in men with coronary heart disease. *Psychology Medicine*, 28, 991–995.

Derogatis, L., Abeloff, M., Melisaratos, N. (1979). Psychological coping mechanisms and survival time in metastatic breast cancer. *JAMA*, 242, 1504–1508.

Di Christina, M., ed. (2015). Epigenetics: Descendants of Holocaust Survivors Have Altered Stress Hormones. *Scientific American Mind*, 26(2), 10.

Diederen, K. M. J., Neggers, S. F. W., Daalman, K., Bloom, J. D., Goekoop, R., Kahn, R. S., Sommer I. E. (2010). Deactivation of the parahippocampal gyrus preceding auditory hallucinations in schizophrenia. *American Journal of Psychiatry*, 167, 427–435.

Dodgson, G. & Gordon, S. (2009). Avoiding false negatives: Are some auditory hallucinations an evolved design flaw? *Behavioral and Cognitive Psychotherapy*, 37, 325–34.

Domino, G. (1980). Synesthesia and creativity in fine arts students: An empirical look. *Creativity Research Journal*, 2, 17–29.

Douglas-Klotz, N. (2003). *The Genesis Meditations: Shared Practices of Peace for Christians, Jews, and Muslims.* Wheaton, IL: The Theosophical Publishing House.

Dreher, H. (2003). *Mind-Body Unity: A New Vision for Mind-Body Science and Medicine.* Baltimore, MD: The Johns Hopkins University Press, 155–200.

du Boulay, S. (1991). *Teresa of Avila: An Extraordinary Life.* New York: BlueBridge, 66–68.

du Boulay, S. (2004). *Teresa of Avila: An Extraordinary Life.* New York: Blue Bridge, 46–55.

Ecker, R., Ticic, R., & Hulley, L. (2012). *Unlocking the Emotional Brain: Eliminating Symptoms at Their Roots Using Memory Reconsolidation.* New York: Routledge.

Eigen, M. (2005). *Psychotic Core.* London, UK: Karnac.

Exline, J. J., Yali, A. M., & Lobel, M. (1999). When God disappoints: Difficulty forgiving God and its role in negative emotion. *Journal of Health Psychology*, 4, 363–379.

Eyerman, J. (2013). A clinical report of holotropic breathwork in 11,000 psychiatric inpatients in a community hospital setting. *MAPS Bulletin Special Edition*, 1, 24–27.

Fadiga, L., Fogassi, L., Gallese, V., & Rizzolatti, G. (1996). Action recognition in the premotor cortex. *Brain* (Pr. 2), 593–609.

Falck-Yetter, T. G. & von Hofsten, C. (2006). Infants Predict Other People's Action Goals. *Nature Neuroscience*, 9, 878–79.

Ferrucci, L. M., Cartmel, B., Turkman, Y. E., Murphy, M. E., Smith, T., Stein, K. D., & McCorkle, R. (2011). Causal attribution among cancer survivors of the ten most common cancers. *Journal of Psychosocial Oncology*, 29(2), 121–140.

Fink, G. R., Markowitsch, H. J., Reinkemeir, M., Bruckbauer, T., Kessler, J., & Heiss, W. D. (1996). Cerebral representation of one's own past: Neural networks involved in autobiographical memory. *Journal of Neuroscience*, 16, 4275–4282.

Flach, F. (1988). *Resilence: Discovering New Strength in Times of Stress.* New York: Fawcett Columbine, 15,39 and 40.

Fox, G. (1808). Journal. Vol 1. Philadelphia, PA: Fry and Kammerer.

Francis, L. J. & Robbins, M. (May, 2003). Personality and Glossolalia: A Study Among Male Evangelical Clergy. *Pastoral Psychology*, 51(5), 391–396.

Freud, S. (1901/1958). The psychopathology of everyday life. In J. Strachey (ed. and trans.), *The standard edition of the complete psychological works of Sigmund Freud*, Vol. V1. London, UK: Hogarth Press.

Friberg, T. R., Bremer, R. W., & Dickenson, M. (2007). Diminished perception of light as a symptom of depression: Further studies. *Journal of Affective Disorders*, 108, 235–240.

Fujii, D. & Ahmed, I. (2002). Psychotic disorder following traumatic brain injury: A conceptual framework. *Cognitive Neuropsychiatry*, 7, 41–62.

Gee, L., Pearce, E., & Jackson, M. (2003). Quality of life in schizophrenia: A grounded theory approach. *Health and Quality of Life Outcomes*, 1, 1–11.

Gentz, W. H., ed. (1986). *The Dictionary of Bible and Religion.* Nashville, TN: Abingdon Press, 923.

Gibson, J. J. (1986). *The Ecological Approach to Visual Perception.* New York: Psychology Press.

Goodman, F. D. (1972). *Speaking in Tongues: A Cross-Cultural Study of Glossolalia.* Chicago: University of Chicago Press.

Goswami, S. S. (1980). *Layayoga: An Advanced Method of Concentration.* London: Routledge and Kegan Paul, 78–79.

Greer, G., & Tolbert, R. (1986). Subjective reports of the effects of MDMA in a clinical setting. *Journal of Psychoactive Drugs*, 18, 319–327.

Greyson, B. (1983). In J. M. Holden, B. Greyson, D. J. James (eds). Pleasurable Western Adult Near Death Experiences: Features, Circumstances, and Incidence, *The Handbook of Near-Death Experiences (p.*20). Santa Barbara: ABC-CLIO, LLC.

Grimes, J. (1996). *A Concise Dictionary of Indian Philosophy.* New York: State University of New York Press, 269.

Grof, S. (2001). *LSD Psychotherapy.* Sarasota, FL: MAPS.

Grossarth-Maticek R. (1982). Interpersonal repression as a predictor of cancer. *Social Science and Medicine*, 16, 493–498.

Grudem, W. A. (1994). *Systematic theology: An introduction to biblical doctrine.* Leicester: Inter-Varsity Press, 1070.

Haimerl, C. J., Valentine, E. R. (2001). The effect of contemplative practice on intrapersonal interpersonal and transpersonal dimensions of the self-concept. *Journal of Transpersonal Psychology*, 33, 37–52.

Hammersley, P., Dias, A., Todd, G., Bowen-Jones, K., Reilly, B. & Bentall, R. P. (2003). Childhood trauma and hallucinations in bipolar affective disorder: Preliminary investigation. *British Journal of Psychiatry*, 182, 543-7.

Hammersley, P., Taylor, K., McGovern, J. & Kinderman, P. (2010). Attributions for hallucinations in bipolar affective disorder. *Behavioral and Cognitive Psychotherapy*, 38, 221-6.

Harris, J., Erbes, C., Engdahl, B., Tedeshi, R., Olson, R., Winskowski, A. M. M., & McMahill, J. (2010). Coping functions of prayer and posttraumatic growth. *The International Journal for the Psychology of Religion*, 20, 26–38.

Heidt, P. (1981). Effective therapeutic touch on the anxiety level of hospitalized patients. *Nursing Research*, 35, 101–105.

Helm, H. M., Mays, J. C., Flint, E. P., Koenig, H. G., & Blazer, D. G. (2000). Does private religious activity prolong survival? A six year follow-up study of 3,951 older adults. *Journal of Gerontology*, 53A (7) M400–M405.

Higgins, R. (2001). Buddhists practice forgiveness: Mindful suffering. *Christian Century*, 118, 9–10.

Hileman, L. (2008). The unique needs of protestant clergy families: Implications for marriage and family counseling. *Journal of Spirituality in Mental Health*, 10/2, 119–144.

Hill, R., Darling, C. A., & Raimondi, N. M. (2003). Understanding boundary-related stress in clergy families. *Marriage and Family Review*, 35(½), 147–166.

Hodge, D. R. (2007). A systematic review of the empirical literature on intercessory prayer. *Research on Social Work Practice*, 17, 174–187.

Hollingworth, A., Williams, C. C., & Henderson, J. M. (2001). To see and remember: Visually specific information is retained in memory from previously attended objects in natural scenes. *Psychonomic Bulletin and Review*, 8(4), 761–768.

Holmes, S. W., Morris, R., Clance, P. R., Putney, R. T. (1996). Holotropic Breathwork: An Experiential Approach to Psychotherapy. *Psychotherapy Theory, Research, Practice, Training*, 33(1), 114–120.

Holroyd, S., Currie, L., & Wooten, G. F. (2001). Prospective study of hallucinations and delusions in Parkinson's disease. *Journal of Neurology, Neurosurgery and Psychiatry*, 70, 7347–738.

Honig, A. Romme, M., Ensink, B., Escher, S., Pennings, M., & Devries, M. (1998). Auditory hallucinations: A comparison between patients and non-patients. *Journal of Nervous and Mental Disease*, 186, 646–651.

Iacoboni, M., Woods, R. P., Brass, M., Bekkering, H., Mazziotta, J. C., & Rizzolatti, G. (1999). Cortical mechanisms of human imitation. Science, 286, 2526-8.

James, W. (1960/1902). *The varieties of religious experience.* London: Collins.

Jones, S. R. & Fernyhough, C. (2006). The roles of thought suppression and metacognitive style in proneness to auditory verbal hallucinations in a non-clinical sample. *Personality and Individual Differences*, 41, 1421–1432.

Judge, A. M., Estroff, S. E., Perkins, D. O., & Penn, D. L. (2008). Recognizing and responding to early psychosis: A qualitative analysis of individual narratives. *Psychiatric Services*, 59, 96–99.

Jung, C. G. (1963). *Memories, Dreams and Reflections* (trans. R. Wilson and C. Wilson). London: Collins and Routledge and Kegan Paul.

Kaplan, G. A., Reynolds, R. (1988). Depression and cancer mortality and morbidity: Prospective evidence from the Alameda County Study. *Journal of Behavioral Medicine*, 11, 1–13.

Kaplar, M. E., Wachholtz, A. B., O'Brien, W. H. (2004). The effect of religious and spiritual interventions on the biological, psychological and spiritual outcomes of oncology patients: A meta-analytic review. *Journal of Psychosocial Oncology*, 22(1) 39–49.

Karremans, J. C., Van Lange, P. A. M., Ouwerk, J. W., & Kluwer, E. S. (2003). When forgiving enhances psychological wellbeing: The role of interpersonal commitment. *Journal of Personality and Social Psychology*, 84, 1011–1026.

Keller, E. (1986). Effects of therapeutic touch on tension headache pain. *Nursing Research*, 35, 101–105.

Kelly, C. (2004). *Life Force: The Creative Process in Man and in Nature.* Victoria: Trafford Publishing.

Kingdon, D. G., Ashcroft, K., Bhandari, B., Gleeson, S., Warikoo, N., Symons, M., Taylor, L., Lucas, E., Mahendra, R., Ghosh, S., Mason, A., Badrakalimuthu, R., Hepworth, C., Read, J., & Mehta, R. (2010). Schizophrenia and borderline personality disorder: Similarities and differences in the experience of auditory hallucinations, paranoia, and childhood trauma. *Journal of Nervous and Mental Disease*, 198(6), 399-403.

King-Lenzmeier, A. J. (2001). *Hildegard of Bingen: An integrated vision.* Collegeville, MN: Luturgical Press.

Klostermaier, K. K. (1994). *A Survey of Hinduism.* Albany, NY: State University of New York Press.

Koenig, H. G., George, L. K., & Titus, P. (2004). Religion, spirituality and health in medically illness: hospitalized older patients. *Journal of American Geriatrics Association*, 52, 554–562.

Kraepelin, E. (1919). *Dementia praecox and paraphrenia* (trans. R. M. Barclay, G. M. Roberson (3 ed). Chicago Medical Book Co. (Original work published 1896).

Krebs, P. M., Norcross, J. C., & Prochaska, O. (2011). Stages of change. *Journal of Clinical Psychology*, 67(2), 1–12.

Krieger, D. et al. (1979). Physiologic indices of therapeutic touch. *American Journal of Nursing*, 4, 660–662.

Landrine, H.& Klonoff, E. A. (1994). Cultural diversity in causal attributions for illness: The role of the supernatural. *Journal of Behavioral Medicine*, 17(2), 181–193.

Lawler, K. A., Younger, J. W., Piferi, R. L., Billington, E., Jobe, R., Edmonson, K., & Jones, W. H. (2003). A change of heart: Cardiovascular correlates of forgiveness inresponse to interpersonal conflict. *Journal of Behavioral Medicine*, 26(5), 373-393.

Lawler-Row, K. A. (2010). Forgiveness as a mediator of the religiosity-health relationship. *Psychology of Religion and Spirituality*, 2(1), 1–16.

Le Shan, L. (1990). *Cancer as a Turning Point*. New York: Penguin Putham, Inc.

Lee, T., Chong, S. A., Chan, Y. H., & Sathyadevan, G. (2004). Command hallucinations among Asian patients with schizophrenia. *Canadian Journal of Psychiatry*, 49, 838–842.

Leister, M. B. (2013). Near death experiences and ayahuasca-induced experiences-two unique pathways to a phenomenologically similar states of consciousness. *The Journal of Transpersonal Psychology*, 45(1), 24–28.

Levy, S. M., Herberman, R. B., Lippman, M., d'Angelo, T., Lee, J. (1991). Immunological and psychosocial predictors of disease recurrence in patients with early-stage breast cancer. *Behavioral Medicine*, 17, 67–75.

Levy, S. M., Herberman, R. B., Lippman, M., d'Angelo, T. (1987). Correlation of stress factors with sustained depression of natural killer cell activity and predicted prognosis in patients with breast cancer. *Journal of Clinical Oncology*, 5, 344–353.

Levy, S. M., Herberman, R. B., Maluish, A., Schlein, B., Lippman, M. (1985). Prognostic risk assessment in primary breast cancer by behavioral and immunological parameters. *Health Psychology*, 4, 99–113.

Lindberg, D. A. (2005). Integrative review of research related to meditation, spirituality and the elderly. *Geriatric Nursing*, 26, 372–377.

Logothetis, N. K. (2002). Visual competition. *Nature Reviews Neuroscience*, 3(1), 13–21.

Long, A. A. (2009). How did Socrates divine sign communicate with him? In S. Ahbel-Rappe & R. Kamtekar (eds). *A Comparison to Socrates.* London, UK: Blackwell.

Matsui, H., Nishinaka, K., Oda, M., Hara, N., Komatsu, K., Kubori, T. & Udaka, F. (2006). Hypoperfusion of the auditory and prefrontal cortices in Parkinsonian patients withverbal hallucinations. *Movement Disorders*, 21(12), 2165–2169.

Maunsell, E., Brisson, J., Deschenes, L. (1995). Social support and survival among women with breast cancer. *Cancer*, 76, 631–637.

McCarthy-Jones, S. (2012). *Hearing Voices: The Histories, Causes and Meanings of Auditory Verbal Hallucinations.* New York: Cambridge University Press, 46.

McCullough, M. E. & Witvliet, C. V. O. (2002). The psychology of forgiveness. In C. R. Snyder and S. J. Lopez (Eds.), *Handbook of Positive Psychology.* New York: Oxford, 446–458.

McCullough, M. E. & Worthington, E. L., Jr. (1994). Models of interpersonal forgiveness and their applications to counseling: Review and critique. *Counseling and Values*, 39, 2–14.

McCullough, M. E. (2001). Forgiveness: Who does it and how do they do it? *Current Directions in Psychological Science*, 10, 194–197.

McCullough, M. E. (2008). *Beyond Revenge.* San Francisco, CA: Jossy Bass, 205

McKenzie, C. (2009). *Babies Need Mothers: How Mothers Can Prevent Mental Illness in their Children.* Bloomington, IN: Xlibris.

McKenzie, C. D. (2004). Personal communications.

McMinn, M. R., Chaddock, T. P., Edwards, L. C., Lim, B. R. K. B., & Campbell, C. D. (1998). Psychologists collaborating with clergy. *Professional Psychology: Research and Practice*, 29, 564–570.

Mellody, P. (2003). *Facing Love Addiction.* New York: Harper Collins.

Monroe, R. (1977). *Journeys Out of the Body.* Garden City, NY: Doubleday & Company.

Moody, R. (1975). *Life After Life.* Covington, GA: Mockingbird Books.

Moody, R. (1993). *Reunions: Visionary encounters with departed loved ones.* Kansas City, MO: Universal Press Syndicate.

Moody, R. (1995). Personal communication.

Mosher, L. R. & Hendrix, V. (2004). *Soteria: Through Madness to Deliverance.* San Francisco, CA: XLibris.

Mueser, K. T. & Butler, R. W. (1987). Auditory hallucinations in combat-related chronic posttraumatic stress disorder. *American Journal of Psychiatry*, 44, 299–302.

Murphy, H. B. M., Wittkower, E. D., Fried, J., & Ellengerger, H. (1963). Across-cultural survey, of schizophrenia symptomology. *Journal of Social Psychiatry*, 10, 237–249.

Murphy, M. (1992). *The Future of the Body: Explorations Into the Further Evolution of Human Nature.* Los Angeles: Jeremy P. Tarcher, Inc.

Nadon, R., Hoyt, I. P., Register, P. A., & Kihlstrom, J. F. (1991). Absorption and hypnotizability; context, effect re-examined. *Journal of Personality and Social Psychology*, 60(1), 144–153.

Nave, O. J. (1962). *Nave's Topical Bible.* Nashville, TN: The Southwestern Company.

Newberg, A. & Waldman, M. R. (2009). *How God Changes Your Brain: Breakthrough Findings from a Leading Neuroscientist.* New York: Ballentine Books.

Newberg, A. B., Wintering, N. A., Morgan, D., Waldman, M. R. (2006). The measurement of regional cerebral blood flow during a glossolalia: A preliminary SPECT study. *Psychiatry Research: Neuroimaging*, 148(1), 67–71.

Noyes, R. & Kletti, R. (1976). Depersonalization in the face of life-threating danger: A description. *Psychiatry*, 39, 19–27.

Nyugen, C. (1990). Sthiramati's Interpretation of Buddhology and Soteriology, Ph.D. thesis Harvard University.

Obermeier, A., & Kennison, R. (1997). The privilegins of vision over vox in the mystical experiences of Hildegard of Bingen and Joan of Arc. *Mystic Quarterly*, 23, 137–163.

Ohayon, M. M. (2000). Prevalence of hallucinations and their pathological association in the general population. *Psychiatry Research*, 27, 153–164.

Oman, D. (2010). *Similarity in Diversity? Four Shared Functions of Integrative Contemplative Practice systems in Contemplative Practices in Action*, edited by Thomas G. Plante. Santa Barbara, CA: ABC-CLIO, LLC.

Oman, D., Shapiro, S. L., Thoresen, C. E., Plante, T. G., & Flinders, T. (2008). Meditation lowers stress and supports forgiveness among college students: A randomized controlled trial. *Journal of American College Health*, 56(5), 569–577.

Orem, S. L., Binkert, J., and Clancy, A. L. (2007). *Appreciative Coaching: A Positive Psychology of Change.* San Francisco, CA: Jossey-Bass.

Orr, L. and Ray, S. (1977). *Rebirthing in the New Age.* Berkeley, CA: Celestial Arts.

Pargament, K. I. (2011). *Spiritually Integrated Psychotherapy.* New York: The Guilford Press, 151.

Pargament, K. I., Steele, R. E., & Tyler, F. B. (1979). Religious participation, religious motivation, and individual psychosocial competence. *Journal for the Scientific Study of Religion*, 18, 412–419.

Parrot, A. C., Milani, R., Parmar, R., Turner, J. J. D. (2001). Ecstasy polydrug users and other recreational drug users in Britain and Italy: Psychiatric symptoms and psychobiological problems. *Psychopharmacology*, 159, 77–82.

Parrott, A. C. (2007). The psychotherapeutic potential of MDMA (3,4 methylenediomethamphetamine): An evidenced-based review. *Psychopharmacology*, 191, 181–193.

Perlman, D. (1999). Personal communication.

Perry, J. W. (1999). *Trials of the Visionary Mind: Spiritual Emergency and the Renewal Process.* New York: State University of New York Press, 27.

Persinger, M. A., Roll, W. G., Tiller, S. G., Koren, S. A., Cook, C. M. (2002). Remost viewing with the artist Ingo Swann: Neuropsychological profile, electroencephalographic correlates, magnetic resonance imaging (MRI), and possible mechanisms. *Perceptual and Motor Skills*, 94(3 Pt. 1), 927–949.

PewResearchCenter: Religion & Public Life (May 12, 2015). America's Changing Religious Landscape: Christians Decline Sharply as Share of Population; Unaffiliated and Other Faiths Continue to Grow.

Pickert, K. (2014). The Art of Being Mindful. *Time Magazine*, 183(4), 40–46.

Piedmont, R. L. (2004). Spiritual transcendence as a predictor of psychosocial outcome from an outpatient substance abuse program. *Psychology of Addictive Behaviors*, 18(3), 213-222.

Pitt, L., Kilbride, M., Welford, M., Nothard, S., & Morrison, A. P. (2009). Impact of a diagnosis of psychosis: User-led qualitative study. *Psychiatric Bulletin*, 33, 419–423.

Plante, T. G. & Thoresen, C. E. (2007). *Spirit, Science and Health.* Westport, CT: Prayer, 14.

Platz, W. E., Oberlander, F. A., & Seidl, M. L. (1995). The phenomenology of perceptual hallucinations in alcohol-induced delirium tremens. *Psychopathology*, 28, 247–255.

Poloma, M. M. & Pendleton, B. F. (1991). The effects of prayer and prayer experiences on measures of general well-being. *Journal of Psychology and Theology*, 19, 71–83.

Prigogene, I. & Stengers, I. (1984). *Order Out of Chaos: Man's New Dialogue with Nature.* New York: Bantam.

Puthoff, H. & Targ, R. (1976). A perceptual channel for information transfer over kilometer distances: Historical perspective and recent research. *Proceedings of the IEEE,* 64(3), 329–354.

Puthoff, J. (1996). *Journal of Scientific Exploration*, 10(1), 63–76.

Quinn, J. (1988). Building a body of knowledge: Research on therapeutic touch 1974-1986. *Journal of Holistic Nursing*, 6, 37–45.

Quinn, W. H., Herndon, A. (1986). The Family Ecology of Cancer. *Journal of Psychosocial Oncology*, 4(1/2), 45–59.

Ramirez, A., Craig, T., Watson, J., Fentiman, J., North, W., Rubens, R. (1989). Tress and relapse of breast cancer. *BMJ*, 298, 291–293.

Read, J. Agar, K., Argyle, N., & Aderhold, V. (2003). Sexual and physical abuse during childhood and adulthood as predictors of hallucinations, delusions and thought disorder. *Psychology and Psychotherapy: Theory, Research and Practice*, 76, 1–22.

Redmond, C., Larkin, M., & Harrop, C. (2010). The personal meaning of romantic relationships for young people with psychosis. *Clinical Child Psychology and Psychiatry*, 15, 151–170.

Resnick, H. S., Kilpatrick, D. G., Dansky, B. S., Saunders, B. E., & Best, C. L. (1993). Prevalence of civilian trauma and posttraumatic stress disorder in a representative national sample of women. *Journal of Consulting and Clinical Psychology*, 61, 984–991.

Rhinewine, J. P., Williams, O. J. (2007). Holotropic breathwork: The potential role of a prolonged, voluntary hyperventilation procedure as an adjunct to psychotherapy. *Journal of Alternative and Complementary Medicine*, 13(7), 771–776.

Roberts, B. (1991). *The Path to No Self.* New York: The State University of New York.

Roberts, B. (1993). *The Experience of No Self.* Albany, NY: State University of New York.

Roche, S. M., Mc Conkey, K. M. (1990). Absorption: Nature, assessment and correlates. *Journal of Personality and Social Psychology*, 59(1), 91–101.

Rofail, D., Heelis, R., & Gournay, K. (2009). Results of a thematic analysis to explore the experiences of patients with schizophrenia taking antipsychotic medication. *Clinical Therapeutics*, 31 (Suppl. 1), 1488–1496.

Rogentine, G. N., Jr., van Kammen, D. P., Fox, B. H., Docherty, J. P., Rosenblatt, J. E., Boyd, S. C., & Bunney, W. E., Jr. (1979). Psychological factors in the prognosis of malignant melanoma: A prospective study. Psychosomatic Medicine, 41(8), 647- 655.

Romanski, L. M. (2007). Representation and integration of auditory and visual stimuli in the primate ventral lateral prefrontal cortex. *Cerebral Cortex*, 17, 161–169.

Romme, M., Escher, D., Dillon, J. Corstens, D., & Morris, M. (2009). *Living with Voices.* Herefordshire, UK: PCCS Books, 95–100.

Roud, P. C. (1990). *Making Miracles.* New York: Warner Books.

Ryan, R. M., Rigby, S., & King, K. (1993). Two types of religious internalization and their relations to religious orientation and mental health. *Journal of Personality and Social Psychology*, 65, 586–596.

Rye, M. S., Pargament, K. I., Ali, M. A., Beck, G. L., Dorff, E. N., Hallesey, C., Williams, J. G. (2000). Religious Perspectives on forgiveness. In M. E. McCullough, K. I. Pargament, C. E. Thoresen (Eds.). *Forgiveness: Theory, research and practice*, 17–40.

Saenz, M., Koch, C. (2008). The sound of change: Visually induced auditory synesthesia. *Current Biology*, 18(15), R650–R651.

Salzberg, S. (1995). *Lovingkindness: The Revolutionary Art of Happiness.* Boston: Shambala Publications.

Samarin, W, J. (1972). *Tongues of Men and Angels: The Religious Language of Pentecostalism.* New York: Macmillan, 120.

Samarin, W. J. (1972). Sociolinguistic vs. Neurophysiological Explanations form Glossolalia: Comment on Goodman's Paper. *Journal for the Scientific Study of Religion*, 11(3), 293–296.

Samarin, W. J. (1972). *Tongues of Men and Angles: The Religious Language of Pentecostalism.* New York: Macmillan.

Sandage S. J. & Moe, S. P. (2013). *Spiritual Experience: Conversion and Transformation in APA Handbook of Psychology, Religion and Spirituality, volume 1, Context, Theory and Research,* edited by Kenneth I. Pargament, 411.

Sandage, S. J. & Jankowski, P. J. (2010). Forgiveness, spiritual instability, mental health symptoms, and well-being: Mediator effects of differentiation of self. *Psychology of Religion and Spirituality*, 2(3), 168–180.

Sannwald, G. (1959). Statistische untersuchungen an spontanphänomenen. *Zeitschrift für Parapsychologie und Grenzgebiete der Psychologie*, 3, 59-71.

Schilt, T., de Win, M. M. L., Jager, G., Koeter, M. W., Ramsey, N. F., Schmand, B., & van den Brink, W. (2008). Specific effects of ecstasy and other illicit drugs on cognition in poly-substance users. *Psychological Medicine*, 38(9), 1309–1317.

Schuhmacher, S. & Woerner, G. (1994). *The Encyclopedia of Eastern Philosophy and Religion*. Boston, MA.: Shamgala Publications, 333–334.

Schulz, R., Bookwala, J., Knapp, J. E., Scheier, M., Williamson, G. M. (1996). Pessimism, age, and cancer mortality. *Psychol Aging*, 11, 304–309.

Schwartz, G. E. (2007). *The Energy Healing Experiments.* New York: ATRIA books.

Scurlock, J. & Anderson, B. R. (2005). *Diagnoses in Assyrian and Babylonian Medicine*. Chicago, IL: University of Illinois.

Seligman, M. E. P. (2002). *Authentic Happiness: Using the new Positive Psychology to realize your potential for lasting fulfillment.* New York: Free Press.

Sessa, B. (2010). Shaping the renaissance of psychedelic research. *The Lancet*, 380(9838), 200–201.

Sessa, B. (2012). Shaping the renaissance of psychedelic research. *The Lancet*, 380, 200–201.

Shapiro; S. L. & Walsh, R. (2003). An Analysis of recent meditation research and suggestions for future directions. *Humanistic Psychologist*, 31, 86–114.

Shapiro, S. L., Schwartz, G. E., & Bonner, G. (1998). Effects of mindfulness-based stress reduction on medical and premedical students. *Journal of Behavioral Medicine*, 21, 581.

Shuster, M. A., Stein, B. D., & Jaycox, L. H. (2001). A National Survey on Stress Reactions after the September 22, 2001 Terrorist Attacks. *New England Journal of Medicine*, 345, 1507–1512.

Sidgwick, H., Johnson, A., Myers, F. W. H., Podmore, F., & Sidwick, E. M. (1894). Report on the Census of Hallucinations. *Proceeding of the Society for Psychical Research*, 10, 24–422.

Smith, A. M. & Messier, C. (February, 2014). Voluntary out-of-body experience: An FMRI study. *Frontiers in Neuroscience*, 8, article 70.

Smith, H. (1991). *The World's Religions.* San Francisco: Harper, 126.

So., K & Orne-Johnson, D. (2001). Three randomized experiments on the longitudinal effects of transcendental meditation technique on cognition. *Intelligence*, 29, 419–440.

Sommer, I. E. C., Daalman, K., Rietkerk, T., Diederen, K. M., Bakker, S., Wijkstra, J. & Boks, M. P. (2010). Healthy individuals with auditory verbal hallucinations; who are they? Psychiatric assessments of a selected sample of 103 subjects. *Schizophrenia Bulletin*, 36(3), 633–641.

Sommer, I. E., Diederen, K. M., Blom, J. D., Willems, A., Kushan, L., Slotema, K., Boks, M. P., Daalman, K., Hoek, H. W., Neggers, S. F. & Kahn, R. S. (2008). Auditory verbal hallucinations predominantly activate the right inferior frontal area. Brain, 131, 3169-77.

Spiegel, D., Bloom, J. R., Kraemer, H. C., Gottheil, E. (1989). Effect of psychosocial treatment on survival of patients with metastatic breast cancer. *The Lancet*, 14, 888–891.

Stavraky, K. M., Donner, A. P., Kincade, J. E., Stewart, M. A. (1988). The effect of psychosocial factors on lung cancer mortality at one year. *Journal of Clinical Epidemiology*, 41, 75–82.

Stavraky, K., Buck, C., L., Ott, J., Wanklin, J. E., Stewart, M. A. (1968). Psychological factors in the outcome of lung cancer. *Journal of Psychosomatic Research*, 12, 251–259.

Stern, D. N. (2004). *The Present Moment in Psychotherapy and Everyday Life.* New Yotk: W. W. Norton & Company.

Stokes, D. M. (1997). Spontaneous psi phenomena. In S. Krippner (ed.), *Advances in parapsychological research*. Jefferson, NC: McFarland, Vol. 8, 6–87.

Teasdale, J. D., Barnard, P. J. (1993). *Affect, Cognition and Change: Remodeling depressive thought.* Hove, UK: Lawrence Erlbaum Associates.

Tellegen, A. & Atkinson, G. (1974). Openness to absorbing and self-altering experiences ("absorption"), a trait related to hypnotic susceptibility. *Abnormal Psychology*, 83(3), 268–277.

Temoshok, L. & Dreher, H. (1993). *The Type C Connection.* New York: Penguin Books.

Temoshok, L. (1985). Biopsychosocial studies on cutaneous malignant melanoma: Psychosocial factors associated with prognostic indicators, progression, psychophysiology and tumor-host response. *Social Science and Medicine*, 20, 833–840.

Temoshok, L., Heller, B. W., Sagebiel, R. E., Blois, M. S., Sweet, D. M., DiClemente, R., J. & Gold, M. L. (1985). The relationship of psychosocial factors to prognostic indicators in cutaneous malignant melanoma. Journal of Psychosomatic Research, 29, 139–53.

Tepper, L., Rogers, S. A., Coleman, E. M., & Malony, H. N. (2001). The prevalence of religious coping among persons with persistent mental illness. *Psychiatric Services*, 52, 660–665.

Thalbourne, M. A., Bartemucci, L. & Delin, P. S., Fox, B., & Nofi, O. (1997). Transliminality: Its nature and correlates. *Journal of The American Society for Psychical Research*, 91, 305–331.

The Holy Bible, Revised Standard Version (1952). New York: Thomas Nelson & Sons.

Thomas, L. (2010). *The Encyclopedia of Energy Medicine.* Minneapolis, MN: Fairview Press.

Thomas, P., Mathur, P., Gottesman, II., Nagpal, R., Nigaonkar, V. I., & Deshpande, S. N. (2007). Correlates of hallucinations in schizophrenia: A cross-cultural evaluation. *Schizophrenia Research*, 92, 41–49.

Tolbert, N. (2001). The polarities of consciousness. In I. Clarke (ed). *Psychosis and Spirituality*, 30.

Toussaint, L. L., Shields G., Dorn, G., & Slavich, G. M. (2014). Effects of lifetime stress exposure on mental and physical health in young adulthood: How stress degrades and forgiveness protects health. *Journal of Health Psychology.* Advance online publication. doi:10.177/1359105314544132.

Tross, S., Herndon, J., II, Korzun, A., Kornblith, A. B., Cella, D. F., Holland, J. F, Raich, P., Johnson, A., Kiang, D. T., Perloff, M., Norton, L., Wood, W. & Holland, J. C. (1996). Psychological symptoms and disease free and overall survival in women with stage II breast cancer: Cancer and Leukemia Group B., *Journal of the National Cancer Institute*, 88(10), 661–67.

Tsang, J., McCullough, M. E., & Hoyt, W. T. (2005). Psychometric and rationalization accounts of the religious-forgiveness discrepancy. *Journal of Social Issues*, 61, 785–805.

Vandewalle, G., Schwartz, M., Phillips, C., Luxen, A., Dijk, D. J., & Marquet, P. (2010). Spectral quality of light modulates emotional brain responses I humans. *PNAS*, 10, 1073.

Vazquez, S. R. (2013). *Accelerated Ecological Psychotherapy: ETT Applications for Sleep Disorders, Pain and Addiction.* Lanham, MD: Jason Aronson.

Vazquez, S. R. (2013). *Emotional Transformation Therapy: An Interactive Ecological Psychotherapy.* Lanham, MD: Jason Aronson.

Vazquez, S. R. (Winter, 2001). Ethical Issues in Energy Medicine Caregiving. *Bridges: ISSSEEM Magazine*, 12(4), 15–18.

Vincent, A., McAllister, S. J., Singer, W., Toussaint, L. L., Sletten, D. M., Whipple, M. O., & Low, P. A. (2014). A Report of the Autonomic Symptom Profile in Patients With Fibromyalgia. *Journal of Clinical Rheumatology*, 20(2), 106–108.

Wachholtz, A. B. & Pargament, K. I. (2008). Migraines and meditation: Does spirituality matter? *Journal of Behavioral Medicine*, 31, 351–366.

Wacholtz, A. B. & Pargament, K. I. (2005). Is spirituality a critical ingredient of meditation? Comparing the effects of spiritual meditation, secular meditation, and relaxation on spiritual, psychological, cardiac, and pain outcomes. *Journal of Behavioral Medicine*, 28(4), 369–384.

Wade, J. (2004). *Transcendent Sex: When Lovemaking Opens the Veil*. New York: Gallery Books.

Walker, J. (1999). Personal conversation with neurologist specializing in neurotherapy.

Walsh, R. & Glob, C. (ed.) (2005). *Higher Wisdom: Eminent Elders Reflect on the Continuing Impact of Psychedelics.* Albany, NY: SUNY.

Walsh, R. (2005). Can synesthesia be cultivated? Indications from surveys of meditators. *Journal of Consciousness Studies*, 12, 5–17.

Ward, J., Huckstep, B., Tsakanikos, E. (2006). Sound-colour synesthesia: To what extend does it use cross-model mechanisms common to us all? *Cortex*, 42(2), 264–280.

Watts, A. (1984). This Is It. In J White (ed.). *What Is Enlightenment*. Los Angeles, CA: Jeremy T. Tarcher.

Webb, J. R., Toussaint, L., & Conway-Williams, E. (2012). Forgiveness and health: Psycho-spiritual integration and the promotion of better health. *Journal of Health Care Chaplaincy*, 18, 57–73.

Weihs, K. L., Enright, T. M., Simmens, S. J., Reiss, D. (2000). Negative affectivity, restriction of emotions, and site of measures predict mortality in recurrent breast cancer. *Journal of Psychosomatic Research*, 49, 59–68.

Weisman, A. D., Worden, J. W. (1997). Psychological analysis of cancer deaths. *Omega Journal of Death and Dying*, 6, 61–75.

Welwood, J. (2000). *Toward a psychology of awakening: Buddhism, psychotherapy, and the path of personal and spiritual transformation.* Boston, MA: Shambala.

Whitson, J. A. & Galinsky, A. D. (2008). Lacking control increases illusionary pattern perception. *Science*, 332, 115–117.

WHO (1973). *Report of the international pilot study of schizophrenia.* Geneva: World Health Organization.

WHO (1979). *Schizophrenia. An international follow-up study*. Chichester, UK: John Wiley and Sons.

Wild, T. C., Kuiken, D., & Schopflocher, D. (1995). The role of Absorption in Experiential Involvement. *Journal of Personality and Social Psychology*, 69(3), 569–579.

Wirth, D. (1990). The effect of non-contact therapeutic touch on the healing rate of full thickness dermal wounds. *Subtle Energies*, 1, 1–20.

Witvliet, C. V. O., Ludwig, T., & Vander Laan, K. (2001). Granting forgiveness or harboring grudges: Implications for emotion, physiology and health. *Psychological Science*, 12, 117–123.

Wolf, D. and Abell, N. (2003). Examining the effects of meditation techniques on psychosocial functioning. *Research on Social Work Practice*, 13, 27–42.

Wong, E. (Trans. 1997). *Teachings of the Tao.* Boston, MA: Shambala Press.

Wuthernow, R. (1998). *After Heaven: Spirituality in America since the 1950's.* Berkley and Los Angeles: University of California Press.

Yee, L., Korner, A. J., McSwiggan, S., Mears, R. A., & Stevenson, J. (2005). Persistent hallucinosis in borderline personality disorder. *Comprehensive Psychiatry*, 46, 147–154.

Young, L. E. (ed.) (1899). *The Science of Hypnotism.* Baltimore, MD: Land M Ottenheimer.

Zeiders, C. (2003). The Anthropological and Scientific Case for Psychoenergetic Healing. *The International Journal of Healing and Caring, on-line*, 3(1), 1-32.

Zoll, R. (October 9, 2012). Religious affiliation on decline in U. S., survey shows. *Associated Press, Fort Worth Star-Telegram*, p. 1.

Index

About the Author

Steven R. Vazquez, PhD, is the founder of the innovative Emotional Transformation Therapy® approach to psychotherapy. He is a licensed professional counselor and licensed marriage and family therapist in the state of Texas. Dr. Vazquez has taught his approach in nine different countries and throughout the United States. His work has been cited in several books and he has published numerous articles in peer-reviewed professional journals. Dr. Vazquez holds a doctorate in counseling psychology. He has been in private practice for over thirty-three years.

www.ingramcontent.com/pod-product-compliance
Ingram Content Group UK Ltd.
Pitfield, Milton Keynes, MK11 3LW, UK
UKHW012037150926
475560UK00001B/63